SAVING THE SELF

Consumerism, Freedom and You

For Abigail
and David.

Strong supporters of
the literary
community.

CRISTIAN LACATUS

SAVING THE SELF

Consumerism, Freedom and You

Tiberius
Publishing

Cover photo by Glamour Images

Layout by Infoscan Collette

Printed by AGMV Marquis

ISBN 0-9736981-0-1

Printed in Canada

Tiberius
Publishing

Ottawa – Ontario - Canada

Library and Archives Canada Cataloguing in Publication

Lacatus, Cristian, 1971-
Saving the self: consumerism, freedom and you / Cristian Lacatus.

Includes bibliographical references and index.
ISBN 0-9736981-0-1

1. Self-actualization (Psychology) 2. Change (Psychology)
3. Consumption (Economics) I. Title.

BF637.S4L325 2005 158.1 C2005-900016-3

For my father,

Tiberiu

(1948-1999)

Amor vincit omnia

Acknowledgments

I am grateful to those who have supported, reviewed and encouraged my writing, foremost among them David Staines. Many thanks go out to Seymour Mayne and Ruth Bradley-St.Cyr for their invaluable advice on the practicalities of turning a manuscript into a book. The efforts of my cheerful editor, Mike Heenan, who polished the manuscript, are also much appreciated. Finally, I would like to thank my family for their unwavering support, and especially my lovely wife, Flavia, who believed in me when I doubted myself.

Cristian T. Lacatus

Contents

Introduction ... 1

1. Consumerism: What You Must Save Yourself From ... 3
2. The Seeds of Freedom ... 9
3. Suburban Hell: The Consumer Landscape and the Death of the Community ... 15
4. Freeing Your Body: Breaking Away From Consumer Food ... 25
5. Overcoming Obesity: The Problem with Being Overweight ... 41
6. Your Health ... 49
7. Freeing your Mind (1) Breaking Away From Consumer Entertainment ... 59
8. Freeing your Mind (2) Embracing Knowledge Through Reading ... 65
9. Freeing your Mind (3) Embracing Knowledge Through Education ... 75
10. Sports ... 89
11. Travel ... 103
12. Culture 1: Inherited Culture ... 113
13. Culture 2: The Creative Self. You Are an Artist ... 121
14. Culture 3: Developing a Personal Culture ... 131
15. Business/Finances ... 153
16. The Environment ... 171
17. Sexuality ... 189
18. Spirituality ... 201
19. Death ... 209
20. Not a Conclusion, but a Beginning ... 223

References ... 229

Index ... 245

About the author

Cristian Lacatus, M.A., LL.B., is currently working for the Canadian Ministry of the Environment. He lives with his wife, grandfather and sheepdog in Ottawa, Canada.

Introduction

The purpose of this book is neither to motivate you, nor to demand perfection, nor to change your personality. The advice focuses on tangible means of achieving self-fulfillment through everyday behaviour such as reading, travelling, eating and sex. The goal is to help you discover the self so you may start on your own journey of self-fulfillment.

The road towards saving the self is unique to each individual. The book points out what is wrong with the consumer world we live in, and explores the possibility of a non-consumer existence. It is up to you to carve out that existence in your own particular fashion. It is up to you to choose what you eat, how you will have sex, and where you will travel. This book cannot reveal your self to you, but does point out the concrete, mundane, everyday actions through which the self is revealed.

This book is universal. By that, I mean that the only criterion needed for this book to apply to you is the fact that you are a human being. This book applies to every individual regardless of cultural, racial, sexual, religious, political or philosophical background and is meant to be interpreted in light of your background. All of your particular characteristics form part of your journey in liberating the self from consumerism. All are valid methods of achieving self-fulfillment.

This book is not about self-deprivation. It is about regaining the self and taking, exploring, and expanding what you already have. It is about enriching yourself, about feeling better, even looking better. It will not teach you anything you could not learn on your own. There are no secret nuggets of wisdom mined from some Buddhist monastery deep in the Himalayas. There are no magical formulae, no seven steps to a better you, no Eastern philosophy recast as a palatable Westernized spiritual diet, no meditations, no retreats into the wilderness, no native sweat-lodge. There are no recipes for success, recipes that require more than you are willing to give.

This book is about who you are and about the things you do every day. It is about the life of Everyman, it is about the life of all men and women on this planet. There are no radical proposals; there is only common sense.

This book is also my way of embarking on that journey towards self-fulfillment.

In writing it, I have taken a step closer towards my own goal of self-realization. In helping you find your freedom, I am discovering my own.

Chapter 1

Consumerism: What You Must Save Yourself From

This chapter offers a brief overview of consumerism and its unwitting creators, multinational corporations.

Consumerism, tool of the multinationals[1]

Through the rise to power of the multinationals one of the greatest nightmares of human imagination has come to pass: Man is now being controlled by his creations. From Mary Shelley's *Frankenstein* to the *Terminator* and *The Matrix*, this nightmare scenario has been played out again and again in movies and books. However, in reality, it is not machines or monsters that control you, but multinational corporations - and consumerism is their weapon of choice.

What's wrong with being controlled by multinationals? Multinationals are not human. Even worse, there is no single human entity controlling multinationals. Power is shared among the directors, officers and shareholders, but there is no control locus. This problem stems from the fact that publicly-held multinationals have no definite owners. Does the Ford family own Ford? Does Bill Gates own Microsoft? No. The shareholders are the owners. But who are the shareholders? Impossible to say, as the members of this class change every second a share of the company is traded. The ownership changes every day.

1. Corporations having operations in more than one country are labeled multinationals. My definition of multinational turns on the nature of the company's ownership. Publicly held corporations listed on stock exchanges are multinational by virtue of their shareholders' backgrounds, even if the company's area of operation is limited to one country.

Without a definite proprietor, multinationals lack a human foundation to anchor them, to define a human agenda. No one person controls the company. No one person can do what they want with the company. There are multiple and conflicting interests that seek to steer the company in various directions but there is no unchallenged helmsman. Anybody and everybody associated with the multinationals can be removed. Every human being employed by the multinational works to fulfil the interests of the company and not the interests of a human being.

Consequently, these companies exist in a vacuum, exist only to fulfil certain artificial preconditions. Their sole reason for existence becomes existence itself. The multinationals' function cannot be related to any human need or a human will. Their function cannot be pinned down to any specific human interest. We are being controlled by an entity that has absolutely no human considerations in achieving its aims.

The multinationals are not accountable to human beings. They are only accountable within their own economic sphere. The sole thing they respond to is the stock market. For multinationals, the only moral good is the growth of their market value.

Deprived of the human context, giant corporations are nothing more than amoral, abstract entities functioning in a void. They are a deck of cards made of worthless data. They are completely self-contained worlds without any relational link to the human. They serve as their own reference point, and have meaning only within themselves.

Due to their existence within a fictional economic realm, multinationals treat you in economic terms. For the multinationals, your existence is reduced to numbers. You exist to maximize profits, gain market share, further corporate growth and provide shareholder value. That is your function within the calculus of these giant corporations. In fulfilling their statistical expectations, soulless corporations will care little about what the process will do to you. They have no human compassion, and are utterly indifferent to human suffering. Regardless of how much you might suffer as a result of their actions, multinationals will have neither pity, guilt nor a conscience.

The multinationals have an Achilles heel. They depend on people. Their survival is tied to your purchase of their products. But you, as a human being, are difficult to reduce to mere numbers. You have a will, you have emotions, you have hormones. That just won't do for the multinationals. These variables are apt to screw up their calculations. So the multinationals use consumerism in an attempt to make you predictable. They use consumerism to transform you from a human being into something artificial, something programmable, something more comprehensible to them: a consumer.

Multinationals use consumerism to manufacture consumers. But how does consumerism achieves their aims?

Consumerism is an artificial multinational-created universe composed of consumer products. If you conduct your life inside the virtual reality of Consumer-world then you are a consumer. Within its artificial universe, consumerism exerts absolute control over every aspect of your existence, from birth until death. Consumerism provides as complete a guide to your life as any religious, philosophical or political system. It dictates what you eat and drink. It controls your sexuality, your thoughts, your feelings and your desires. Consumerism is your god and your conscience, your hope and your dream.

In exercising absolute control, consumerism transforms you into a puppet for fulfilling the interests of the multinationals. At its simplest, this means that everything you do or think or want involves the consumption of goods manufactured by multinational corporations. These goods can be physical ones, such as food, drink, clothes and cars, or they can be non-material goods such as movies and music. When your whole existence is dependent upon the consumption of these goods, you have been *consumerized.*

Consumerism is very efficient in capturing you within its net. Endowed with protean malleability and flexibility, it is capable of swallowing and incorporating anyone and anything within its structure. Consumerism has no enemies. Consumerism is not against any religion, race, ethnicity or gender. Consumerism is everyone's friend. As such no one is safe from its clutches. White, Asian or black, you will still be consumerized. American, Brazilian or Korean, you will still be consumerized. Catholic, Muslim or Jewish, you will still be consumerized. No matter your class or social status, consumerism is after you and, if you fall prey to its charms, you will become a consumer. Consumerism functions like a ubiquitous supervirus, infecting all with its presence, yet adopting infinite outer coats to deceive its victims as to its actual nature.

So what's wrong with being a consumer? Why not live in Consumer-world?

A consumer is a faceless, mindless and indistinguishable creature. It has no gender, ethnicity, nationality or means of identification beyond its work and its consumption. It is a creature to be kept in a state of utter imbecility except perhaps for a very narrow area of specialization: its profession. It is not an active but a reactive creature whose every need and desire is to be controlled through advertising and satisfied through predetermined means. Its only choice in life is to choose between competing brands. Is this what you want to be?

If you are a consumer you cannot be yourself. All of your talents, abilities, potential, all that you may be or could be, will go unfulfilled because of your consumer slavery. Everything that nature, God or your parents gave to you will be wasted as long as you allow yourself to be trapped in a consumerized existence. Consumerism buries the self.

The purpose of every human being on this planet is the same. Each one of us lives for the possibility of fully achieving our potential, of fully realizing the self. As a consumer, instead of realizing the self, you will only realize profits for the multinationals. But if all you exist for is to fulfil the needs of corporations, how can you justify your existence?

Labouring to consume

Consumerism is often thought of as a measure of an individual's success, achievement, wealth, well-being or prosperity. The acquisition of consumer products is portrayed by the multinationals as a good thing. In fact, the process of consumption ultimately begets pain and suffering rather than happiness.[2] Every single consumer product that you acquire or experience serves only to undermine your potential by denying you the opportunity to express the self.

Not only does consumerism harm the self, but it is also arduous work.

Consumerism makes you work needlessly in two different ways. On one hand, you put in long hours to make the money needed to maintain and increase your consumption levels. On the other hand, the actual process of consumption is a chore in itself, often more wearisome than creating the underlying wealth. The multinationals make you work harder in spending your money than in earning it.

Buy, buy, buy, watch, watch, watch, eat, eat, eat: there's always something you must do to satisfy the consumerist gods. And just when you think you can do no more, you find out about the new store that is having its grand opening or the Pizza Hut special or the new satellite system that lets you have 1,000 channels. In the end, you are driven to

2. If you cannot afford certain consumer goods, you are frustrated and envious of those who have the potential for greater consumption. Alternatively, consumption becomes meaningless, a desperate attempt to hide your own failings and deficiencies. It serves as an illusion providing synthetic joy that deep inside you know is utterly fake but choose to cling to in a futile attempt to deny the harsh truths of existence.

desperation, and no wonder. The availability of consumer products has far outstripped your capacity to consume. Your self is being overwhelmed in the barrage. The potential for consumption is endless; you are not. Whether you get 10 or 1,000 channels, you still have only one pair of eyes, and there are still only 24 hours in the day.

If consumption is hurting you why keep on doing it? One reason is the external pressure from consumer advertising. You are constantly browbeaten towards ever growing levels of consumption. The pressure on you to consume is relentless and ubiquitous. The multinationals constantly seek to control your every living moment by whipping you into a consumerist frenzy. Consumer advertising creates a state of barely controlled madness where you are running from one consumer chore to another. As such, consumption becomes devoid of pleasure but a hard taskmaster.

Second, there is the insidious internal pressure to consume. The multinationals have created within you an artificial need for consumer products. You have betrayed the genuine needs of the self by substituting consumer needs in their place. Satisfying these ersatz cravings is no easy matter since the pressure you put on yourself is just as relentless as the external advertising.

These artificial needs for consumer products are completely independent from the external pressures of consumer advertising. You will act on your internal needs even if you are never exposed to an advertisement for that product again. Regardless of whether you see another McDonald's commercial in your life, you will still go to their restaurants for your Big Mac since it is something you are programmed to need.

Third, multinationals have made consumption an end in itself. As such you do not consume for pleasure. You consume solely for the sake of consumption. You consume because you simply don't know what else to do with your time. Why do you constantly shop, if you already have more than you need? Why do you shop for things you don't need? It is just a meaningless exercise designed to fill up your time, to order your existence.

Consumption and waste

Since consumption has far outstripped necessity, it has become more than just conspicuous consumption; it has become waste. How ironic that multinationals, whose business culture has made efficiency the eleventh commandment, care so little about their products once they are out of corporate hands. Multinationals might be the most efficient and productive business entities on earth, but they are also the most wasteful, producing infinitely more than you can consume.

The more important aspect of waste has to do with you, the consumer. Encouraged to acquire more consumer products then you could possibly need or want you are left with the need to dispose of this excess. That is why the bigger the consumer, the bigger the waste.

Waste is food portions that are much too big for any human being to consume but a restaurant's badge of pride. Indeed, it has become a hallmark of good business to serve the patron more than he could possibly eat and throw the rest away. Waste is purchasing consumer goods you do not need, use or even want. Waste means leaving the lights on and the tap running and the car running and everything else running. Waste means not employing available technology or common sense to reduce energy consumption, but intentionally, purposefully and proudly producing energy-wasting objects or using them in a wasteful manner.

Consumption engenders more than physical waste. Live in Consumer-world and waste becomes a psychological need. You revel in waste as a form of escapism from the consumerist taskmaster. You are crying out to escape. You want the pressure to consume to stop, you want to put a halt to the cycle of work and consumption, but, just like a drug addict, you feel imprisoned within this lifestyle. So you waste more and more, you plunge ever deeper, looking vainly to bottom out, looking vainly for a measure of consumer satiety. You feel that if you just waste enough, then perhaps the pressure will cease, then perhaps you will stumble onto a path out of the consumerist prison. But there is no escape through excess, there is no salvation through waste. The road to freedom is simple. Stop the consumption. But how can you step out of Consumer-world?

Chapter 2

The Seeds of Freedom

Freedom cannot be given or taken, bought or sold.
Freedom can only be learned and expressed.

The answer lies with **individual expression**. Individual expression is the fundamental building block of your existence. This is the method through which you, as a human being, regardless of age, gender, race, religion and ethnicity, location and class can break free from consumerization. Freedom means uncovering the buried self and using it to fight back the forces that seek to reduce you to a mindless consumer slave.

Individual expression is not a negative resistance, a denial of consumerism. It is above all a positive affirmation of your individual self, the unfolding of those unique qualities that make you who you are. Individual expression is not just a method of self-preservation, of preventing your self from being taken over and controlled by the multinationals. Individual expression is the means towards self-fulfillment, towards realizing your full potential as a human being. The best way to escape Consumer-world is by letting your true self shine through the darkness of consumerism, by affirming your independence as a human being, by reaching the pinnacle of your abilities. That is individual expression. It is about you, it is about ensuring that your actions represent your desires and your will, and not the desires imposed by consumerism, not the will of the multinationals.

Individual expression is the only path to global freedom. It counters the multinationals' vision of a global consumer peace with a myriad of different voices, with a multiplicity of individuals. Universal peace and solidarity may only be achieved by allowing each human spirit unbound freedom in developing its potential. Individual expression fragments the consumerist monolith sliver by sliver until nothing is left. Individual expression does not require alliances, does not require dogmatic adherence to any ideology, does not require that you follow anyone or anything. The only thing to be followed is your path to self-fulfillment.

Individual expression means accepting the fact that the sole thing you need to make this world a better place is to achieve your potential. In achieving your potential you will make your family better, you will best serve your friends, your creed, your race your nationality, the earth. Achieving your potential is truly the road towards earthly salvation for both your self and the earth. For all the evils and wrongs that arise on this earth stem from people seeking to effect changes in others rather than making the changes within themselves.

Individual expression is a holistic attempt to live your life outside the grasp of the multinationals. It forms a complete guide for evading their tentacles, for existing outside consumerist structures, or at least, for a minimal amount of interaction with consumerist structures. The manifestation of the individual self within daily life is reconfigured to reflect the needs of the self and not the needs of corporate entities. The goal is to live in a human society, not in a multinational one.

Individual expression is freedom

Although freedom from consumerism is the key towards self-development, the very process of extracting your self from consumerism's grasp is itself a means of self-development. Since resisting consumerism is self-expression and self-expression is inevitably self-development, in acquiring your freedom you simultaneously fulfil your individual potential. Indeed the process of self-fulfillment begins the moment you are aware of the consumer control exerted upon you. For you cannot break free until you know that you are imprisoned.

Freedom starts with assuming two basic responsibilities: 1.Think for yourself. 2. Care for yourself.

Using your brain to think for yourself means using your brain to think how you can best achieve your potential. That means thinking outside the consumerist box. That means looking at your naked self[3] in the mirror and asking what do I need to achieve my emotional, physical, intellectual and spiritual potential? Do I need consumerist offerings? No. So then what would truly make my mind, body and spirit happy? It seems a simple question. It is the hardest question of all to answer. It becomes much harder to answer in the face of consumer propaganda whose sole purpose is to create within you artificial needs and artificial happiness.

3. By naked I mean not only physically, but also intellectually, emotionally, spiritually and psychologically as well. See yourself as objectively as possible for who you really are.

You must care for yourself. This is not an encouragement towards narcissistic self-love. It means, at its most basic, not harming your self. And you harm your self, daily. You harm your self through the consumer food and drink which poisons your body. You harm your self through the purchase of needless consumer products and the consumer waste they generate, waste that pollutes your living space. You harm your self through the vehicles you drive, metal monsters that taint your air and your lungs. You harm your self through the chemicals used to clean your house and keep your lawn green. You harm your self through the television and the video games that you wallow in, meaningless consumer entertainment that corrodes your intellect and spirit. You do it. Willingly. Nobody is forcing you. True, you are brainwashed into enjoying these harmful activities. Yes, you can plead ignorance, but most of the time it is just a question of laziness or indifference. Whatever you plead, it doesn't matter. The ultimate responsibility rests with you. You are the one inflicting the harm. You are the only one who can stop it.

Re-discovering your needs

You must embark on a project of reclamation. The time has come to reclaim your original self, to discover your genuine needs. The ideal state you aim towards, whether you call it happiness or perhaps a more modest satisfaction, cannot be achieved through brand-name consumption. Mindless consumption is the world of illusion, of artificial joy, of an ersatz contentedness. If you are to take the right path, if you are to have even a chance of being truly satisfied, then you must discover your true needs. These are not served by the crowded highway of modern consumerism, but by the road less traveled. But what are your true needs?

Your body has needs. The need to drink, to eat, to breathe, to procreate are some of humankind's basic impulses. Your mind also has needs. You need pleasure, love, respect, joy, admiration and a host of other emotions. Through individual expression you use your abilities and talents to fulfil your needs. In the process you are helping the self towards achieving its potential, you are growing as a human being.

Discovering your true needs is a two-step process. First, you must free yourself from the world of artificial needs, the world of consumerism. Second, through contemplation and experience, you must discover and nurture your own true needs. Only then will you successfully revive the self that now lies buried under the consumer avalanche.

Escaping artificial needs

Through constant exposure to consumer advertising, your mind has been programmed to function is a passive/acceptance mode. In the passive/acceptance mode, you unquestioningly absorb consumer impulses and then choose among them. Choosing among consumer impulses means choosing among artificial needs. For the truth of the matter is that the self does not **need** any consumer products. Your need for consumer products has been implanted in your brain through relentless advertising. Freeing yourself from these artificial needs requires questioning your needs and determining which are real and which are not.

Switching your mind from a passive/accepting mode to an active/critical mode is the first step in discovering your true needs. In the active/critical mode, the mind sifts through the incoming consumer impulses and determines if they have any value for you. Being in the active/critical mode does not require enormous effort or deep philosophical thinking. Most of the time, being mentally active involves asking yourself earth-shattering questions such as: What sort of pants do I like? What sort of pants am I comfortable in? What sort of pants do I feel more attractive in?

Questions about your pants might sound ludicrous but they refer to a very important and profound concept, that of personal freedom. Listen to your own mind, follow your own tastes, stand by your aesthetic sensibilities. Do not allow consumer brands to define you. Define your self. This is the essence of freedom. This is what your forefathers struggled to achieve. Freedom. Those who fought to achieve and preserve your freedom were not fighting for the rights of corporations to run your life.

Multinationals and their consumer propaganda are similar to totalitarian regimes. However, there is a crucial difference between the two. If you raised your voice in opposition to a totalitarian regime it was very likely you would never be seen again. But you can escape the chains of brand-name slavery without fear of reprisal. All you need do is think for yourself.

Discovering the true self

Freeing yourself from consumerism's artificial needs is the easy part. Figuring out your actual needs is another matter. Discovering your genuine needs is not as easy as it may sound. If, like most people in the Western world, you have been raised on a daily stream of consumer propaganda, your real needs are underdeveloped or perhaps unknown to yourself.

How will you know what your true needs are? You will have stumbled onto a true need when you have discovered a way in which you want to express yourself. We all want to be attractive, but how do you want to be attractive? What makes you attractive in your own opinion? Similarly we all need to eat, but what do you want to eat? Do you really crave that Big Mac or is that craving the result of decades-long propaganda? True needs can only be generated from the self. Only by contemplating your being using your rational and imaginative faculties will you arrive at an answer. The question might be as simple as: "What is my ideal pair of pants?"

Chapter 3

Suburban Hell: The Consumer Landscape and the Death of the Community

This chapter explores the nature of modern suburban life, how it harms rather than helps the self towards fulfillment. The chapter ends with proposing methods for re-establishing control over your living space by choosing to live within a community.

How has consumerism come to rule your life? The first act of control has been determining the nature of your living space. Consumerism has decreed the ideal consumer shall live in endlessly replicating soulless suburbs, and so it has come to pass. The United States and Canada are the sole countries in the developed world with both rapidly growing populations and exceedingly large territories. The combination of these two features has led to the phenomenon of urban sprawl and, more importantly, the predominance of suburbia.

North Americans have migrated to the suburbs, leaving the city cores as hollowed-out ghettoes or skyscraper-filled financial centres. The suburban lifestyle, however, lacks an essential ingredient: a communal identity. Suburbia is an impersonal world, a world where communication can only be effected through technological methods, principally the car and the phone. Suburban sprawl has killed the idea and the reality of the community. Suburbia is a world of strangers.

The impossibility of establishing a sense of community in suburbia is revealed by the isolationist arrangement of the suburban landscape. Suburbia is designed to entrap the individual within Consumer-world by minimizing all human contact. This is achieved in a number of ways.

Separation of commercial and residential districts

In the suburban milieu, residential and commercial districts are carefully separated. On one hand you have large residential neighbourhoods, where all you will see are houses, houses and more houses. These neighbourhoods are usually served by a single, central commercial district, the shopping centre. Sometimes an endless array of strip malls lining a highway or a main street passes for a commercial district.

The schizophrenic separation of residential and commercial spaces has destroyed any chance of creating a community by denying you and your neighbours the place and opportunity to gather and socialize. The residential/commercial dichotomy ensures that you and your fellow suburban residents will remain strangers to each other.

Distance

There is a reason why they call it urban sprawl. The explosion of urban populations, the existence of the car, and the desire for single residential homes has resulted in urban centres with enormous geographical dimensions. Major population centres such as New York, LA and Toronto are ringed by gigantic suburbs that take half a day to cross in moderate traffic.

Regardless of the size of the city, the individual suburban community is itself dispersed. Whether at the level of a whole suburb or just for a particular subdivision, the focus is on providing space and privacy to the individual homeowner. This desire for space has made it impracticable if not impossible to have a community. The sheer spread of a suburban neighbourhood works against community interaction; a single suburban housing subdivision can cover the area of a small European city.

Lost in this vast suburban expanse, the car becomes your sole viable mode of transport. You forsake walking as utterly impractical. So does everyone else. In suburbia you will never meet your neighbours strolling down the street. You will not see kids playing around the neighbourhood. As a suburbanite, you can only entertain yourself within the confines of your property. When you return from work or shopping, and that garage door closes, it closes to the outside world, to a community life. You become a prisoner within your own house. Suburbia is an endless spread of single-family prisons.

Lack of amenities

Were you brave enough to walk around your neighbourhood, it would be a disappointing outing. First of all, a significant number of suburban communities lack a sidewalk. As such, you are likely to walk on the side of the road, a potentially dangerous proposition especially at night or in poor weather. The other option would be trespassing on other people's property, again not a particularly interesting or wise choice.

More importantly, even if you had a sidewalk to walk on, you would have nowhere to walk to. Not only are the nearest shops miles away, the closest recreation facilities are also beyond walking distance.[4] All of which brings me to the original point, namely that suburbia is BORING. Its landscape is lifeless, repetitive and forbidding to the would-be pedestrian. There is nothing to see and nothing to do. A walk around the suburban neighbourhood will get you little more than an unhealthy dose of the dust and fumes left by passing SUV's, and the puzzled stares of motorists wondering what happened to your car.

Migration and immigration

A constant parade of new faces and exploding populations ensure that suburbs lack the demographic stability to ever develop, much less maintain, a community identity.

Migration

As suburbs have no identity, there is no sense of place in the suburban world. Consequently, there is no attachment to the neighbourhood. You do not buy into a neighbourhood identity when you buy a house. Yes, you want a crime-free neighbourhood or perhaps one with cachet if you've got the money, but ultimately what you care about is having a place to live. This indifference towards your surroundings encourages migration and a relatively rapid turnover of residents. Suburban life is the revolving-door lifestyle.

Another reason for the constant flux in the composition of the suburban population is the ease of human movement. Today's world is one of unprecedented social and geographic mobility. Picking up and leaving is not the earth-shattering decision that it was in the old days, but often a requirement of the job. Work-based moves bring up a third reason for suburbia's demographic instability namely the hunger to experience Consumer-world. Constantly searching for a better consumer lifestyle, modern professionals are much more nomadic than their parents and grandparents, much more inclined to a change of address.

---

4. That is, if there are recreation facilities in the first place.

The lack of communal roots means that many people have no emotional attachment to the "family home". In the impersonal suburban milieu, the family home is a long-term hotel room, another consumer item that will be upgraded one day. It is unlikely to serve as the foundation of the family. It is even less likely that subsequent generations will remain there. The ancestral family home is a thing of the past.

Immigration

To this already unstable communal mix we must add a constant stream of immigrants. Immigrants of different cultures, races, religions and traditions will prefer to communicate and form communities within their own ethnic group. Some of these communities congregate to specific neighbourhoods, such as the Chinatowns and "Little Italies" found in most large North American cities. Other ethnic communities are dispersed throughout the city as a whole.

Suburbs usually include a variety of immigrants. These immigrants feel no particular attraction to the suburban neighbourhood, which they view as something new and foreign. Their sense of displacement makes it virtually impossible to integrate them within the suburban neighbourhood, even if there was a community within which they could integrate. Immigrants maintain a sense of communal identity by interacting with other members of their own ethnic group, to the detriment of the local neighbourhood.

Consequences of suburbia

What is the end result of the suburban living arrangement? Avoiding boredom has become the quintessential suburban predicament. Trapped in the tedious and lonely suburban lifestyle, you are forced to turn to the multinationals to make it bearable.

The multinationals have kindly offered you two avenues for escaping boredom:

Consumer technology

The first and easiest way to avoid boredom is through consumer technology. Consumer technology has become an indispensable part of your daily life. Plugged into one of the electronic apparatuses through which multinationals control you, you forget about the tedium of your existence. The earphones have become outgrowths of your ears, the television is always blaring, the video game console helps while away the hours before sleep finally comes. TV's, CD's, DVD's, MP3's, take your pick. Electronics spewing consumer entertainment preoccupy your leisure time. Machines ensure you stay closeted inside rather then enjoy the great outdoors. Machines ensure you never develop a communal identity but remain in a neighbourhood of strangers.

The mall

If the house gets to be too much, there's always the shopping centre. This is the other escape avenue that the multinationals have made available to you. But you will not develop a communal identity at the mall. Dominated by transnational franchises, malls are designed to promote a relationship between you and the multinational, not to develop social relationships or strengthen existing friendships. Malls want to create consumers, not form communities.

If everyone came to the mall for socializing purposes or with socializing purposes in mind, malls would quickly go under. These temples of consumerism are designed to prevent the creation of community spirit by focusing your attention exclusively on consumer goods. While you may consider shopping a social experience and go with family or friends, shopping centres are not designed to promote socializing behaviour. You do not go to shopping centres to meet people or see your neighbours. You do not go to the mall to play cards and drink coffee. No one does that. Yet that is what happens in living communities. That is what you don't have. That is what consumerism has stolen from you.

In order to ensure maximum consumption, malls are planned to function as impersonal creations. The mall experience is premised on a number of anti-communal tactics.

Crowds: Malls attract huge numbers of clients and employees in order to ensure that you are constantly in the company of strangers. In the mall, you can be in the middle of a crowd, and yet be all alone.

Variety: Malls seek to attract business from as far away as possible. By bringing in a wide variety of customers from as dispersed a geographical region as possible, you can be confident that the people you see on a visit to the mall will never be seen again.

Turnover: High turnover rates for clients, employees and even businesses prevent the formation of community. Malls operate to move people in and out as efficiently as possible. They are not places for gathering and socializing. You are encouraged to consume to your heart's content… and then leave. So much for communal identity.

Anti-communal policing: Mall management invariably frowns upon any attempt to use the mall to generate community identity, as forlorn suburban teenagers often try. Malls across America have taken measures to dispose of the "mall rat" problem, which is really the attempt of teenagers to form a community within the mall. It's not that malls don't want teenagers. It's just that they don't want teenagers to socialize in the mall. They want teenagers who consume.

For adults, who wish to socialize at the mall, slightly subtler tactics are employed.

Removal of socializing space: Benches and other places where you can sit down are greatly reduced in number and size. The idea is to deny people the place and opportunity to gather.

Time limits: If you have found a spot in the mall where you could socialize, your socializing opportunity will be curtailed by incoming clientele. Mall management will quickly and politely tell you to give your seat to a new client who is in search of seating.

Banning social activities: Mall management will generally forbid the use of mall premises for social activities such as cards or backgammon.

Saving the Self

The first step on your road towards freedom is establishing a foundation for the self. Escape the consumerized suburban life and find a place where the self can thrive. It is time to move from Consumer-world to a human society. How can this be done?

Find your community

Wherever you live, or wherever you wish to settle, make sure it's within a community. Is it a place where everyone knows each other? Are there kids playing outside? Do the locals have a favourite hangout? Can you walk down the street and meet people? Can you walk to the grocery store? Can you walk, period?

Communities have a heart and a personality. Communities are not simple geographical delineations, not just some builder's development. Laying down a few hundred houses on some farmland does not make a community. People do. You can belong to a rich and rewarding community living in a forlorn but closely-knit hamlet on the side of the mountain. On the other hand, you can be living in Manhattan and be the loneliest human being on earth.

If your neighbourhood is a genuine community, even if you have just moved in as a stranger, you will soon become part of it. On the other hand, if you have lived all of your life in a soulless suburb, one of the infamous "builder's communities", you will die as you live: among strangers.

If the place you live in is not a community, you have one of two choices:

Build a community

Work with those who live beside you to fashion a communal identity. Help organize community events such as a "bring your own food" barbeque, a community crime watch project, a joint garage sale or a kids' day. There are a myriad of activities that can be done with little preparation and are relatively inexpensive or even free, that will help kindle the community spirit. Give everyone a chance to participate and you will see the bonds forming, you will see the community born before your eyes. Make people want to stay in the neighbourhood. Break down the suburban walls of loneliness and estrangement.

Move

Find a true community and enjoy its benefits.

Find your place - the family home

A man's home is his castle, goes the old saying. Do you have your castle? Forget about the upwardly-mobile lifestyle, disregard the financial advantages of constantly buying and selling your homes to turn a quick profit. What your self needs, more than money or prestige, is stability. The self needs to know it has a stable home base, a comfy lair to call its own.

By setting roots within the family home, you are also helping to create a community within your neighbourhood. You are acting as a pillar upon which the communal spirit can be built. The stability you project can influence others to settle down here. It is upon familiar houses and familiar faces that the identity of the neighbourhood is formed.

The importance of the family home is validated and strengthened by ownership. Make sure you own the home. Be certain the bank cannot take it away from you. Purchasing the home should trump any other priorities, especially consumerist ones. While you might not have the money to buy your home outright, you can try to pay it off as soon as possible.

If you can, build your own house. While it would be ideal if you could physically construct your own dwelling, if not, make sure it is custom-built to your tastes. Determining the nature of your dwelling is a primary form of self-expression. Let the stamp of your individuality be firmly embossed on your dwelling. Project the self outwards through your abode.

If you buy, avoid purchasing a home in a subdivision. The monotonous, repetitive architecture of these consumer dwellings annihilates community identity. Buy into an older neighhbourhood, where each house tells a story. Make sure your house is unique.

Whether you buy or build, it is crucial that you personalize your home. Invest in the home to make it the best possible dwelling, namely the dwelling that most closely reflects the needs of your self. Working on the family home will keep consumer temptations at bay. In doing things like renovating and gardening, not only are you maintaining and improving your place, you are putting your personal imprint on the house. The house becomes an extension of the self, a manifestation of your identity. As such the house becomes a distinct, recognizable part of the community. Communities are not created by house numbers and street names. Communities are created by people's homes. When you know the houses by the names of the owners rather than by the house numbers then you are living within a community.

Find your neighbours

Once you find a place to settle down, do not remain a stranger. Knock on some doors, find out who lives beside you. Get to know your neighbours and if there are any you like, befriend them. At the very least, have cordial relationships with those who share your communal space.

Inserting yourself within the community will confer distinct advantages:

Borrowing things: You can borrow things from your neighbours, be it a wrench or a BBQ starter.

Favours: You can ask favours from your neighbours, like feeding the cat when you are gone.

Increased safety: If your neighbours know and respect you, they are likely to act if they see strange goings-on at your house while you are away.

Consumer freedom through social interaction: Best of all, if you share a drink with the neighbour you won't be wasting your time on consumerist pursuits.

Find your local businesses

In order to socialize, people need a common space. Most often, this space is provided by a local business, such as a café, grocery store or bar. Neighbourhood businesses serve as the hub of a community and facilitate the development of a communal identity. The local business is where you will meet the same faces every day, from the proprietor to your various neighbours. It is the place where the locals hang out.

True communities have local, family-owned businesses embedded within their residential spaces. If you can find the local bar or café, you will have found the heart of the community. This is where you can melt away the stress of day-to-day life without relying on the consumerist crutch. Besides serving better products than the multinationals, family-owned businesses serve something much more precious: companionship. Local family-owned businesses help both the mind and the body take a break from consumerism. If your community does not have a local hangout, perhaps it is time to consider moving to a place that does.

Chapter 4

Freeing Your Body: Breaking Away From Consumer Food[5]

Controlling your food means controlling your body. This chapter explains how you have lost control over your food intake and what steps you should take to re-establish it.

Consumer food is one of the methods through which the global consumer, that docile, mindless creature, is created. The multinationals use consumer food to make you fat. Why do they want you to be fat? A good consumer is a fat consumer. Fat tames your body by depriving it of energy and stamina, by transforming you into a near motionless pachyderm, barely able to shift your bulk from the car to the restaurant. Fat also tames your mind by damaging your self-esteem and encouraging indolence. In fattening you like a pig, multinationals keep you in a state of easy manipulation.

The multinationals will protest vehemently that it is ridiculous to accuse them of promoting obesity. In a way, it is true. Consumer food producers do not specifically set out with this goal in mind any more that the tobacco industry propagates lung cancer or emphysema. But, just like the tobacco industry, the consumer food multinationals know full well the consequences of their products. And, unlike the tobacco industry, which gains little profit from lung cancer, the consumer food industry directly profits from fatness: fat people tend to consume increasing amounts of the products that made them fat in the first place.

---

5. Consumer food is food produced and marketed by the multinationals. It can be roughly broken down into two categories: 1. Fast food, such as burgers and pizza, served at multinational franchises such as McDonald's. 2. Junk food, served in convenience stores often owned by multinationals. Junk food includes candy bars, chips and various chemical concoctions such as licorice.

How do the Multinationals Succeed in Addicting you to Consumer Food?

Indirect advertising

The secret of the multinationals' success lies in the nature of their advertising. The multinationals have perfected the tactic of *indirect advertising*. Indirect advertising does not focus on praising the product, but rather on creating an artificial need for the product within you. The artificial need for consumer food products has nothing to do with the products themselves. Consumer food multinationals know the poor quality of their products and, as such, seek to distract your attention from the products themselves. The artificial need for the multinational's product arises from things that have nothing to do with the quality of the food.

The McDonald's example

One of the primary reasons for McDonald's success is its undisputed status among kids.[6] But how does it attract the kids? If you think it's the "great food", think again. McDonald's attracts kids with the games and prizes on offer. It is no coincidence that McDonald's, the world's most successful and well-known restaurateur, is the sole restaurant chain with a kids' Playland. McDonald's strategy is to get its customers as early as possible and to keep them for life. They do that with toys, games and giveaways. Food has absolutely nothing to do with it.

Kids are not the only ones attracted by side issues when it comes to consumer food, and McDonald's in particular. For adults, McDonald's propaganda[7] advertises four basic things, none of which have anything to do with the quality of the food:

Convenience: With over 30,000 outlets, worldwide, you will be hard-pressed to find a place without a McDonald's. Wherever you live, it's a pretty safe bet that the nearest McDonald's is just around the corner.

Speed: "Thirty seconds or its free", says the billboard nearest my house. You do not have to wait to get your order filled as at a restaurant. McDonald's does not subscribe to the saying, "all good things take time".

---

6. You can never start the brainwashing too early when it comes to consumer food. Unlike other addictions such as alcohol or nicotine there are no legal age limits to prevent multinationals from indoctrinating you while you're still in the cradle.
7. Lately, McDonald's seems to associate itself with a permanent state of happiness – which is, not coincidentally, a feature shared by cults and psychedelic drugs – through the insidious creation of the McHappy meals.

In serving you quickly, McDonald's encourages you to treat the food as something to be consumed with similar alacrity. The idea is if you eat something fast enough, preferably some take-out on the go, you won't really have time to consider the taste, but will be satisfied that your stomach is full.

Value: You go to McDonald's because they promise to give you the greatest amount of food for the least amount of money. Their infamous Supersize meals have single-handedly created an obesity epidemic. Even if McDonald's will phase out Supersizes, the fact remains that your stomach, accustomed to large portions, will still benefit from the ridiculously small prices of McDonald's menu items, allowing you to binge eat to your heart's content.

Comfort: Indirect advertising also transforms the consumer food outlet into something that belongs to you. Your attraction to McDonald's is partly underpinned by its comforting familiarity, a familiarity purchased through multi-billion dollar advertising campaigns. McDonald's has succeeded in penetrating your life and becoming an indispensable part of it. It has acquired the status of your second kitchen, your other dining room. You feel at home there.

One reason you do not eat consumer food is for the culinary experience. I do not think that in the history of McDonald's, two people have had a conversation like:

Jane: Oh have you heard about the new McDonald's restaurant?

Jerry: No, how is it?

Jane: You've just got to try it. They have these exquisite Big Macs you just can't forget.

Saving the Self

Know what you are eating

The key to the success of the multinationals is that you must never think about consumer food as food. As indirect advertising floods your mind, you fail to register the blandness of consumer food, its chemical sweetness, its artificial flavors and the terrible damage they do to your body. The time has come to shut the propaganda floodgates. It's time to care for your self. Examine carefully what you are putting into your body. You owe it to your self to know what you are eating.

Food has two qualities you must keep in mind when planning your next meal:

Food is intimate

Food is the most intimate of all things. It is the only thing you ingest into your body. It travels through the whole of your body and engages many of your organs, from the stomach to the digestive tract. Considered in the light of its intimacy a lackadaisical attitude towards food is incomprehensible. Think about this for a moment.

You believe in the autonomy of your body. You believe in a personal space around your body that you do not want to be invaded by others. You do not want strangers or even co-workers to invade that personal space. It makes you feel uncomfortable, perhaps even frightens you and yet you will allow a soulless corporation to pour its poisons down your throat, to enter your body with its products and mercilessly damage your organs. How can you explain that? How can you justify granting a multinational access to the deepest recesses of your body when you will not allow a human being to touch you? There is no explanation. It is only a matter of realizing how you have surrendered your body to the multinationals. This realization is key, for this is the first step in your journey towards reclaiming your body, and freeing it from the perils of consumer food.

The intimacy of food means that only food of the finest quality will be accorded the honour of entering your body. You value your body too much to allow anything else to disturb its intimacy. It must be awarded the highest respect, the highest reverence possible, through the daily ceremony of the three meals.

The intimacy of food means that controlling what you ingest is one of the self's greatest acts of freedom. If you do not have control over what you put into your body, if you consume whatever the multinationals tell you, not only have you failed to respect your own body, you also have failed to respect your self. Respect the body and unleash the self. Take responsibility for your food choices. Do not allow anyone else to determine what you put into your body.

Food keeps you alive

It is not enough to control your food choices. You must know the nutritional value of the food that you eat. Educating yourself on what your body needs to keep you alive and healthy is simply a matter of life and death. This education has two aspects:

Basic components: These are the building blocks of your life. You must know what your body's daily requirements are in terms of calories, proteins, dietary fiber, fats, minerals and vitamins. These needs are unique to you depending on your age, gender, ethnicity, lifestyle and physical condition.

The right foods: Once you know what your body needs in terms of basic components, you must learn the foods that provide these basic necessities. The goal is to have the necessary information to determine your own diet, rather than have some corporation make that determination for you. Knowing the right foods means discovering different menu choices or even developing new dishes yourself. Not only will your health and well-being see a marked improvement when your diet is oriented towards your needs, but you are establishing control over your most basic responsibility, keeping yourself alive.

Adopt the right mentality

Consumer food kills

You know smoking kills. But do you know consumer food kills as well? If not, it's time to acknowledge the fact that consumer food can hurt you in a whole lot of ways. Consumer food kills you with the bad cholesterol that is slowly blocking your arteries. Consumer food is responsible for the dangerously high levels of salt and carbohydrates in your diet. Gastrointestinal problems have reached endemic proportions as a result of this. Enormous invisible damage is being done to your internal organs every time you eat at McDonald's, damage that you can't see in the mirror.

Most of all, consumer food kills you with the damage you can see, namely fat. Being overweight puts you at a higher risk for a number of afflictions such as diabetes, hypertension and various types of cancer. Do you think it is a coincidence that heart disease is America's number one killer? Or that obesity-related diabetes is an epidemic waiting to happen? Have you wrapped your mind around the fact that obesity is an even bigger killer than tobacco? If you think a few extra pounds are just a comfy addition to the old belly, you're missing the point. Fat is not about how you look. Fat is not about being happy with your body. Fat is about life and death.

Once you recognize consumer food for what it really is - a health hazard - deal with it in the same way you would deal with smoking: try to quit. It won't be easy. You're addicted. We all are. But the key is to realize that it's an addiction and to treat it like an addiction. Acknowledge yourself an addict and start on the road to recovery. For one common feature of all addicts, regardless of the nature and degree of their dependency, is the desire to quit. Once you acknowledge your addiction you have just taken the first step towards recovery.

Since it is an addiction, you probably don't have the willpower to quit cold turkey. The consumer food industry is working very hard to make sure you remain addicted to their products. It is hard to resist the convenience and propaganda of the consumer food industry. Finally, there's something else that makes kicking the consumer food habit much harder than quitting tobacco: you can live without smokes, but you need to eat.

Recondition your mind

The solution to quitting lies in developing the right mental approach. Here are a number of mental strategies for beating the fast food addiction:

Consumer food as tobacco

The best way to resist the multinationals is by treating consumer food like tobacco. Every cigarette is seven minutes off your life. So is every Big Mac. Keep that firmly in your mind the next time you've got the munchies and the Golden Arches are beckoning.

See the enemy

View fast food as the enemy of your body, as an intruder that has attacked your mind. Be angry, be combative, be your own drill sergeant. It's a war out there!

Consumer food as sickness

Look at consumer food and bring to mind not the associations of pleasure that consumerism has programmed within you, but the medical associations of high cholesterol, early-onset diabetes, cancer-causing chemicals and stroke. One particularly effective method of doing this is by renaming your favourite consumer foods after the diseases they bring. Rename the Big Mac the Colon Cancer, and it will not seem as tempting.

Consumer food as a social faux-pas

Another weapon for winning the consumer food wars rests in social censure. Smoking has become a faux-pas in many social circles. Lighting up can turn off many people for a number of reasons that go beyond health issues. Smoking is just not as socially acceptable as it once was. It is time to do the same with consumer food. I'm not asking you to change other people's minds. It is just a matter of your own perception. By viewing consumer food as socially unacceptable you can pass on invitations to the local Burger King. In fact, you are more likely to develop an aversion towards consumer food.

The temptation will also subside if you treat your friends' consumption of such foods as a social negative and tell them so. Non-smokers make their dislike for cigarettes known. Why not do the same for consumer food? Make people uncomfortable with eating or even mentioning consumer food in your presence, and they won't try to tempt you with it again.

Find the alternative

Good food is healthy food

Getting rid of consumer food is the easy part. Staying off consumer food on a long-term basis requires finding an alternative. Otherwise, you'll go back to the same old thing.

What sort of food do you need to keep your self in tip-top shape? First, you need food that will make your body feel better. Few people in North America do not know that fruits, vegetables and grains help their bodies. The problem is that your mind also desires pleasant sensations. Your mind also wants to enjoy the food that you eat: the sort of enjoyment that comes from pizza and donuts. As such, most people prefer to eat consumer food, because they view the alternative as "health foods". Consumer food might be boring and bland, but health food is a term synonymous with tasteless vegetarian offerings more fit for cattle. The choice does not lie between Big Macs and Tofu burgers. There is another way. It's called **holistic food.**

Holistic food satisfies the needs of mind and body. Simply put, holistic food tastes good and fulfills your nutritional requirements.

It is impossible for me to define holistic food, because the person who makes that decision is you. Since one of the qualities of holistic food is pleasant taste, you are the one who decides what specific recipes you like, the foods and drinks that you prefer. I cannot tell you that Chinese cuisine is good, or even that a specific Chinese dish is good, because while the stuff might be good for your body, you might not like the taste. So then it's not holistic food for you, although it might be holistic food for others.

Although your taste buds might be the sole arbiter of good taste, holistic foods share a universal basis in terms of fulfilling your nutritional requirements. Only certain types of foods can help your body. As such, all holistic foods possess the following features:

Quality ingredients: Without quality ingredients there can be no holistic food. What is quality? Quality means freshness, quality means organic produce, quality means processed without chemicals or preservatives, quality means natural.

Good preparation: The food must be prepared well. This involves two aspects: Good preparation means food fresh from the oven, barbeque, rotisserie, or stovetop. That means no irradiation, no prepackaged, frozen, or microwaved food, and certainly nothing sitting under a heat lamp for hours on end. Good preparation also means food prepared in a hygienic environment. The tools used to prepare the food and the actual ingredients used should be up to the highest standards in terms of sanitary conditions.

Good presentation: The food needs to look appealing in order to excite your senses. If it looks like crap, you'll tend to think that it tastes like that as well.

Conclusion:

How these three features combine to satisfy your self is what makes you an individual. For each of you, the chemistry will be different in terms of taste, texture, arrangement, and colour. As long as the underlying basis of physical satisfaction is there, you needn't worry.

The French Cuisine example

Holistic foods are not deprived of any of the ingredients that you like. It's just that the quality of the food will not harm you. French cuisine, widely considered to be among the best in the world, is full of butter, cheeses, pates, pork, and fats of every kind. French desserts are so rich they can make you sick. Yet the French are healthier than North Americans. Obesity, a notorious killer in North America, is relatively rare in France.

Not only are they thinner, but the French also live longer. French women are among the world's longest-lived. How can their singular longevity be explained considering the high amounts of fats and carbohydrates in their diets?

There are two key ingredients to the Gallic recipe for a long life:

Quality fat

Although French cuisine uses numerous high-calorie ingredients, they are also quality ingredients. The French use fresh butter for cooking rather than the three-day old, tar-like oil that sits in the fryers of most fast food chains. French pates and cheeses are natural and prepared using traditional methods that stretch back for centuries. Consumer foods such as Kraft processed cheese or the infamous Cheez Whiz are the products of chemical experiments rather than of nature's bounty.

Your body needs fat. The question is whether it gets the right sort of fat. French cuisine has what doctors term good fat, while consumer food gives you only the artery-hardening, heart-attack-causing bad fat. Nor it is only the French who benefit from a fat-laden cuisine. Many European and Asian cuisines contain significant amounts of fat; yet if you look at Europeans and Asians, they are much slimmer than their North American counterparts.[8]

Alcohol

The second ingredient of the Gallic recipe for healthy living is moderate alcohol consumption. French meals are not complete without an accompanying bottle of wine. While consumer food addicts begin and finish their meals with soft drinks, French cuisine lovers start with *aperitifs*, down a couple of glasses of red wine and perhaps even finish off with a *digestif*. One thing is for sure. The wine helps dilute the fat they have just eaten. It cleanses their vessels and prevents atherosclerosis. What do consumer drinks such as Coca-Cola or Pepsi do for you? The gas will make you belch, the sugar will ruin your teeth and the caffeine will keep you awake at night.

If the French splurge on fat-filled diets, down it with gallons of booze, and outlive their fellow humans by a decade, then surely they must be doing something right. That "something" is catering to both the needs of the mind and the body. That something is eating holistic foods. It is what you need to do. Find out what caters to your body and your mind, whether in terms of food or anything else in your life. Always remember that your needs are not only the product of your pleasure but also of the body's desires for good maintenance. Ultimately, your choice is not

---

8. Although obesity rates are rising in European and Asian countries, the culprit, once again, is consumer food rather than traditional ethnic cuisines. Brainwashed by the multinationals, the planet's youth has embraced consumer food, unwittingly poisoning themselves with its terrible offerings.

between fatty and healthy foods. Your choice is between holistic food and consumer food.

The necessity of cooking

The revolution begins in the kitchen. Cooking is one of the most basic acts of independence. It is also one of the most neglected. Not only does most of the modern world rarely cook, an increasing number does not know HOW to cook. And don't complain that you don't have the time! Such arguments are easily dismissed. A trip to the restaurant can occupy more time than cooking and eating a simpler, cheaper and healthier meal. Moreover, any time you save by not cooking is often wasted on consumerist leisure activities such as watching television, which only cooks your brain into a stinking mess.

Why should you cook?

Cooking is essential for a number of reasons:

Holistic food: The best way to ensure you have holistic food every night is by making it yourself.

Family unity: From ancient times, when families gathered around the cooking fire, cooking has been a unifying force. A family working together in preparing the evening meal is a family communicating directly with each other and not through the hypnotic common medium of the television. In today's hectic lifestyle, cooking provides the kitchen equivalent of a family outing. What better opportunity to bond, what better way to show each member of the family how important their contribution is to the household than through the basic act of preparing a meal? A busy kitchen is often the sign of a cheerful and cohesive family.

Variety: The diets of North American are not only extremely poor, but for a large segment of the population, they are also mind-numbingly dull. Too often, your eating experiences are limited to fast-food outlets and convenience store junk food. Cooking provides you with the opportunity to choose from an almost infinite array of recipes. It allows you to sample the tastes of many regions, cultures and nations in the comfort of your own home. When you are cooking your meal, every night can be a different culinary experience, every evening can provide gastronomic delights.

A large variety of foods is recommended as part of a healthy diet. Every fruit, vegetable, cereal, meat, and dairy product contains its own mix of needed vitamins, minerals, fats and fibers. The more variety you have, the more likely you are to meet all of your body's needs. You can achieve optimum variety when you decide what to eat for your meal.

Quantity control: Multinationals thrive by encouraging the overconsumption of their food. They flourish as you eat yourself to death. And eat yourself to death you will as long as they decide the size of your meals. Through cooking, you are re-establishing at least a partial control over your body's food intake. Rather than being forced to choose among the excessive-sized offerings of the consumerist giants you alone decide the quantity of food you put into your body. No more Supersize meals designed to tempt you into stuffing yourself by offering better "value" for the dollar. No more doggy bags to take home and eat as a late night snack.[9] No more pressure to clean your plate so that you don't waste your money. You control the portions.

Quality control: Consumer food is mostly a chemical experiment and has little to do with food. Who knows what they put in it? Who knows who made it? Can you vouch for the quality of the ingredients? Rest assured that the multinational is primarily interested in the bottom line and will purchase the cheapest supplies available in order to prepare its products. When you do the cooking, you can pick the best and freshest ingredients available. Your body and your mind deserve the best and it is up to you to ensure that's exactly what they will get.

Cooking also ensures that the food is stored and prepared in hygienic conditions. Did the McDonald's employee really wash his hands? How clean is the kitchen area? How is the meat stored? Are they using ingredients past their expiry date? Every time you have consumer food, you roll the dice. Every time you cook at home you know exactly what you are getting.

Economics: You can cook a healthy meal for a family of four for less than the price of four McHappy meals. How can you go wrong with that?

You owe it to your children: By cooking, and by teaching your children how to cook, you are preventing them from becoming McDonald's addicts, faithfully flocking to that temple of culinary crap for their daily cholesterol overdose, complete with a worthless gewgaw. Soaring childhood obesity rates show that parents have abnegated the responsibility of feeding their children and have entrusted the multinationals with doing the job. The consequence is unhealthy children who grow up into unhealthy

---

9. Nothing is more depressing than seeing the steady stream of patrons exiting from mall eateries carrying a doggy bag. The doggy bag is a symbol of consumer excess, of prizing quantity above quality and of the ideology/scripture of waste preached by the consumerist globalizers.

adults, many of whom will be prematurely killed by a lifetime of consumer foods. Through home cooking you can ensure your kids will avoid that terrible fate.

Cooking teaches children to assume control over their own bodies and choose what they put into their bodies. It is a lesson in self-sufficiency, but also a lesson in freedom, for cooking acts as a bulwark against the vapid charms of the consumer food industry.

Creativity: Cooking is a creation. It is a combination of craft and artistry. The simple act of preparing a meal not only saves you from eating consumer food; not only takes you away from consumer entertainment, but it gives you the chance to employ your creative abilities. Cooking is a valid method of self-fulfillment.

Controlling your ingredients

Buy directly from the farmers

Most urban centers have open door markets where local farmers sell their products. You can buy fruits and vegetables from them during the summer and fall months when their produce is available.

If there are no markets within the city, you can be sure there are nearby farmers who have produce to sell. Drive to the city outskirts and you are sure to find local farmers who sell their bounty directly to the customer.

Advantages of buying directly from the farmer

Freshness: Local farmers sell fresh produce. Multinationals offer products that are picked unripe, frozen and trucked in from thousands of miles away.

Information: The farmer is best positioned to provide you with the necessary information to help you decide whether a particular produce is something you want to put into your body. There is an infinitely greater potential for assessing the value of your produce if you are face to face with the man or woman who grew them. Only the farmer can confidently discuss the produce in terms of the agricultural methods used in raising the produce (i.e. did they use chemical fertilizers, or GM seeds?), how the produce should be consumed (i.e. are they best boiled rather than fried?) and what recipes the produce is best suited for (i.e. stews, side dishes or soups?).

Value: Local farmers tend to sell cheaper than any supermarket, even more so if you buy directly from their farm. Farmers are anxious to unload their produce before it rots in the field.

Flexibility: Farmers are ready to accommodate you in a number of ways including:

Giving you what you want: In supermarkets you must buy prepackaged produce or produce by the pound. Farmers will sell it to you the way you want it, whether it's by the case, or as a mix of produce, if that will help the transaction go through.

Business hours: Farmers will often have flexible hours in terms of dealing with clients.

Deal-making: You can haggle on price with farmers, especially if you seek to buy in greater quantities. Try to do that with the local supermarket.

Buy organic

Not only are organic farmers usually individual, human farmers rather than multinational corporations, but their produce is also beneficial to the environment. More importantly, these products are beneficial to you, being free of nasty chemicals and genetic modification.[10]

Buy from independent, specialty stores

If you cannot purchase directly from the farmer, you have to decide from whom you will purchase your cooking ingredients. Here again is your opportunity to help another class of threatened small businessman, namely the small grocers. I am referring to the greengrocers, the bakers, the butchers, the fishmongers and the specialty food stores that offer specific ethnic products.

Why should you help the small businessman? Because it's your self that reaps the benefits. Although large grocery outlets conveniently combine all of the small grocers' produce under one roof, small grocers compensate with better prices, a larger selection and superior quality. Furthermore, many of these small establishments are personally run and supervised by their owners. That means the person who serves you has a personal interest in your satisfaction. That means the person who serves you is most knowledgeable about the produce on sale. In any case, the small business owner is better placed to answer your questions than some 19-year-old running the deli counter at your local consumer supermarket.

10. On the importance of organic products to the self, please see the Environment Chapter.

Grow your own

Most municipal bylaws prevent the raising of domestic animals in urban areas. However, there are few bans on establishing your own vegetable garden in a corner of your backyard. Growing your food is the optimal method of controlling what you eat. A well-tended organic vegetable garden goes a long way towards improving the quality of your food.

Not everyone possesses the necessary prerequisites for growing their own food. What if you don't have the land? What if you don't have the time? What if you don't have the knowledge? What if you don't have a green thumb? Here are three solutions:

1. Subcontract: Many chefs at top-notch restaurants have custom vegetable gardens to supply them with the best produce. You deserve the same.

   Find a farmer who will grow your vegetables and provide your dairy and meat products according to your specifications (i.e. grain-fed, hormone-free poultry, organic heirloom tomatoes, etc). This is not as difficult as it sounds, and everyone wins. Hard-pressed farmers are eager to make a bit of cash on the side and you get your own personal, custom-ordered food supply.
2. Rent some farmland. If you have the time and the inclination rent some nearby land from a farmer and work it yourself to grow fruits, vegetables, even raise animals; whatever your heart desires. Consider it your own little plot of paradise.
3. Purchase some land. Buy your own hobby farm, or your own garden plot. You don't need a lot to satisfy the needs of yourself and your family. You might even end up making some money by selling the extra produce on the market.

The communal option

If you can't subcontract, rent or buy land by yourself, do it with others. Think communally. Pool your money and talents with a few friends and share the bounty.

Pick your own

As long as you live near nature, you can profit from its bounty. Learn what edible wild fruits, nuts and plants grow in your area and then take the time to explore, discover and pick nature's bounty.

Before you turn your nose up at the idea that you would want to eat anything growing wild in the fields, consider Jean Georges. One of the most expensive restaurants in New York, it offers common weeds such as nettles and chickweed on the menu. Why pay top dollar at some fancy restaurant for things you can find in almost every green field? Nature is free. Whether it's wild blueberries or chickweeds, pick your own ingredients and then treat your self to a Jean Georges' meal at a McDonald's price.

If you absolutely can't cook, choose your restaurant wisely

What of the times when you just do not have the time or opportunity to cook? You are tired, you are sick, you are overwhelmed by work, or you are travelling. What then?

Pick restaurants owned by people, not corporations: If you must choose the restaurant option, avoid consumer food outlets. Why should you eat pizza at Pizza Hut or Domino's when you can have it at a family-owned pizzeria? Do you really feel the need to add those extra dollars to finance their global ambitions? At the independently-owned pizzeria you are rewarding a family that works hard every day to maintain their heads above water in such a competitive business. By rewarding their efforts you will be rewarded with good food and a good time.

Ensure the restaurant you pick serves holistic foods: Ask about the ingredients, what they use and how they use it. Are these the sorts of foods that cater to both your taste buds and your body's needs?

Find out who's doing the cooking: Don't be afraid to poke your head in the kitchen. Talk to the chef. Is that a person you would trust to care for your body?

Never sit down and mindlessly stuff yourself with what they put on your plate. Inquire, demand, observe and test. Remember, as soon as you enter a restaurant you are in a situation of dependency where you have given your trust to others. Make sure that trust is well-deserved.

Chapter 5

Overcoming Obesity: The Problem with Being Overweight.

Although you might successfully break away from consumer food, perhaps consumer food has left you with a parting gift: extra pounds. If you are one of those persons hauling around the consumer food bounty, this chapter is for you.

Deceptions of the consumer food multinationals

The consumer food industry has three principal aims.

The first aim is to prevent any characterization of its products as detrimental to health. Consumer food giants are desperately seeking to recast their foods as parts of a healthy diet. KFC made a recent attempt to argue that its fried chicken was good for you. It would be laughable if not for the tragic fact that many people do buy into the advertising.

The second aim of the consumer food industry is to prevent any link between its products and obesity. Multinationals try to pin the blame on other factors for obesity, such as sedentary lifestyles. While it is true that lack of exercise is a factor in the obesity epidemic, the principal culprit remains consumer food.

The third aim of the consumer industry is to prevent obesity from being treated as a health issue. Multinationals have dedicated enormous effort to shaping your views on obesity. Since they want to create a consumer universe full of fat people, they seek to control your attitude towards being fat.

In order to successfully resist their attempts at manipulating you, there are two things you need to know about being fat: First, it's about *what* you eat not *how much* you eat. I've already discussed this issue in terms of holistic food. Second, it's a *health* issue, not an *esthetics* issue. This chapter deals with the health versus esthetics distinction.

By making obesity a question of esthetics, multinationals take advantage of those angst-ridden, overweight people suffering from low self-esteem due to their bloated bodies. The frustration, even rage, felt by the grossly overweight has become another weapon in the multinationals' consumerist arsenal. But why are obese people enraged? It is the advertising of the multinationals that lies at the source of the problem.

Taunted by thinness

The ever-increasing gap between the thin yet perfectly shaped models advertising consumer products and the pudgy reality of modern society has created a schizophrenic divide in the social psyche. On the one hand there is you, the individual, on the other hand, embodiments of human perfection. The message is you can only be beautiful if you look like the consumer models. There is no middle ground, such as being a healthy individual. There is only you, the failure, and them, the successes. This consumer-induced dichotomy makes your body feel like a trap and promotes self-loathing.

In telling you that you cannot be fat and beautiful consumer advertising has made you angry, and rightly so. As such, your natural reaction is to redefine "beauty" to include being overweight. Unfortunately, this backlash against idealized consumer images has been exploited by the consumer food industry to the hilt.

Multinationals have profited from and manipulated the backlash to their own advertising. They have enthusiastically supported your misguided attempts to embrace obesity, to accept the overweight body, even to rejoice in it, as a counter to the multinationals' definition of beauty. Multinationals have jumped on the bandwagon leading the charge against the very thinness their ads promote. Fat is good, they trumpet! Fat is beautiful! Fat is indeed beautiful for the multinationals, their bottom lines and above all, their consumerist vision. But is fat beautiful for you?

If you see excess weight as a badge of resistance against the advertising industry and patronizing images of femininity, you are missing the fundamental point. Fat is a danger to your health. Fat should not be celebrated. Celebrating your excess weight is like a smoker celebrating a two-pack a day habit.

In thinking obesity is acceptable you are not only lining the pockets of corporate giants but also promoting your own illness. Remove fat and body image from the battlefields of sexual equality and rebellion against "mainstream" culture. Damaging your health is not the way to promote individual expression, especially if in resisting one aspect of consumerism (the various fashion magazines and the brand name advertisers), you are helping another (the consumer food industry).

Saving the Self

Losing weight is all about your health

It is essential to separate the polemic of the ideal body image from the health question of weight. If you are a feminist or a social activist, by all means criticize the means through which multinationals construct the feminine model via advertising, but please leave the weight issue out of the debate. If you hold the obsession with thinness responsible for the explosion of eating disorders in young girls, mention in the same breath that the reverse of the coin, obesity, is just as dangerous to women's health and infinitely more widespread.

Consider your weight exclusively in terms of your health. If you are one of those people torn between the unreachable idealized images paraded in advertisements and your own excess weight, remember one thing: you don't need to look like a model to be healthy. Your weight goal is to be within the range suggested by medical literature. You can ask your doctor what that range is. That is where you need to be.

By separating the esthetics from the health issue I am not trying to deny there are no esthetic consequences to being fat. There are esthetic consequences to smoking, such as yellow teeth and fingers, ashtray breath and even smoker's cough. The difference is that people wish to quit smoking primarily because they are aware of its deadly effects. When it comes to losing weight, the primary reason is body image.

Losing weight and shedding the consumer food habit must be founded on the dangers it poses to your health and not on any esthetic concerns. The message is lose weight to be healthier, not to look better. If you think losing weight makes you look better, use that as a secondary motivation. Your priority must always be your health.

By treating obesity as a health problem, you can never be comfortable with being overweight. Ergo you can never be comfortable with eating consumer food. Being comfortable with excess weight is what the consumerist food industry desires. They want every North American, and indeed every human being, since their reach is now global, to be a jolly fat person. If you are comfortable with being fat, then you are unlikely to take any action to reduce or change your poor eating habits. You are thus unlikely to trouble the bottom lines of the consumer food multinationals.

Revolving-door diets: the perils of weight-loss programs

Even if you decide you are not comfortable with being overweight, and many of us are not, the consumer food industry has a backup plan. They have an ally of sorts — a most unexpected one. It is the weight-loss industry.

The two industries operate in what biologists would refer to as a symbiotic relationship. Symbiosis is a term applied to two or more different organisms that are in a relationship where each benefits from the other. So it is between these two industries. Weight Watchers needs McDonald's just as much as McDonald's needs Weight Watchers.

The weight-loss industry has a deep dark secret they don't want anyone to know: weight-loss programs are designed to help you lose weight temporarily. I emphasize **temporarily.** The weight-loss industry wants, needs and depends on repeat clients. Even if you don't come back to the same weight-loss program, as long as you come back to the weight-loss industry as a whole, they're happy. They will help you take off the weight, knowing that over 90 per cent of you will put it back on. How do they know you will put it back on? They rely on their good friends in the consumer food industry to get you back up to an unhealthy weight.

The weight-loss industry needs consumer food. Think about it. If everybody were a normal weight, then the whole industry would just ... disappear. And so, most weight-loss programs treat the symptoms of obesity and not its root causes. In other words, they deal with removing excess weight, and not with the reason you became overweight in the first place. You can lose all the pounds you want, but until you make a permanent diet and lifestyle change, the pounds will just keep coming back.

When you embark on a weight-loss program, whether it's just a special diet or a combination of pills and dieting, your first question should be: how does this diet help me maintain my desired weight for the rest of my life? The answer, invariably, is not a bit. Which is exactly how the weight-loss industry wants it to be.

This does not mean you should never enrol in a weight-loss program or go on a diet. It just means that you'd better choose the right program. The right program is the one designed to make you a healthy person for the rest of your life. How will you know what that program is?

Saving the Self

Salvation starts with the family doctor

First of all, forget the advertising. The right program is a program accepted and promoted by health professionals. If you really want to deal with your weight problem, start by consulting your family doctor. There are a number of advantages to seeing your family doctor before you embark on a weigh-loss program:

Knowledge: Medical professionals have a deeper understanding of the medical causes of obesity. They are familiar with the psychological and neurological underpinnings of food cravings and with the whole host of factors underlying your excess weight. Consequently they are eminently more capable to deal with your weight-loss problem than some fad diet.

Perspective: Due to their medical perspective, the physician does not view obesity as shedding a few pounds to fit into a bathing suit. The doctor treats your weight problem as an illness, as a danger to your health. Physicians know it's not about pills or diets, which treat only the symptom (excess weight), and not the cause (why you gained the excess weight in the first place). Physicians will thus caution you against weight loss programs and crash diets that stress the body's immune system and end up causing more damage than good. A doctor's main focus will be to wean you off your consumer food addiction, the root cause of your weight problem.

Trust: A doctor is bound by the Hippocratic Oath and strict professional codes to help you rather than keep you as a return customer. Moreover, from your perspective, you are likely to have established a relationship with your doctor, having entrusted him/her with your health.

No financial interest: A further reason why doctors are unlikely to treat you as a return customer is they do not have the same financial interests as weight loss clinics. Businesses depend on a steady stream of clients to be profitable. Few doctors are likely to engage in such callous and reckless behaviour for the sake of a few extra bucks. Multinationals such as Weight Watchers will not be quite as scrupulous about their practices.

Physicians want to make you a healthy person: Becoming a healthy person is not about some fad diet, it's about living a healthy life. You should only have to lose weight once. That requires a doctor who will deal with your weight problem organically and monitor your weight just as he or she monitors your blood pressure and heart rate. A doctor will give you the tools necessary to maintain a healthy weight for the rest of your life. Physicians will help you towards a healthier and lighter self through a combination of healthy diet, exercise, and psychological fortitude. You trust your doctor with caring for all of your other ailments. Why should your weight be an exception?

Personal attention: There are two aspects of personal attention:

a) Your weight problem, your weight solution. Getting your diet tips from books can be dangerous. Their suggestions apply generally, and they might not be right for you. You might have special requirements that no diet book can take into account and deal with, such as lactose-intolerance or diabetes. Even if following the prescribed diet is not dangerous, you might be a vegetarian who does not care for diets high in animal protein such as Atkins. Only the family doctor, fully aware of your medial conditions and personal preferences, can craft a dietary program that is specifically designed with your unique needs in mind.

b) Person to person care. Enrolling in a Weight Watchers' program means you will be part of a group, lost in the crowd. The family doctor deals with you, the individual, and you alone. During your appointment, all of the doctor's concentration is focused on helping you become a healthier person. Nobody in the weight-loss industry can hope to match the personal attention lavished upon you by your doctor.

Weak minds/weak bodies

The vicious cycle of consumer food-induced weight gain followed by a temporary weight loss is difficult to break because consumerism has weakened your mind. Cherished character traits such as restraint, temperance, discipline and self-control have been devalued by the propaganda of the corporate giants. Multinationals exhort you to indulge in all of your cravings — cravings they manufacture for you in the first place. The idea of achievement through effort is frowned upon. You are encouraged to take the easy way out, embodied by the magic pill or magic diet mentality[11].

Multinationals have succeeded is numbing your conscience and destroying your willpower by creating a society that refuses to engage in personal responsibility. In the consumer world there are two basic truths: "It's never your fault/problem," and "The multinationals have all the solutions." Everything is arranged so that you have no worries. But you do have to worry and you do have to take responsibility.

11. The latest trend seems to be surgical procedures such as stomach stapling.

Personal responsibility is the key to escaping your prison of fat. It is up to you to take the weight off. Physicians can point out the way, but you must walk through the door. You must change your eating habits, you must exercise and you must persevere. Until you find the strength to do what is best for your self, you will be condemned to do what is best for others.

By shifting the burden of blame onto someone else, by abdicating responsibility over your own body, you are allowing the consumer giants free rein. You must work towards fulfilling yourself and your potential. You must strive towards overcoming your consumer food addiction by spurning the obesity-causing products of the multinationals. As with everything else, freedom begins with you.

Chapter 6

Your Health

Before there was Pfizer, Merck and GlaxoSmithKline, people still managed to cure themselves of a host of diseases and maintain a healthy body and mind. This chapter is dedicated to protecting your health without recourse to consumer medications.

Health is wealth, but the method of keeping healthy has been consumerized. Multinational pharmaceuticals dominate your understanding of sickness and health. As with food, we have surrendered control of your body to corporations.

In order to comprehend the necessity for natural healing, it is important to understand the problems associated with consumer medicines:

Chemical problems/chemical solutions

Multinationals present illness as a chemical imbalance that can only be treated with consumer chemicals. Consumer treatment invariably takes the form of chemical medications for even the most minor ailment.

Multinational pharmaceuticals are developing medicines for symptoms and ailments that are easily treatable by natural healing. Before consumer medicines, a cough was treated with honey and lemon juice. Now there are medicated lozenges, Tylenol Cold, Neo-Citran and a myriad of other consumer products.

Ironically, one of the main advertising points of such consumer medications is their natural medicine content. Halls' lozenges, for example, contain honey and lemon to help alleviate coughing and sore throats. Why settle for minute amounts of honey and lemon, lost among chemicals, additives and preservatives, when you can just take the lemon and honey itself?

Health is achieved through pills

If the consumer path to health is a chemical one, the ultimate consumer symbol of health is the pill. The pill is the condensed solution to your every health problem. The pill is the culmination of millions, even billions, of dollars of research. It is something you can trust. The pill neatly encapsulates the consumer message that you need the multinationals to make you feel better.

Multinational advertising revolves around the pill. Since you are a consumer, you do not have the patience or interest in comprehending the science behind the treatment. As such, the multinationals neatly summarize their message in the pill. Depressed? Take the pink pill. Impotent? Take the blue pill. Whatever your problem, a coloured pill provides the solution.

Redefining sickness: the shrinking definition of health

Multinationals are distorting the field of medicine by redefining health. Each year it becomes harder to be healthy. Each year the circle of health shrinks. Multinational-supported studies are transforming slight, natural variations in your body and mind into full-blown illnesses requiring consumer medical treatment.

Your body is a perpetually changing organism. It is only natural to encounter various fluctuations during this evolutionary process. Consumer medicine cannot admit this variation. Consumer medicine has redefined health as a constant, unchangeable state of being. If you are deemed to be outside the consumer health norm, regardless of your actual state of health, you are ordered to gobble up consumer medicines to revert to that optimum state. For example, if you are affected by changes in the weather that does not mean you are an unhealthy human being. It simply means that your body is reacting to its environment. The multinationals cannot permit this deviation from the norm. According to them, any symptoms associated with these weather changes, from depression to rheumatic pains, must be treated with consumer medicines.

Consumer health is a medicated utopia wherein your body is kept in a fictitious state of "health." However, this perfect health concept invented by the multinationals runs athwart the body's natural rhythms and cycles, predicated on change. By following the prescriptions of the multinationals you end up being nothing more than a drug addict, using consumer medicines to achieve your artificial health Nirvana.

Consumer health also denies the body the opportunity to engage with the surrounding environment and draw sustenance from it. Nature not only mends sickness, it is the key to shaping and maintaining your health. Keeping healthy is a function of living within the natural world, not of ingesting consumer pills.

Saving the Self

When faced with minor sickness you have a number of options before reaching for the consumer medicine cabinet:

"Body, heal thyself"

Do nothing. If it's an inconsequential matter such as a headache, minor aches and pains, bruising, small cuts, indigestion, nausea and the like, let the body heal itsself. Given time these problems will disappear. Here are three ways by which the body has the opportunity to heal itself:

Sleep: If the discomfort is more than you can bear then a nap is in order. Sleep is an excellent method for the body to recuperate and heal from illness.

Exercise: For headaches and even minor pains, a workout is the ideal prescription. Exercise will dissipate stress-induced migraines and limber up sore muscles and joints.

Meditation: Deep meditation can help relieve the underlying stress that is responsible for many of our illnesses. By re-establishing the mind-body balance and affirming the union of the self, meditation is an effective method of preventing and curing many common ailments.

Nature

Air

Fresh air cleans and filters the lungs from all sorts of man-made pollutants, from cigarette smoke to car and factory emissions. A few hours spent in a park or a forest can help you maintain a clean bill of health. Pollutant-free air is a priceless, even lifesaving boon for asthmatics and allergy-sufferers. Fresh air also prevents illness by ensuring the optimum functioning of your lungs. Other benefits of air include improved concentration, strengthening the immune system, facilitating the elimination of toxins and dispelling headaches, stress, fatigue and neurasthenia. Fresh, clean, crisp air, rich in oxygen energizes the body giving it that extra boost needed for optimal physical and intellectual performance.

Water

Swimming

Swimming toughens the body, increasing its resistance towards colds and the flu. In Russia, some parents dip their babies in freezing water to build up their immunity at a time when the human body is at its most vulnerable. Swimming is an effective form of physiotherapy that helps cure many pains by allowing your body to exercise in a weightless environment, thus working out stiff joints or injured muscles without gravitational stresses.

Drinking

Drinking fresh water provides the body with its needs without any unnecessary sugar, caffeine, aspartame or other damaging additives of consumer drinks. Drinking fresh cold water is what the body needs to keep healthy. Beyond the necessity of drinking, water has a number of therapeutic effects.

Hydrotherapy

There are numerous hydrotherapies in existence, using water in all of its forms.

From the ice pack to relieve pain and inflammation to the hot bath for melting away the day's cares, hydrotherapy is a part of life. The salutary effects of water therapy extend beyond these common uses. Hydrotherapy can help treat numerous ailments if done properly. The following breakdown of some common hydrotherapies and their benefits will illustrate how you can save the self through water rather than consumer medicines:

Douches are a jet or stream of water gently applied to cleanse or stimulate an internal or external part of the body.

External douches function in helping blood flow. They are applied to various parts of the body such as knee, chest, arm and face. The various types of external douches are used to relieve a host of symptoms and conditions including headaches, insomnia, varicose veins, poor circulation, bronchitis, angina pectoris, bronchial asthma, multiple sclerosis, toothaches, vertigo, tinnitus, back pains, neuralgia and rheumatism. Internal cleansing douches involve a stream of water directed into the vagina or anus for cleansing purposes.

Baths: The therapeutic effects of bathing have been recognized as long as civilization itself. The ancient Greeks, Romans and Chinese all used baths to help maintain the health of mind and body. Baths can be hot, cold or lukewarm and can involve either partial or full immersion of the body. Tepid baths are useful in treating fevers, common colds and back pain. Hot baths are perfect for stress relaxation, reducing muscle soreness, helping rehabilitate injured muscles and alleviating labor pains. Cold baths treat a number of ailments including varicose veins, susceptibility to edemas, headaches, low blood pressure, circulatory problems, sleeplessness, proneness to the common cold, sweaty feet, or a contused ankle.

Steam Baths: Steam rooms and saunas are recommended to open the skin pores and cleanse the body of toxins. Steam inhalation is prescribed for respiratory infections. A sauna is an eliminative procedure; it stimulates blood flow, increases the heart rate, has an immune-modulating effect, promotes hormone production, encourages mucosal secretions in the respiratory system, opens the airways, reduces resistance to respiration, regulates the vegetative system, relaxes and can improve mental outlook. Like most other forms of heat-based hydrotherapy, saunas and steam baths are excellent methods for relieving stress.

Compresses: There are two types of compresses, cold and hot. Compresses are prepared by soaking a linen cloth in cold or warm water and then placed or wrapped around the affected area. Compresses should be changed regularly, as soon as they reach room temperature. Cold compresses reduce fever and inflammation and treat headaches and sprains. Warm or hot compresses are valuable in treating abscesses, muscle aches and respiratory problems.

Sun

Heliotherapy

The treatment of illnesses by exposure to the sun began as early as ancient Egypt. From speeding up wound healing to combating serious illnesses such as breast cancer, heart disease, multiple sclerosis and osteoporosis, the sun has blazed a path to human health. Although the thinning of the ozone layer has made tanning a potentially dangerous proposition by allowing a greater proportion of UV rays to penetrate the atmosphere, moderate exposure in the early morning or late afternoon can still prove enormously beneficial.[12]

12. The sun can damage skin, from wrinkles to sun burns to melanoma, but even water can make you ill if you drink too much. The wisdom of the Ancient Greek

Sunlight increases the body's Vitamin D content by catalyzing calcium metabolism and strengthens the bones of young and old alike. Deprived of sunlight, you could be liable to Vitamin D deficiency, a condition responsible for a number of ailments.

Sunlight lowers cholesterol, stress, heart rate and blood pressure while increasing muscle strength, white cell function, sex hormones and toxin elimination. Sunlight increases resistance to infection and kills bacteria, viruses and fungi. The sun helps set your biological clock by synchronizing your circadian rhythms.

Beyond its many abilities to prevent and cure bodily diseases, the sun is essential to your mental health. People living in sunlight-drenched climates nearer the equator tend to have, if you will pardon the pun, sunnier dispositions. If, by contrast, you live in a place where sunlight is at a premium, you are liable to be affected by seasonal affective disorder (SAD). SAD is a seasonally-based depression that strikes when sunlight is in short supply, such as during long winter months. If you get the January blues, it's probably because you are not getting enough sun. No wonder you save up your money for a tropical holiday during wintertime. It is just your mind's natural desire to benefit from the restorative powers of sunlight. You need the sun to maintain a positive attitude, to raise your mental energy and to regenerate your desire for self-fulfillment.

Nature's products

Nature is the world's greatest medicine cabinet. All of the ingredients needed for your health are found within nature. Natural products are at the root of virtually every consumer medicine. In fact, for the most part, consumer medicines are chemical imitations of naturally occurring ingredients.

The ability of nature to heal has been rediscovered by the Western world through the rise of alternative medicines such as the extremely popular herbal remedies. However, in many non-Western cultures, natural products exist side by side with consumer medicines, and in many cases are the preferred form of treatment.

There are two types of natural products that can benefit your health:

Herbs/roots/plants: There are thousands of plants and roots in existence used to treat an infinite number of problems. Their uses must be

---

aphorism "nothing too much" holds true to this very day. Apply this maxim to sun exposure, and indeed to everything else in your life, and the self will be the better for it.

researched or discussed with an expert in alternative medicine and above all with your physician.

When you think of herbal remedies you tend to think of the bottled products sold at your local pharmacy. In fact, those products should be only your last herbal resort for a number of reasons:

1. They are increasingly being produced by multinationals.
2. They contain minute or non-existent quantities of the essential ingredient.
3. They contain additional chemicals and preservatives.
4. They may have consumer medicines, some of which are highly dangerous.
5. They are unregulated by the FDA and as such you have no guarantee as to their efficacy.

Rather than choosing manufactured and often consumerized herbal remedies, fabricate them yourself. Establish control over the healing process. Become your own pharmacist. Here's how:

Acquire your own ingredients

Purchase needed herbs and essential oils. Whether in herbal stores, markets or even over the Internet, medicinal plants are available for sale.

Establish your healing garden. Even a small apartment can still hold a wide variety of potted medicinal plants.

Prepare your own medication

Unlike over the counter herbal remedies and consumer medicines, almost exclusively available in caplet or tablet form, healing herbs can be prepared in a number of ways.

Tinctures are prepared by soaking your medicinal plants in drinkable alcohol such as vodka or brandy. The mixture is placed in a jar and let sit for at least a week to extract and preserve the desired properties of the herbs. Tinctures can be taken internally, hence the need for a potable type of alcohol, or applied externally to the skin.

Infusions involve the soaking of your botanicals in either cold or hot water. Teas are essentially a form of hot infusion. Cold infusions are also applied externally in what is called a wash. Hot or cold, infusions are less concentrated than tinctures.

Decoctions are water infusions made of tougher vegetal material such as bark, roots, seeds and nuts.

Poultices are nature's bandages. They are made by mashing or bruising herbs and spices into a paste, moistened with hot water, and applied to the skin as a dressing. Poultices may be applied directly to the affected area, or they may be wrapped in linen cloth. When separated from the skin they are often referred to as plasters.

Infused oils use base oils such as olive, soy and canola, in which herbs are soaked. Again, they can have both internal and external applications.

Healing foods

Hippocrates, the founding father of medicine, stated: "Let food be your medicine and let medicine be your food." Nearly 3,000 years later, despite enormous advances in the medicinal field, the axiom still holds true. Common whole foods such as apples, honey and nuts are medicines in themselves. They heal minor ailments and can help alleviate the symptoms of more serious medical conditions. Best of all, a diet rich in healing foods is your best defence against disease, especially the two biggest killers of Consumer-world citizens: cancer and heart disease. Another staple consumer disease, diabetes, is also effectively prevented through healing foods.

Healing foods are best consumed raw, or with as little cooking as possible to preserve their beneficial effects. Heavy processing tends to destroy many of their beneficial qualities. Leafy greens such as spinach and cruciferous vegetables such as cauliflower and broccoli are some examples of foods that lose their healing properties when overly cooked.

Educate yourself on the wealth of literature available on healing foods. Knowing their beneficial qualities will permit you to fashion a dietary regimen that will ensure optimum health.

The following list is a basic guide to some common illnesses that can be combated with healing foods:

High blood pressure - Garlic
High cholesterol – Barley, Beans, Garlic, Spinach
High blood sugar- Nuts, Oats
Coughs and colds – Lemon, Lime, Garlic
Diabetes – Grapefruit, Nuts
Cancer – Broccoli, Carrot
Acne - Cucumber
Acidity –Honey, Bananas
Constipation – Prunes, Beets
Diarrhea – Yogurt
Inflammation - Pineapple
Asthma – Garlic, Onion

CAUTION: Consult your physician:

Before undertaking any alternative healing practices, you need to consult your physician for a number of reasons:

Diagnostic: Natural treatments are useful for many conditions, but first you must discover what ails you. Before embarking on the path of natural healing, let your physician determine what exactly must be healed.

Treatment: Physicians are usually informed about natural remedies and can recommend the best course of treatment. Treatment is very important for three reasons. First of all, you wish to make sure that your natural treatment is the most efficient possible. Second, natural methods of healing, although infinitely preferable to consumer chemicals, can be potent medicines with a number of side effects. Unless you know how to use them properly, you could end up doing more harm than good. Third, some treatments, while beneficial for an existing condition, are not recommended if you have secondary health problems or conditions. Saunas are not recommended for those who have heart disease or are pregnant. Herbal treatments should not be taken at least two weeks prior to surgery and should be resumed afterwards only with the doctor's consent.

Persistent symptoms: Persistent symptoms can signify a serious illness that cannot be effectively treated by natural healing alone. Examples include Aids, cancer and diabetes. It is best to go for a medical examination of apparently non-life-threatening problems such as headaches that cannot be cured using natural healing methods.

Conjunctive treatment: As mentioned above, some medical conditions cannot be effectively treated by natural healing alone. Consulting with a physician will allow you to employ natural healing methods as a complement to other medical treatments. Natural healing may be used in conjunction with chemical treatments to help combat the disease or the after-effects of those treatments. Thus natural healing may be used in conjunction with chemotherapy to help combat the powerful side-effects of that treatment.

Chapter 7

Freeing your Mind (1) Breaking Away From Consumer Entertainment

A mind is a terrible thing to waste — especially when it is yours. This chapter outlines the devastating impact of consumer entertainment on the brain and offers some suggestions for taming television.

Consumer entertainment acts on the mind in the same way consumer food acts on the body, by making it flabby and inefficient. The chief weapon in the arsenal of consumer entertainment is television.

The television

If you are like most people, your leisure life is patterned by the *TV Guide*. Every channel gives you something to watch. Must see TV, can't miss Thursdays, all new episodes, world television premieres: do these things sound familiar? Perhaps you are not taken in by such advertising. Perhaps you have your own favourite shows, shows you watch religiously, just as religiously as you eat your Big Macs. How much of your life is determined by the *TV Guide*? How many of your living hours are consumed by television? How often do you think about what's on the tube tonight?

If you cannot conceive of a life without television, it's because you do not know how to fill up your spare time. Regardless of how that leisure time could be filled, one thing is certain — denied the possibility of consumer entertainment, you are forced to find other means of preoccupying the self. Without the crutch of consumerism you must apply your mind and innate talents in order to divert the self. Imagine being forced to come up with a non-consumer method of entertaining yourself. Imagine if there were no consumer entertainment topics to discuss with your fellow workers, friends and family. What would you talk about?

The fear of free time drives your addiction towards consumer entertainment. It is a fear created by the boredom of the suburban lifestyle. It is a fear encouraged by the multinationals. Above all it is a fear of the self. Consumer entertainment prevents you from asking the questions that really matter, namely how to satisfy and improve the self. Consumer entertainment serves only to deceive the self into fearing self-expression. The reason we fear free time is because we simply don't know what to do with it.

Television and your kids

For your children, television is particularly pernicious since their minds are at a crucial development stage when they absorb the knowledge that will serve them during adulthood. By filling their minds with the moronic offerings of television we stunt their intellectual and physical development, hamstringing them for the rest of their lives.

Television watching denies kids the opportunity to play. Play is the essential means of "practicing" for adulthood in terms of social, intellectual and pragmatic skills. Play is also the primary method through which the child can manifest and fulfil the self. If you love your kids, you won't permit television to stunt their development by keeping them in a stupefied silence. Much better they run around the house and neighbourhood, being loud, playful, gregarious and even annoying. At least then, they are being kids. At least then, they are being themselves.

How television affects you

Television attacks the mind in three ways:

Passive intellect: A vegetative torpor is the preferred state of avid television watchers. You do not have to think any longer, only absorb the information stream presented to you. The need for thought becomes obsolete, except for the few neurons required to interpret the transparent cretinism of most television programs. After all, just how much do you really need to think when watching the parade of trailer park trash duking it out on *Jerry Springer*?

When thought becomes unnecessary, the mind suffers. Brain functions atrophy due to lack of use. You lose perspicacity, inventiveness, and logical ability — essentially all that is necessary for the progress of the self. Without an active mind, discovering your needs becomes a moot point.

Pop culture: Television fills the mind with a host of useless facts and trivia. Precious memory space is taken up with names of television characters, actors, singers, episodes, videos and other consumerist trivia. All of this brain space should store information that is essential to intellectual and physical needs.

Identifying your needs is not only a subjective process, but also an inward journey of self-discovery. Your needs exist in conjunction with the objective world and not in a void. The more you know about the world around you, the greater the chance your ability to express and satisfy your needs. If your knowledge is limited to the prison box of Consumer-world, you will know nothing of the objective world, and the process of self-discovery will be irredeemably harmed.

Brainwashing via commercials: Television is the principal source of consumer advertising. Television commercials account for many of your consumer product purchases.

Anatomy of the commercial

Slogans

Most of the products advertised have accompanying slogans. Pepsi used to be "the choice of a new generation" and "things went better with Coke." A perfunctory assessment of these slogans is sufficient to show them as utter nonsense. Nonetheless, multinationals persist with these ridiculous slogans, investing enormous amounts of money to make them omnipresent. Why? Because they work. Advertisers have taken to heart the lessons taught by Goebbels and Mao's little Red Book. If your message is simple and you repeat it often enough, you will inculcate that message in people's minds, no matter how outrageous it is. Goebbels convinced a whole nation that genocide was a good thing. Mao had widespread, fanatical support for the "Great Leap Forward" even as it impoverished and killed millions of his adherents. Surely, it cannot be so difficult to convince consumers that using a particular product enhances their lives.

Only a brief application of critical thought is required to counteract this insidious propaganda. Stop for one moment and ask yourself why are corporations telling me such ridiculous things? I know my life will not be improved by choosing a particular soft drink. Take Pepsi for example, and their "Pepsi generation" ad campaign. I challenge Pepsi to name one person who seriously considers himself part of the "Pepsi generation." Have you ever met any "Pepsi generation" people?

The corporate slogans of today are so farfetched they shame the mountebanks of yesteryear with their magic potions and snake oils. If advertising slogans are so ridiculous, why do people keep on buying consumer products?

Artificial needs

Commercials construct an artificial need for the product by tying the product to an actual need of the consumer. Consumer products such as perfumes, clothes and cars are linked to making the consumer more attractive to the opposite sex. Are Polo shirts really the key to romantic success? They would certainly appear not to be for the models that advertise them, models whose esthetic perfection would be evident in rags. What it is going to do for you is an entirely different question, especially if you are among the 99 per cent of the population who does not look like those models.

Blinding you with the stars

Another way the television commercial creates artificial needs is by using consumer entertainers. Here advertisers rely on two things.

First, in modern times, the people who are respected, admired and idolized are consumerist confections of mass entertainment and professional sports.

Second, imitation is the sincerest form of flattery.

Put the two together and voila: instant consumer success. If Britney Spears drinks Pepsi and I love Britney Spears, then I will be closer to her if I down it by the gallon. Few people stop to ask themselves if the stars hawking corporate brands actually use the products. In fact, even if they do use them, it's only because that forms part of the multi-million dollar contracts they have signed with the respective multinational. The stars get millions to promote and use a particular consumer product. What will you gain from using that same product?

Saving the Self

Freeing the mind: overcoming television addiction

The best way to overcome consumer entertainment is by gradually weaning yourself off of it. Reduce the time spent in front of the tube and your mind will be sharper, clearer and better placed to determine how it can best fulfil the self. Here are some methods for achieving that reduction:

Prioritize

If you have a favourite show you can't bear to miss, watch that show. But pick out a couple of favourite shows and limit yourself to them. For example, you do not need to catch every reality-based TV series out there. One will suffice.

Watch with a purpose

Avoid watching TV as an activity in itself. Turn on the set with a purpose, not just to see what's on. Too many people watch television as a means of escaping boredom. If you have nothing to do, think of something. Don't just reach for the remote. Moreover, when you do turn on the TV, make sure it is with *your* purpose, not the purpose imposed by the *TV Guide*. In other words, there is something on television that has aroused your genuine interest. Do not turn on the television because some tabloid magazine says you need to watch a show.

Choose your programming wisely

Change the type of programming you watch. It goes without saying that a lot more people watch pro wrestling, music videos and *Jerry Springer* than the evening news or educational programs. This is a sad comment on the state of modern culture. Nonetheless, television does offer some opportunity for intellectual stimulation. Specialty channels devoted to worthy subjects such as nature, history, arts, medicine and science are available in some cable packages. Even the networks offer the occasional program that demands some sort of mental activity on the viewer's part. Finding the right channel or picking the right program could really make television worth watching.

Even if you do watch purely for entertainment value, make sure the programming has some entertainment value in the first place. Search out the innovative and the intelligent, regardless of the genre. *Monty Python* and *Mr. Bean* showed that comedy does not have to be in the prefabricated sitcom format. If you prefer movies, choose movies based on great works of literature over comic book adaptations. *A Christmas Carol* or *Les Miserables* not only entertain, but also educate and enlighten.

Avoid the commercials

Here are four methods for sidestepping this nefarious weapon of consumer propaganda:

a) Watch television channels without commercials. A number of cable and satellite channels allow you to enjoy commercial-free programming.
b) Tape shows so the commercials can be automatically skipped.
c) Switch to a non-commercial showing channel. Check out the weather channel during commercial breaks.
d) Have a back-up activity. Whether it's a newspaper or a book, or something from work, have something ready for commercial breaks. Press the mute button and keep yourself busy for the two minutes of consumer advertising.

Question the slogans, question your needs

Next time you walk into a mall to act out advertising-induced consumer impulses, ask for some proof of what the commercials show. Where are the experiment results? Where are the scientific studies showing that wearing Gap khakis will improve your lot in life? Demand to see the empirical data correlating Ralph Lauren perfume to a significant increase in sexual activity. Inquire how exactly that Tommy Hillfiger shirt will make you happy. If the customer service rep stares at you in a wide-mouthed stupor, and you've already bought the product, ask for your money back and try to figure out what you really need.

Seen in the light of reason, consumer advertising might seem ludicrous. But, of course, you cannot look at matters so reasonably, so dispassionately. For, as the multinationals know, you will do anything to fulfil primordial needs such as attracting a partner. Perhaps the clothes do not work, perhaps it is ridiculous to think that they do, but just on that off chance they do, can you afford not to have that consumer product?[13] Until you can escape this sort of thinking do not ridicule commercials, because the next time you buy a consumer product, the laugh will be on you.

---

13. Artificial needs have also become a self-fulfilling prophecy. Please see the chapter on Sexuality to discover how consumer products have come to play a prominent role in the modern relationship, with devastating consequences for the sexual self.

Chapter 8

Freeing your Mind (2) Embracing Knowledge Through Reading

Consumerism enslaves the mind by killing its need for knowledge. Reading is one of the means by which you can resurrect your need for knowledge and achieve freedom of thought.

The assault on knowledge and the retreat of the intellect

In order to discover your needs, you need to think. In order to think, you need a basis. The basis of all thought is knowledge. Unfortunately, knowledge has been taking a beating lately, replaced by consumer misinformation. You might be living in the Information Age, but the only information you are receiving is produced and marketed by the multinationals.

The paradox of existence is that the more you know the less you know. Traditionally, this meant that knowledge[14] is a gradual awareness of the infinite depths of ignorance. Consumerism has changed the meaning of that paradigm to signify that the more consumer information you absorb, the more ignorant you become.

Life in the consumer universe has brought about a retreat from knowledge. Knowledge is increasingly irrelevant beyond professional needs. It is ironic that in the age of universal schooling and public

---

14. My working definition of knowledge is "non-consumer information." This includes both intellectual fields of knowledge (biology, history) and practical fields (cooking and sewing). However, in this chapter I am dealing with the intellectual or academic fields of knowledge.

libraries, people reject and disparage knowledge. How did we end up in this sorry state?

The key to the downfall of knowledge rests with a paradigm shift in the definition of human achievement. For as long as recorded history, knowledge was both a means and a mark of achievement. People admired and consulted with the knowledgeable. Knowledge made you a somebody and gave you a privileged social, economic and political position. The great achievements of Ancient Greece stem from that society's appreciation and admiration for knowledge. The Delphic Oracle acknowledged Socrates as the wisest man in Greece. When Plato founded the Academy, young men flocked to his side, eager to partake of his wisdom. Men of genius were also esteemed at royal courts. Aristotle, for example, was the teacher of Alexander the Great. The custom of the powerful seeking the advice of the learned persisted well into the 20th century.

Consumerism has changed all that. Consumerism has degraded the value of knowledge by showing you that knowledge is not necessary to achievement in modern society. For the first time in history, ignorance is revered. Consumer propaganda has completely overturned the scale of human achievement so that stupidity has become a prerequisite for success. For the first time in history, people are practicing intellectual self-abnegation, suppressing their intellect for social acceptance or economic prosperity. We are living in the Age of Cretinism.

As the value of knowledge diminishes, knowledgeable people are steadily eliminated from our consciousness. Shut out of the consumerist-run mass media, men of knowledge have fallen into obscurity, condemned to irrelevance. Consumerism has erected new heroes. Scientists and scholars have been replaced with consumer idols, actors, singers and professional athletes, as the individuals worthy of your admiration and respect. Their irresistible combination of wealth and fame cannot be achieved through knowledge. No doctorate degree, no published treatise, no great scientific discovery will gain global fame, adulation and respect. But if you are a consumer idol, if you are Brad Pitt or Britney Spears or David Beckham, then you will be at the forefront of popular consciousness.

The consumer propaganda machine guarantees universal recognizability for its idols. Television, magazines and newspapers detail the often banal activities of the new "great men". These idols are extensively quoted and their image and importance constantly inflated by populist sycophants who pass for journalists and reporters. Indeed, the amount of television time and newsprint devoted to the monosyllabic ramblings of these intellectual non-entities is wholly disproportionate to the value of their utterances.

None can escape the fascination with consumer idols. The weakest among us merely absorb as much as possible of this mind-numbing diet. Countless others struggle to achieve this much-vaunted "star" status. The consumer propaganda machine is relentless in selling this brittle dream. Consumer propaganda constantly urges you to imitate consumer idols and their stupidity. Children are particularly vulnerable. How many kids all over the world grow up fantasizing to be like or even meet, a famous actor or professional athlete?[15] How many children in this world grow up wishing they could be a Dante, a Newton or a Mozart, not to mention recent, mostly obscure geniuses.[16]

The sad truth is that consumer idols are unworthy of your admiration. They have done very little to advance the human condition. Not only do the "achievements" of Madonna dwindle into insignificance when set beside those of Einstein, Madonna's achievements only have value within the parameters of Consumer-world and are illusory. The "greatness" of Madonna is measured by consumer statistics such as records sold, or Top Ten hits. Consumerist actors are judged on the basis of Oscars. At an even cruder level, all consumer idols are judged by the size of their contracts and their lavish spending habits.

The only measure of judging of another human being is how much can they contribute to the advancement of your self. Judged by this measure, interest in consumer idols is harming rather then helping your self. Rather than seeking out the knowledgeable, we have chosen to quench our mental thirst with the bubbles of consumer stupidity. This choice is not wholly our fault. Being stupid is something we learned in school.

Choosing to be stupid: the lesson consumerism taught

High school turned millions of people against knowledge. Once an institution of learning, school has become the exact opposite, an anti-knowledge monster. The only lesson learned in high school is that knowledge is bad and stupidity is good.

High school is the birthplace of adolescent culture. But the culture it gives birth to, ironically, is a culture that rejects knowledge. Knowledge is a branding iron, a mark of condemnation and social isolation within

15. "I want to be like Mike" ran one popular ad, urging kids to "imitate" Michael Jordan by purchasing consumer products.
16. I would like to see the results of a survey that asked people to name three Oscar winning actors and three Nobel prize winners.

adolescent culture. Destructive terms such as geek and nerd are used by North America's youth to isolate their more knowledgeable peers. But in labelling scholarship as geeky or nerdy, adolescents isolate themselves from knowledge.

How did the pejorative terms of geek and nerd arise and what accounts for their pervasiveness in adolescent culture?

These terms are the tools of consumerism. They are the perennial weapons used to frighten youth away from education and knowledge. They are used to create a culture of stupidity and ignorance by promoting hostility towards any individual who belongs to a culture of intelligence, a culture marked by intellectual curiosity, academic excelence, scholarly pursuits and encyclopedic knowledge. Consumerism has encouraged placing intelligent individuals on the lowest rung of the high school hierarchy.

During the formative period of adolescence, when personality and character undergo the difficult transformation from childhood to maturity, self-image and self-esteem are at their most vulnerable. The pressure to belong, to fit within your peer group, is intense. But fitting in comes with a price. It means forfeiting intellectual pursuits frowned upon by the "in crowd," the high-school aristocracy.

Fitting in means a wholehearted and absolute embrace of consumer entertainment and the individuals it promotes. Fitting in means discussing the private lives of pop singers, actors and professional athletes. Fitting in means memorizing trivial details about movies, TV shows and professional sports. Fitting in means wearing Gap clothes and Nike shoes and being a consumer brand addict. Fitting in means absolute obeisance to the multinationals.

The alternative is a form of internal exile within your high school. "Branded" as a social misfit, you are doomed to loiter about at the periphery of the school's social activities. Technically considered as part of the student body, your existence goes unnoticed by your peers. To paraphrase James Joyce, "you are cast out from life's feast," through no fault or intention of your own. Your sole crime was affirming your individual self. You transgressed in seeking to explore the knowledge at your fingertips. You are guilty of daring to fulfil your intellectual potential. In the high school microcosm, that is an unpardonable sin.

The punishments are swift and many. You will not be invited to parties or any other social events for that matter. You will not be considered attractive to the opposite sex. Indeed, you will not even have a common ground for communicating with the fairest members of the opposite sex. How many teen models or cheerleaders appreciate academic excellence or prodigious ability in the game of chess? How many football jocks are coupled with math whizzes?

Consumerism promotes fear and scorn towards knowledge not out of malice but out of necessity. The survival of the consumer industry depends on its clients, the consumers, being kept in a maximum state of imbecility. The more knowledgeable people are, the more the multinationals' bottom lines suffer. Educated people prefer intellectual pursuits such as reading[17] over watching television or going to the movies. Reading in particular is a prime enemy of the multinationals, directly competing with consumerism for your leisure time. To ward off the consequences of knowledge, multinationals have invented the concept of "cool," of what it means to be "in" and saturated the youth with it.

Consumerism actively sows divisions among young people, punishing the uncooperative and rewarding the adherents. Friendship, popularity and sex, all that the adolescent heart desires, is premised upon adhering to the will of the global conglomerates. You must live the life they wish you to live. You must conform or suffer the consequences. Consumer giants are directly responsible for the ruin of millions of lives, for making the adolescent experience one of endless misery and suffering. Untold adolescents have suffered, not because they were intelligent, but because they dared to show it. They dared to manifest their intellect. A ruined youth is the price many have paid for resisting the multinationals. It is a dear price indeed.

The true tragedy of the situation is that regardless of where you placed in the high school hierarchy, consumerism still harmed you. A cursory exploration of high school's three broad social classes reveals how youth is victimized.

The three types of students that make up high school society are the popular kids, the kids who want to be popular and the geeks/nerds/misfits/outcasts.

Do not envy the popular kids. Theirs is a hard lot. If you were a popular kid, you know what I am talking about. The popularity struggle is perpetual warfare. Those at the top of the pile fight to maintain their status while others seek to knock them off their pedestals. Popular kids, with their self-esteem dependent on their status, also live in constant fear of losing their position. They are victims of their own "success."

The modern day popularity struggle is just another consumer concoction. The measure of popularity is based on how closely you adhere to the consumerist ideal, on how effectively you ape the concept of "cool"

---

17. Or attend cultural events such as the theatre, opera, symphony, ballet etc.

established by the multinationals, on how closely you match the perfect consumer. As such, the victory is a hollow one. The most popular boy or girl is often the furthest from their true self. They have obliterated their true personality and replaced it with a multinational manufactured one.

If you were one of those kids who struggled to be with the "in crowd" you are perhaps the greatest victim of high school consumerism. Your life was part tragedy, part farce, but all acting. You played out your existence because you would not suffer the consequences of manifesting your intellect and your love of knowledge. Your frightened adolescent soul willingly hid and submerged its intelligence, its true self, as if it were some hideous disease. You were living a lie, constantly working to maintain the illusion of stupidity, constantly chasing away any hint of learnedness. You lived in constant terror that you would be found out and punished by the consumer secret police, also known as the popular kids. You had nightmares of being chased out from that circle and condemned to suffer in the social limbo populated by the geeks and freaks.

If you were a "geek," you were closest to your true self, right? You expressed your intelligence, you manifested your true self and damn the social torpedoes! You paid a bitter social price but it was worth it! You had the courage to rebel against the tyranny of adolescent consumer decorum. You had the courage to rebel against the consumer lifestyle.

Before you pat yourself on the back, realize things are not as simple as that. The multinationals are too wily to get boxed in. Remember they want every single one of you to be a consumer, even if you hate Britney Spears or Disney. They have seized upon the potential for adolescent rebellion against the uniform, routine lifestyle they promote. As such, they have moved quickly to co-opt the inherent rebelliousness of teenagers and turn it to their own profit. Multinationals have transformed teenage rebellion into an aversion towards intellectual pursuits. Simultaneously, consumerism has inextricably linked rebellion with its products.

Everything and everyone that could serve as a means of resisting consumerism has been consumerized, or as the euphemism goes, "brought into the mainstream." The multinationals have branded rebellion and made it into a consumer product. Even the terms of "geekiness" and "nerdiness" have been re-molded by the multinationals to signify not intelligence or knowledge, but merely a particular type of consumer, one with preference for certain types of consumer entertainment. If you thought you rebelled by listening to alternative music, you were wrong. You were still living in a consumer world. From punk to grunge to Marilyn Manson, the music of rebellion is owned, marketed and distributed by the same multinationals who sold Vanilla Ice, New Kids on the Block, and Britney Spears. You can break out of the ordinary, you can rebel, you can tell authority to f*** off. The way you did that in high school was by consuming the multinational's products, not by expressing the self. In the end, your social status was determined by what you consumed, not by who you were, making you no different from the popular kids, making you just another consumer victim.

Saving the self

There are two ways to acquire intellectual knowledge. The first is through self-education via reading. The second method is through formal education, such as high school, college or university courses.

Reading yourself to freedom

Young or old, start opening books. Reading is a key to breaking the consumer entertainment stranglehold that multinationals have upon society. Reading helps the self in a number of ways:

Liberating thought: Your thought processes have become atrophied or rendered sluggish by years of functioning in the passive consumer mode. Reading will give the mind a booster shot and awaken both intellect and imagination.

Increasing knowledge: Along with formal education, reading is the premier method of increasing your knowledge base.

Self-education: Choosing to read and choosing your books, means choosing your education. When you make the conscious decision to read, you are making a decision to be your own mentor, to control and determine the nature of knowledge your self needs to absorb in order to progress.

Personal culture: Reading improves the self in terms of a developing a personal culture. Knowledge civilizes the self and elevates it above the plateau of basic instincts.

Reading might seem a simple prescription for acquiring knowledge, but in fact, things are not as they seem. The process of choosing what to read is just as important as the act of reading itself.

The key to a rewarding read is planning ahead. In the old days, men of genius spent years planning the ultimate library, setting down the essential books for a complete education. While you do not have to spend years formulating such plans, you must have a reading plan in mind before cracking a book. There are four crucial steps to a reading plan that rewards the self.

Start with introductory textbooks

Your first reading choices should give you a general grounding in those disciplines where you have either forgotten everything or never learned it in the first place. By reading relatively short introductory texts you will have a basic introduction to the sum of human knowledge in that particular field.

Introductory textbooks sketch out the history, the jargon and the basic principles of a discipline. They also serve as a stepping stone, opening new vistas of knowledge for study, blazing new paths for your mind. Thus, an introductory textbook in philosophy serves as a barebones summary of conceptual approaches towards questions such as the nature of existence and the meaning of truth, while providing you with definitions of basic philosophical terminology. It is then up to you to decide which of these questions are most relevant to your self, and how far, or how deeply, you wish to pursue the answers. But you must test the waters before plumbing the ocean's deep.

Introductory textbooks also give you the option of stepping back from the water's edge. Let's say you've read an introduction to philosophy and this is not a particular field you wish to pursue. You can stop with the introductory text, and move on to another field. However, you will have still gained the benefit of acquiring at least a basic knowledge in that field, of understanding that particular facet of human knowledge. Your mind will always be able to use that information, perhaps unconsciously, to advance the self towards fulfillment.

On a very practical level, introductory textbooks point the way towards further reading. An introductory text will reveal the names and works of pre-eminent importance within that field. These seminal texts are then used to form your reading list. By reading a brief introduction to philosophy you will then know which are the most important books on philosophy, the books you must read first. Introductory textbooks winnow the reading list so you can read the cream of the crop.

Read original sources/The men of genius

Someone once said that all Western philosophy is a footnote to Plato. As such, if you are going to explore the philosophical field you are obligated to read Plato first. You will not, cannot truly understand anything that comes afterwards until you read Plato. The men of genius, the original sources for the discipline you are studying, are luminaries in their field. They form the foundation of that discipline of knowledge. They must be read first in order to understand what the discipline is all about.

A second reason for beginning with the masters is that you are getting the best. You have a limited life and a limited amount of time you can devote to reading. How can you make the best of it? If you are only able to read three philosophy books, they should be the three best possible books.

Seminal texts represent the fulfillment of genius' potential. They are a mark of both that individual's fulfillment and of mankind's fulfillment as a whole. They are the texts that have the most to offer to you, that can best provoke your self to stir and awaken from its consumerist doze. What makes these texts important is not some scholarly decree, but their time-tested ability to help the individual self, to help you. Each of these texts, each of these authors, presents a universal perspective. The writings of Newton, Darwin, Einstein, Shakespeare, Plato, Buddha and Jesus have value precisely because these are people who have dug deepest into their exploration of the self, have travelled farthest along the road towards self-fulfillment. By following along their paths you too may explore the deepest reaches of your self, you too may uncover your own potential and let it shine through.

Move to the lesser lights/contemporaries

Below the top echelon of mankind's genius lie other geniuses, perhaps not as bright, but luminaries nonetheless. The third step in your reading plan is to flesh out the discipline with these other worthy contributors. Beyond Plato and Aristotle, beyond Kant and Descartes, there is Russell, Heidegger and Kierkegaard. Then there are notable contemporary philosophers, more obscure, but who reveal the state of philosophy in our present day. These men of genius, famous or obscure, help broaden the discipline and your understanding of it. They are invaluable aids to enhancing your knowledge base.

Refer to the academic commentators

Academics are the people who explain and comment on the great texts. They should be your last reading choice rather than your first.

It's not that explanatory texts and commentaries don't have value: there is genuine textual criticism, there are the fields of hermeneutics and exegesis. Annotations are valuable in explaining abstruse passages. Criticism and differing interpretations should be evaluated for their potential worth. However, that worth amounts to nothing more than an intellectual's opinion. Do not allow an intermediary to rehash a great philosopher's or spiritual figure's thoughts, or even a great politician's or artist's. No matter how difficult the original work seems, try to make some sense of it. If there are things you do not understand, refer to explanations or critical commentary. However, such critiques should serve either as a companion to your own interpretation or as an aid in developing your own interpretation, nothing more.

The crucial aspect of reading remains your individual understanding of the original text, no matter what that interpretation may be. If you agree with an academic's interpretation of the text, it should be because your understanding of that text coincides with the academic. Do not simply adopt another's opinion without formulating your own. There can be no substitution for individual self-expression. Remember, you are reading for your own benefit and nothing else.

Chapter 9

Freeing the Mind (3) Embracing Knowledge Through Education

Formal education is the other method for expanding your knowledge base ... if you can manage to stay away from consumer learning.

The second method of acquired learning is within the formal confines of an educational institution. That means going to school to become smart rather than stupid.

Taking a course or a program of studies in a selected discipline can be enormously helpful in expanding the boundaries of the self. Just as with reading, you must plan ahead in order to ensure the maximum benefit to the self. For consumerism has invaded the sacred halls of learning and, unless you are prudent and wise, the only education you will receive is a consumerist one.

Before selecting your courses there is an important factor you need to address: Know your language. The language of knowledge is the language you speak. Unless you know that language, you will not be able to properly absorb and understand the knowledge offered to you.

Learning how to speak: English, a dying language

Consumerism has slain the word.

The rapid consumerization of society is sounding the death knell for the English language. It will be a slow and painful death. Only remnants will survive, locked away in the ivory towers of universities, but ultimately the rot will claim it even in those last refuges. Its death seems inevitable even as it marches triumphantly across the world. How can this paradox be explained? How can English, the planet's language of choice, be dying?

Consumerism is slowly killing the English language.[18] It is a process analogous to the global destruction of the environment. Just like countless animal and vegetal species, so the words of the English language are disappearing, condemned to extinction through non-use. Words are dying, words are disappearing every day. Words have become curiosities, relics existing only in dusty, forgotten dictionaries and in the esoteric preoccupations of a dwindling number of academics. The beauty and majesty of the English language, as encapsulated in the Oxford English Dictionary, is lost to the overwhelming amount of people.

Consumerism has killed the language by decreeing that you shall communicate at the lowest possible common denominator. You are constantly urged to pare down your vocabulary. Consumerism preaches that in simplicity you will find your authentic voice. But this simplified language is not used to express your self, but to express artificial consumer needs. What authenticity can be found in meaningless consumer lives? What deeper truths can be mined in expressing consumer needs?

Newspapers and magazines are willing participants in the process of language simplification. Even respected publications such as *Time Magazine* and the *New York Times* have begun reducing their vocabulary, using the most prosaic and trite language possible. I will not even mention the abysmal depths of consumer entertainment. Consumer society is engaged in a massive process of self-imbecilization and, at its most basic level, this process is reflected through the dismemberment of the English language.

Not only are words disappearing, the relatively few words that comprise our vocabulary are often used in a grammatically incorrect way. Many of the most basic rules of grammar and orthography are falling by the wayside. Something as banal as a properly structured sentence has become a rarity.

Why does consumerism seek to destroy language? So it can be replaced with Consumer-speak. By ensuring that you have a minimal vocabulary, consumerism frees up a lot of brain space in your mind. To fill up that available space, multinationals have developed Consumer-speak.

Consumer-speak is the new universal language. Consumer-speak will bring the human race together under the brand umbrella by limiting every human being to two types of words:

Consumer proper nouns: The endless creations of the consumer industry occupy the greater part of your vocabulary. While your non-consumer vocabulary is a few hundred words at best, you have thousands

---

18. Just as it is killing all languages.

of consumer proper names stuck in your head. Your brain matter is filled with names of actors, actresses, television shows, movies, pop singers and pop songs, not to mention the endless array of consumer brands and goods.

Consumer vernacular: These are the words required to connect consumer proper names in a sentence, or a comprehensible semblance thereof, and to communicate your desire for consumer products.

To make the connection between consumer proper nouns, you employ a very limited range of words or phrases concocted by the multinationals or already existing words that the multinationals have decided to pervert. This is the multinationals' *lingua franca.* Consumer vernacular is composed of words and phrases culled from mainstream movies (i.e. "show me the money!"), pop music - especially the rap lingo which takes delight in bastardizing the meaning of just about every word it adopts - and various commercials. This vernacular changes rapidly so that the "rad" and "gnarly" of yesteryear are soon replaced with the "boo" and "fronting" of today, and those who quoted Dirty Harry now quote Neo. Changes aside, Consumer-speak's influence is constantly growing as the multinationals lower the language bar in an effort to extend their dominion.

The rot goes deeper than mere words or phrases. The very framework of self-expression has been distorted by consumerism. Whereas before people referred to religious, historical, natural or cultural figures or events when seeking to articulate their thoughts, now the sole frame of reference is Consumer-world. Before the onslaught of consumerism, when someone wished to make a comparison, devise an analogy, illustrate by example, or fashion a metaphor or a simile, there were certain basic universal sources they relied on. Some of the sources used in the West were the Bible, Ancient Greek and Roman figures, myths and historical events, and the natural world. So, for example, people would say, "that man has the strength of Hercules". In today's Consumer-speak, the terms of reference are consumer products, from food to entertainment to brand name items. Today, people say, "Like, that guy's strong like the Hulk."

How much longer can the language decline continue? It is unbelievable that language, which has evolved and grown over many millenia, from the first intelligible guttural uttering of the early hominids, should now undergo such a rapid regression, such an alarming decomposition. If this process is not stopped, language shall soon revert to those atavistic howls and growls. The triumph of Consumer-speak means communicating in Neanderthalic mutterings interspersed by the occasional consumer product name.

Learn the language, save your self

In forsaking the language, you are denying the self. The sum of our desires, needs, dreams and disappointments is expressed through language. Language is the quintessential form of self-expression. Consequently, language is the key towards personal fulfillment.

The first step towards self-fulfillment is articulating what you want to achieve both to others and, most importantly, to your self. When you ponder what you are and what you wish to be, you ponder in words. Every word gives meaning to the self by affording it another form of expression. The more limited the words, the more limited the thoughts. The more limited the thoughts, the more limited the self.

Unless you master the language, your ideas, inventions and approaches to a particular problem, be they novel, bold, spectacular and unique, will remain the prisoner of your mind. If you cannot effectively convey your self to others you are denying it an opportunity for advancement. Forsake language and you become the jailer of your self.

Language is not only about helping you express the self. Language also helps you achieve very real needs. Language is key to success in your profession, no matter what that profession is. Perhaps an anecdote will illustrate the problems that arise due to an inability to communicate effectively. One of my friends, a computer engineer, often complained about the meetings of his working group. According to him, these meetings would last for hours without anything getting done. The root of the problem? People could not make themselves understood. Someone would seek to explain their approach to a problem, but either due to their own lack of linguistic ability or the others' lack of comprehension, they would not be understood.

If professionals working in the same technical jargon cannot communicate with each other how can they achieve team goals? In my friend's case, his high-tech company, which at one time was the largest in Canada, lost significant man-hours and precious time better spent working due to its employees' inability to make themselves understood.[19]

Beyond your work, a command of the language will help you achieve all of your goals. From gaining the respect of friends, the admiration of strangers and the love of a chosen one, language is the medium that serves your purpose. Words define your person for both the self and for others.

---

19. Living in the self-proclaimed Silicon Valley North, I happen to know a significant number of computer engineers and even a technical writer. Several of them also complained about their difficulty in understanding and communicating with co-workers.

Language shows the world the type of person you are. Do not allow the multinationals' Consumer-speak to brand you as "one of theirs."

By allowing multinationals to determine the meaning of language you relinquish control over a fundamental instrument of your freedom. You may be free to say anything you want, but what if you do not know how to say it? Freedom of expression is worthless unless you can express yourself. Language is the basis of freedom of expression. When you are walled in by Consumer-speak, where is the freedom of expression? Will you let the multinationals limit you to a few measly words when the English language is rich with hundreds of thousands of words? Will you allow consumerism to sell your self short like that?

Saving the Self

There are four critical steps involved in reclaiming your language:

Know your grammar and spelling: Use words in their proper sense and meaning in a grammatically correct sentence. If you cannot, take a refresher course in grammar and sentence structure.

When writing, make sure each word is spelled correctly. Don't rely on spell-check to do it for you. A spell-checker's sole function should be to correct inadvertent mistakes like typos. It is your responsibility to know and verify the spelling of the words you are using.

Get a vocabulary: The English language has over half-a-million words.

Try to learn a couple of thousand at least. Get a dictionary, even a Pictionary, but expand your vocabulary. A new word a day will keep consumerism at bay.

Once you've learned a word, use it. Don't be reticent to use a word because your friends, co-workers or family won't understand it or will laugh at you for being pretentious. Use newly learned words in everyday language and you will enrich your self.

Learn how to write essays: Habituated to formulating thoughts only in snippets, you never get to exercise your mind for more than ten-second spurts. Three-word sentences underpin most of your daily communications. The mind is like a muscle; if not exercised, it will become flabby. Essay writing provides that exercise by requiring active thinking for a prolonged period of time.

Essay writing also helps the intellect by forcing you to develop a thought or an argument. It's not just a matter of thinking a subject through, it's a matter of depth. Essays force you to delve deeper into the self, to dig for nuggets of wisdom and understanding, to bring the potential of your wondrous mind to the surface.

Crafting a good essay demands a mastery of the language. Essays fuse the need for a good vocabulary with good grammar and thus provide a complete package. Finally, essay writing helps you communicate better in your daily social correspondence, such as e-mails to friends.

Master the practical side of the English language: Excel at the type of writing that can help you in your profession: i.e. business writing, technical manual writing. If you engage in business correspondence on a regular basis, if memos are part of your work routine, make sure that your correspondence will be an asset and not a liability.

Choosing the right course/program

The consumerized university[20] *and the problems of picking a good course*

The trend towards courses analyzing consumer culture is rapidly gaining ground in universities. The preoccupations of university professors tend to evince a fatal attraction to the infantile world of consumerism. Academics are comparing consumer products with everything from literary masterpieces to philosophical tracts. The attempt to canonize rock stars alongside great classical composers and the comparison of world literature with tawdry Hollywood movies are only some of the examples of this trend.

Increasingly, academics research and teach courses that seek to imbue consumer culture with non-existent meaning, to validate it through the academic setting. For some professors this represents a desperate attempt to find relevance within modern society, to familiarize students with some theory, philosopher or artist via the familiar framework of pop culture. Many other professors have fallen into the consumer trap and now believe that consumer products can provide you with a valid source of knowledge, with a fertile terrain for exploring the human condition.

Other academics have gone even further, wholly embracing modern consumer culture. These academics have abandoned knowledge altogether, in an ultimately vain and self-defeating attempt to extract meaning from the meaningless artificial construct that is consumer society. These people disparage Shakespeare as an irrelevant dead white man, but find meaning in studying Pepsi commercials. The mere existence of university courses on such important subjects as *The Simpsons* and video games shows the decay of our institutions of higher learning. These bastions of

20. This applies equally to colleges.

knowledge, which should act as bulwarks against the streams of imbecility spewed by the consumerist giants, are being overrun themselves. Unless drastic action is taken to remedy the situation and control both the curriculum and the quality of the faculty, the value of a university degree will continue to decline.

What lies at the root of this tragic process? Why is the university declining as an institution? Once again, we must look to consumerism for the answer. Consumerism is applying both external and internal pressure on institutions of higher learning in order to control their curricula.

External pressure

The external pressure on universities to consumerize comes from a familiar source: you. Consumer advertising has not only stultified your mind, it has also infantilized you. We are becoming a very infantile society. Consumerism encourages you to treat things superficially, to act in a childish manner. The multinationals want you to be a spoiled brat, constantly asking for a new toy, a different product, which they will most happily provide.

Perfectly content in this infantile universe, you have no wish to change it when you go to university. You expect and desire more of the same within the university environment. In order to accommodate you, some multinationals have set up their own educational centres. McDonald's, for example, has a "university". Whether or not they possess their own university, multinationals eagerly seek to invade already existing ones. You are the battering ram used by the multinationals to ensure that the consumer universe is replicated within the university environment.

What are the results? When you attend university seeking consumerism instead of knowledge the universities feel your pressure. They have begun to relent *en masse*. Instead of countering the noxious effects of years of consumer pollution through their curriculum, many universities now offer you the chance to fully embrace consumerism as part of their study programs. Validated at the university level, consumerism has become a comprehensive and universal system of knowledge.

Internal pressure

The insidious nature of pop culture and its constant propaganda will leave its mark on anyone, regardless of that person's intelligence. Even the tenured professor, a person who has comprehensive knowledge of his field of study as well as remarkable intelligence, is nonetheless prey to the childishness of consumerism.[21] Concomitant with his studies he is also a keen watcher of television shows. He discusses them with his graduate students or perhaps mentions them during his classes.

Consumerism begins to infect his teaching. It gains acceptability. It is accepted as a subject, if only for the sake of comparison, of an essay or a seminar. Slowly, it seeps into academic discourse; surely it pollutes the scholarly mind. After all, aside from the mentally ill, few men completely compartmentalize their experiences. It is difficult to be a Shakespeare scholar and an avid fan of *Star Trek* without drawing parallels between the two. Keep in mind that we are dealing with extremely intelligent people, people who have trained their critical faculties to the point of searching for meaning in almost every activity. Once they turn their attention to consumerism, it is inevitable they will find "meaning" in its products. In fact, they are only practicing a form of intellectual self deception, uncovering meaning where there is none.

So arises this terrible and destructive fallacy, whereby men of great intellect and knowledge bend their attentions towards utterly unworthy subjects, and through their own efforts and abilities, imbue these meaningless creations of consumer culture with artificial significance. For all the articles that have filled academic journals, for all the unmerited reverence accorded to a Bob Dylan or a *Matrix*, the simple fact remains that the emperor has no clothes. No amount of accolades and honest intellectual effort, no amount of reading in all kinds of philosophies or drawing literary analogies, will cloak the naked truth of consumer culture's meaninglessness. In seeking to mine consumerism for genuine academic relevance professors are not only deluding themselves and unwittingly masking the worthless nature of this enterprise, but are in effect engaged in a process of self-destruction. By placing their own academic knowledge on an equal level with the insipid offerings of consumerism, professors condemn the very knowledge which has consumed so much of their life and intellectual passion to irrelevance.

21. During my graduate studies I have overheard many discussions involving persons of otherwise impeccable academic credentials, where the topic was some episode of a puerile TV show.

Saving the Self

Selecting your courses

Choosing your courses is the most important aspect of your university education. Selecting the right course involves a number of considerations:

No consumer courses: The main concern in choosing your course load is to avoid consumer-influenced courses. Choose courses that make no reference to consumer products. Courses in sciences, engineering and math are least likely to be poisoned by consumerism, although, as I will argue later, they are not as crucial to developing the self.

Theory first: Focus on theory and serious analysis. Keep away from anything that discusses the literary qualities of superheroes or analyzes the psychology of gangsta rappers. If you take business courses, choose courses that will help you to become a business owner, not an employee for a multinational. Considering the huge amounts you or your parents are spending on your education, and the huge debt load many of you are assuming, shouldn't you derive maximum profit from your educational opportunity?

Benefit from electives: If you are studying for a degree, try to benefit from your electives. Choose electives in subjects different from your major to broaden your education. Engineers, take English courses. History majors, try biology. If you have a specific ethnic background, then take a course in the culture or politics of your country of ancestry.

Too often, students prefer to fill their elective slots with "easy credit" courses, courses where you do little work and learn even less. Other students, more conscientious, only choose electives within their field, giving them a very narrow band of knowledge. Both choices are missing the mark. The point of electives is to enable the student to experience as many disciplines and fields of knowledge as possible. Don't sell yourself short.

Embrace the Arts and Humanities: Courses in these fields are essential to unlocking the potential of the self.

Whether in schools or universities, the value of an education in the arts and humanities is fading by the year. We live in a pragmatic age, where pragmatism is measured by the income that a particular college degree can bring. Arts and humanities degrees translate poorly in terms of financial rewards. They are consequently thought of as useless in today's society, desperate for the money needed to fully partake in consumerist delights.

Another reason for the slow demise of arts and humanities courses is that these types of courses tax the creative self. For today's mentally lazy students, raised on a steady diet of instant consumerist gratification, the creative self has seriously atrophied. Students either do not know or do not want to revive the creative self. Furthermore, people today love the security and reassurance of science and technology. The idea of a right answer, of an unshakable foundation, of mnemonic exercises and of formulaic responses is very comforting. In short, everything that arts and humanities is not.

If you are one of those who did not like history, or did not like English courses, the problem was not in the books themselves, but rather in your approach towards them. The reason you were turned off by the arts and humanities is that they require your individual expression. This is also the reason why you must embrace them. Embracing this type of knowledge will not be an easy task. Consumerism has frightened you away from expressing your individuality. Consumerism has prevented you from giving of your self. Consumerism has only taught to take, absorb and mimic, never to create, give or share.

Consumerism has also presented you with the means of "outwitting" teachers and professors with rehashed versions of Coles Notes. In using Coles Notes, you are only cheating your self. Few in the teaching profession are interested in what others have to say about a particular work. The major thing professors care about is what the student has to say. More importantly, the only thing *you* must care about is what you have to say.

You must change your mindset when approaching arts and humanities courses. You cannot read a novel as a science manual. There are no right answers in fiction. In fact, there are no answers whatsoever. There are only opinions. Even the professor's opinion is only that, an opinion. You must have the courage to develop and present your own opinion of a work, whatever it may be. The professor's job is not to give you answers, but to provide context and a basic analytical framework for making your interpretations. You are the one who must determine what the work is trying to say. You must give meaning to the work by considering it within your self, by stating how it affected you.

Arts and humanities courses demand that the self interacts with the work, and does not treat it as some foreign object. By giving meaning to other works, by interpreting the other, the self gains meaning and understanding.

Arts and humanities courses offer you the most freedom in developing the self through formal knowledge. Whereas math and physics are governed by their own laws and rules, and are only functional within those boundaries, in the arts and humanities there are no rules. Yes, an essay must have a beginning, a middle, and an end, but do not confuse structure with formulae. What you write in that beginning, middle and end cannot be learned, taught or memorized. For what you must write is your self.

Arts and humanities courses also offer a breadth of scope for self-expression that is missing in rigidly logical fields of knowledge such as mathematics and physics. While the opportunity for self-expression is also alive there, these disciplines of knowledge fail to consider the emotional and spiritual aspects of the self and, as such, are somewhat restricted in their creative potential. Within the arts and humanities, the self has potential to express all aspects of its being, to unfurl its creative capabilities to the utmost. No branch of knowledge provides a more complete stimulation of the self, no branch of knowledge advances you higher on the ladder of self-fulfillment.

Save the children: help them embrace knowledge

In embracing knowledge, it is important not to forget your children. It is your responsibility to protect and nurture their young minds by orienting them towards the acquisition of knowledge. Do not abandon them to the slavery of consumerism. Most of all, do not automatically assume that school will educate your kids. Today's schools are not what they used to be.

The consumerization of schools is the most insidious attack yet upon education.[22] It signals the complete dominance of the multinationals, which already have in their thrall so many of North America's youth. Consumer giants already act as surrogates for busy parents, raising children on a steady diet of its food, culture and entertainment. Well in control of the so-called leisure time of today's youth, multinationals now seek to extend their domain into the classrooms.

The process of learning, the almost sacrosanct acquisition of knowledge, is filtered through the consumer prism. "Educational" television programs have invaded the classrooms. Soft-drink machines are on every corridor. Product advertisements cover the walls. When will it stop? Only when education has been completely consumerized and the school curriculum will be offering courses in MTV, the history of the Super Bowl, and Disney movies.

---

22. Just to be clear, I am not referring to consumerism's domination of adolescents, which I have already addressed, but to the consumerization of the actual learning institution itself.

Saving the Self

Your child deserves better

Your child deserves at least a chance to be educated. But how can you counteract consumerism's corruption of education?

Find your child the right school: Finding the proper school for your child is one of your most important parental duties. As a parent, it is your responsibility to ensure that your child receives the best possible education. If that school is a forty-five minute drive away, so be it. Your child deserves the best. The right school will have the following three attributes. First, the emphasis is on academics and substantive learning. Second, the school has a Consumer-free learning environment. That means no corporate ads on the wall, no "educational" TV in the classroom, no junk-food dispensers down the hall. Finally, school programs deal with your child's aptitudes and needs. Some schools specialize in precocious students; others offer curricula customized for the needs of artistically, scientifically or athletically gifted children. If your child shows a particular talent or just sheer brilliance, even more reason to find a school that will cater to these abilities.

Hire good tutors: Often, school does not offer enough grounding in a particular field of knowledge, or fails to teach certain branches of knowledge due to funding cutbacks. To remedy these lacunae, tutors are an excellent option.

Tutors will provide the close attention and nurturing support children need if they are to avoid falling prey to consumer temptations. By establishing a personal relationship with the child, a private tutor will be in a much better position to influence the child towards a love of knowledge and learning.

Invest the money: Private schools cost a lot; so does tutoring. Stop shelling out money for useless consumer products and invest in your child's education instead. Make a down payment on the fulfillment of their potential, not on an X-Box.

Invest the time: School, tutors and money will only do so much. The ultimate responsibility rests with you. You must be a mentor for your child.

Be there for your child in order to help with schoolwork. Show them you care about knowledge. If you will not fight alongside to help them in the sometime difficult process of learning, why should they bother? This is not an invitation to do the child's homework by any means. Rather, discuss their work and point them towards a solution or towards acquiring the necessary tools for a solution.

Be active in the learning process. See what they are being taught, and by whom. Go to the parent-teacher interviews. Attend a class; although your child might be mortified by your presence, it's worth their pain to reassure yourself that they are being taught properly.

Instill them with a love of learning. If you do not read, why should they? If you do not care about knowledge why should they? By setting the example yourself and taking your children to libraries and museums you remove them from Consumer-world to a place where knowledge is precious. Once introduced to the world of knowledge, your children will learn to prize it as well.

Love for knowledge does not necessarily mean love of school. True success comes when your children seek to increase their knowledge by studying and reading on their own initiative, not just when they are being forced to learn. If you create the right conditions, your child's fascination will be with knowledge and not with consumer products.

Chapter 10

Sports

Consumerism has denatured sport from athletic activity to a consumer orgy. Saving the self entails recapturing the true meaning of sport, before multinationals ruled the day.

Consumer sport, consumer athletes

Their achievements are endlessly replayed. They are remembered as modern legends. Consumer athletes have become the equivalent of mythical heroes, modern day knights in shining armour. Games have the status of battles, and former sport greats are venerated as great warriors. This is no coincidence. Athletes have supplanted the role of military heroes because in the consumerist idyll there are no wars and consumers are not interested in prosecuting them. Man's aggressive impulses are now vicariously satisfied through fandom. Fans are the war host and athletes the commanders, except that these soldiers do not follow their commanders into battle but only cheer them on.

While athletes have competed before spectators since ancient Greece, consumerism has transformed professional sports into an addiction. Due to a multitude of sports channels and the increasingly busy calendars of professional competitions, sports aficionados have metamorphosed from amateur athletes into remote-wielding couch potatoes. Fewer and fewer people play sports, more and more people watch them. Consumer sport has mutated the idea of physical activity from an objective to a subjective act. The elevation to sainthood of consumer athletes, the constant praise of their abilities, has convinced many that their own efforts in the same sport are superfluous, being pale, awkward imitations of the pros on TV. People prefer to watch their consumer heroes rather than engage in what they regard as pathetic attempts at emulation.

The abhorrent culture surrounding consumer sport has made many people turn away in disgust from sports altogether. Consumer sport is associated with brutishness, boorishness, a lack of education, low intelligence and violence, sexual or otherwise. For those who hate consumer sports, sport has become something practiced and appreciated only by morons. Sport-haters reject physical activity as a symbol of a despised social group. Tragically, people are punishing their own bodies to affirm their opposition to consumer sport culture.

Consumer sport: 99 per cent consumption, 1 per cent sport

As the popularity of consumer sport has mushroomed, sport itself has lessened. Since for the multinationals sport is only a revenue source or a vehicle for promoting their products, they cannot rely on the actual sport to provide the so-called "entertainment value." That's one business risk they are unwilling to take. Unhappy fans will not come back. Unhappy fans will not watch the game. So the new message disseminated by the multinationals is simple: you don't have to *watch* the actual game to have fun. The game has become secondary to the "entertainment value."

The WWF, which has understood this better than anyone, has experienced great success in creating consumer entertainment through its soap opera storylines. The wrestling (fake as it is) is only a minor part of its "product." The NFL has succeeded in making the Super Bowl half-time show as talked about as the game. Indeed, multinationals have successfully transformed the Super Bowl into an event for watching new television commercials.

Whole "entertainment value" industries have grown up around consumer sport events, from cheerleaders, to mascots to half-time performances. Your senses are dulled by these garish spectacles so that the actual game becomes irrelevant to your enjoyment. A constant barrage of consumer advertising alternated by consumer music ensures that you will be kept in a consumerist stupor.

The multinationals have also latched onto sport as a perfect vehicle for increasing consumption. The overwhelming message of consumer sports is: consume! You are constantly urged to indulge in consumer food from the hordes of concession-stands lining the halls of various sports arenas. You are constantly urged to buy products associated with your favourite team. Whether on television or in the arena, the message of consumption is relentless.

The reason multinationals can get away with this perversion of sports is your inability to watch a whole game without distractions. Consumerism has reduced your attention span and powers of concentration to virtually nil. You always need different impulses, you always need something to distract your attention. Even if you miss an exciting part due to these distractions, you can always watch it on replay.

Attending consumer sport has also become a method of making employees happy and of doing business. The game serves as a backdrop for partying or deal-making. In both cases, the value of the actual sport is being diminished.

What should be an act of appreciation of a physical spectacle has become a circus and an excuse for even more over-consumption. No wonder North American arenas are full of spectators whose gross obesity prevents them from participating in their favourite sport.

Consumer control

How did the multinationals get their corporate hands on sports in the first place? In a number of ways:

Purchasing the teams outright: A number of multinationals own professional sports teams. Cablevision and Fox Sports, for example, own the New York Rangers.

The corporatization of teams: In Europe, some of the continent's most prestigious soccer teams, such as Manchester United and Borussia Dortmund, have become listed companies, issuing shares to increase their value. Once publicly-listed, teams such as Manchester United do not belong to the people of Manchester anymore, but to the shareholders. They are well on their way to becoming multinationals themselves, if not already there.

Merchandizing: Merchandizing allows multinationals to make big bucks from the fans. Multinationals have transformed team merchandise into a fashion statement. Teams such as the New York Yankees, the Los Angeles Lakers and Real Madrid have become consumer brands in themselves. People who've never seen one of their games or care little for the sport as a whole, wear their products. To increase their revenue, teams have sought an ever-expanding array of ventures with multinationals, selling their athletic soul in the process.

Sponsorship: Sponsorship contracts are pervasive in all professional sports. Advertising billboards dominate the arenas where sports are being played. Sport arenas have been renamed after multinationals (i.e. the Pepsi Centre in Denver). Sporting events have also been named after their sponsor (i.e. the Pepsi 400 in NASCAR racing).

Sponsorship has taken control of the players themselves. Most athletes are beholden to their sponsorship contracts in terms of the products and equipment they must wear while playing. The sponsor has precedence over the team. Athletes have allowed themselves to be turned into walking advertisements for consumerism, stepping out on the playing field in Nike shoes or Adidas shirts. Others have gone further still; some professional boxers paint their bodies with their sponsor's name before stepping into the ring.

The damage done

Beyond the conspicuous consumption now associated with pro sports, multinational control has caused enormous damage to both professional and amateur sports. Here is what they've done:

Destroyed competitiveness: Professional sports are heading towards a crisis. As the distance between rich and poor clubs grows, competition lessens. Professional sports leagues are becoming hopelessly predictable. Rich teams are clustered at the top, poorer ones hug the bottom. Money decides the fate of a team's standing. The team with the biggest payroll, the team with the largest merchandizing empire, the team controlled by the largest multinational, inevitably triumphs. In every European football league, the same two or three clubs jockey for the league championship every year. In North America, financial concerns threaten to destroy professional NHL hockey in the birthplace of hockey, Canada. Canadian clubs, suffering from a weak Canadian dollar and high taxes, are condemned to wallow around the bottom of the NHL, and have lost a number of teams to U.S. hockey hotbeds such as Phoenix.

Distorting the game: One method of distorting the game is by increasing the number of teams within professional leagues. This dilutes the talent pool and makes for second-rate sports leagues with second-rate games. Boring games play into the hands of the multinationals, who kindly offer you a host of consumer distractions to while away the time.

League over-expansion has also destroyed traditional rivalries. Shifts in divisions, conferences, schedules and the like have made traditional rivals meet once in a blue moon. Fans no longer have a hated opposition team. Everything has been smoothed away into a placid amorphous mess. There is your home team and there is everyone else, and they are too many to know or despise.

A second method of distorting sports involves the forced expansion of sports with limited geographical appeal. In an attempt to please the multinationals, the National Hockey League commissioner has undertaken a massive expansion of the NHL in America's sunbelt, where the only skates you'll find have rollers on them, and ice only comes in cubes. The multinationals will not and cannot accept the natural limits of hockey, even in the face of half-empty arenas. The multinationals understand sports only in terms of economics. They believe that all professional sports leagues must be present in large markets (i.e. large urban centres) regardless of whether the sport is actually played, or even capable of being played, within that market.

Globalizing the game: This is perhaps the most destructive interference of all. Multinationals use your money to globalize the game in two distinct ways:

a) Globalizing the player base. Gone are the days when a team's players were the products of the team's city or region. Now, especially in the case of European football, but increasingly in North American professional sports such as the NBA, NHL and MLB, teams are lucky if players in the starting line-up come from the same country.

   Gone also are the days when a player would have a career with the team that first chose him. Player's team affiliations are as fickle as the wind. Team rosters have lost any sense of constancy. The composition of a team now depends on an athlete marketplace where multinationals do all the buying and selling. Identifying with your team roster is difficult since it becomes unrecognizable from year to year. That hated player on the opposition might soon play for you. Sports rivalries and team pride are hard to build on such shifting sands.

b) Globalizing the fan base. A constant team roster is but one aspect of a team's identity. A second aspect is a settled fan base. The fans give the team its *raison d'etre*. They provide, develop and maintain team identity. As the multinationals globalize the fan base, this sense of identity erodes. People from different countries, from different continents, now cheer for what used to be the local team. The Yankees are no longer New York's team. Manchester United does not belong to Manchester. They are global teams with a global fan base. According to the consumer propaganda, as long as you purchase the team's merchandise you are on an equal footing with the most rabid fan from that team's city.

   This is completely missing the point. Only the local fans can truly understand the meaning of the team. For them, the team is inextricably tied up with the place and history of their city. What do all of these things mean to someone in another country, someone who does not share the culture, the mentality or the idea of place associated with the team? What can it mean to be a fan of a television screen? Real fans are embedded in the context of the team, the stadium, the town and its people. Television fans are mere consumers.

Destroying team identity: In North America, arenas are being renamed after multinationals. In Europe, team jerseys are proudly emblazoned with the sponsor's name. Professional sport teams no longer play for their fans, they play for their sponsors. Team identity is now decided by the sponsor. They control the fortunes of the team and they dictate how the team will look and function. When the sponsor changes, so does the identity of the team. Teams have been stolen away from their fans, transformed into consumerist tools. Unless they produce for their multinational masters, they will be moved away or closed down, with complete disregard for the fans' wishes.

Sponsors have also taken control of national teams. The legendary Brazilian national soccer team signed on with Nike. The sponsorship contract forced the Brazilians to play five games per year at Nike's request. The team was also required to field a full-strength lineup for these games, even if the coach wanted to rest his best players for more important fixtures. Perhaps the most egregious, although unproven, allegation is that Nike forced Brazil to play its star striker Ronaldo during the final of the 1998 World Cup, despite the fact he was injured and against the will of the coach. Brazil lost the final 3-0 to France. This was Brazil, where soccer is the unofficial religion. Nike taught the Brazilians a lesson in effectively telling them: this is no longer your team, it's ours.

Destroying the athletes: Through sponsorship, consumerism has transformed sport into a means to an end for elite athletes. The reason most talented youngsters dream of professional sport is not the excitement of playing at a top level or the roar of the crowd, but rather the sponsorship contracts. Sport has become a business venture for athletes. The fans do not matter. Their team does not matter. Even their country does not matter. Their consumer sponsor is the absolute master. Kim Clijsters, a Belgian tennis player, one of the best in the world, refused to play for Belgium because of sponsorship conflicts. Athletes will betray their very country if their consumer sponsors so decree.

The ultimate reduction of professional athletes is the reduction to brand status. When the athlete becomes the brand, he loses his humanity. When Real Madrid purchased David Beckham from Manchester United they bought a brand, not a soccer player. Purchasing David Beckham was a business transaction designed for profit and not for sport. The value of Beckham as a brand is infinitely greater than his value as a player or as a human being. That is the result of consumerism.

The consumerization of professional sport and its consequences

Ever since the multinationals have decided that sport is a perfect consumer vehicle they began pouring enormous amounts of money into it. As sports revenues grew, so did operating costs, principally players' salaries. This created a vicious consumerist cycle. In order to keep or acquire players, teams were forced to find extra sources of revenue. Consequently, they ceded ever more of their identity to the multinationals, the only source of money in town. Multinationals addicted professional sports to their money and in their need for a fix, professional sports became a consumer slave.

Ironically, the consumerization of sport has been highly destructive to the business of sports. No matter how much money rolls in, more money is rolling out. The process has resulted in many professional teams losing money. Teams are groaning under huge debt loads as multinationals expand the game and feed the greed of the athletes. Whole leagues are in trouble from the NHL in America to the Italian Serie A.

The consumerization of amateur sport

The reach of the multinationals has extended beyond professional sports. Multinationals now effectively control national teams as well as important amateur competitions, such as the Olympics. The taint of consumerism has infected every last athletic refuge.

Money has poisoned amateur athletes even more than their professional counterparts. For amateur competitors in fields such as swimming, gymnastics or Greco-Roman wrestling, sponsorship contracts represent the sole chance of snagging significant economic benefits from the years of hard work and dedication spent in their sport. Many of these amateur athletes' greatest wish is to rise to a level where they can become mouthpieces for consumer propaganda. The multinationals have fashioned a new dream for the world's elite athletes: being the ideal consumer slave.

Saving the Self

Who will re-establish the purity of sport? Who will push back the poisonous influence of consumerism? Only one person who can do that: YOU.

Play, don't watch: Remember that sport is meant to be played. It is only during the past few decades, with the rise of the multinationals, that sport has been consumerized and transformed from a physical activity into a passive spectacle. Children, whose enthusiasm and ebullience has not been completely extinguished by the consumer propaganda, prefer to play sports rather than watch them. Reawaken the child within you. Immerse your self in the athletic experience.

Sport elevates the self. Every moment spent playing is infinitely better than hours of vegetating on the couch. As such, do not allow traumatic school experiences or the perfection of professional athletes to turn you away from your needs. Be selfish. You need sport. It's all about you. Disregard any insufficiencies or inherent awkwardness and play.

Sport is not mere physical exercise. Sport fuses the needs of mind and body. When you play sports you are much more whole than in your normal life. The modern lifestyle is schizophrenic. Work is almost invariably a sedentary occupation where you exercise, if at all, your mind. Then, after work, you can "work out" to exercise your body. That is not how you were conceived. This is not a normal operation of the self. You are a whole being and your being exists most when the totality of its self is being used and being challenged. In hunter-gatherer societies, mind and body needed to be simultaneously exercised in order to ensure one's survival. In today's world, where hunting and gathering is confined to a few lost Amazon tribes, sport provides a rough equivalent of that total experience of being.

Sport requires intelligence, cunning, concentration and creativity to maximize your performance. While there is no substitute for athleticism and natural talent, the mind can help mitigate some athletic failings. Thus you might not be a good basketball dribbler or shooter, but you can use your mind to spot the open man, construct plays or make the right play at the right time.

When playing, you are constantly faced with an array of options such as which teammate you should pass the ball to in soccer, or where to hit your next groundstroke in tennis, or how to pitch to the next batter. Your mind thinks, your body executes. Both are applied to the same objective. Both work in concert. The result is not important. Victory is achieved through the experience.

Don't use consumer sport equipment: Playing a sport does not require purchasing consumer products. You DO NOT need $200 Nike shoes to play basketball. Stop wasting your money. Brand equipment will not improve your ability one iota. Perhaps wearing the best equipment money can buy is essential to the professional players. For the millions who play just for fun, it will not make any difference in your enjoyment and ability to play the game. Don't buy into the consumer propaganda.

There is no need to make yourself a walking advertisement for brand name products.

Sport has nothing to do with consumer sports equipment. There is no association between the two. Do not let the association drawn by the consumer giants poison your attitude towards sport and make you turn away from activities that can benefit your body and mind. Your slogan for Nike should be: Just ignore it.

The only thing you need to do when picking sports equipment, is to pick what you need. If the shoe fits and is comfortable, buy it. Often, you do not need specialized equipment to play. You do not need basketball shoes to play basketball; any pair of athletic shoes will do. Before you rush out to buy expensive soccer shoes, remember that Pele, the greatest soccer player of them all, played barefoot on the beach.

Sports equipment is neither fashion nor casual clothing

The second you choose sports equipment based on the brand name you surrender your individuality and become a consumer. Such is the case with an increasing number of people for whom sports equipment has become a fashion statement. People buy the best sports equipment to be seen in it; they do not actually play the sport. If that is you, better throw your shiny new sports gear away, grab a pair of cheap no-name running shoes and a ball, and start playing. Sports equipment's sole function is to enable you to participate in a sport. Sports is not about looking good, it's about feeling good. Your body cares little for what you wear, but would greatly appreciate some exercise to help it feel better.

If you do watch sports, watch for the love of the game: Too many so-called fans have little or no actual knowledge of the complexities, strategies and tactics involved in the game. Educate yourself in the sport of your choice so that you will watch with understanding and genuine appreciation. Become a sport connoisseur and the consumer propaganda attached to the event will fade into meaninglessness. Understand and appreciate the complexities of the game, and you will no longer need "entertainment value" or conspicuous consumption to make the game exciting.

Consumerism has perverted the process of watching sports in two crucial ways:

The purpose

Because many fans do not understand the subtleties of the game and because in Consumer-world superficiality and brevity is prized, multinationals have reduced sports from a whole game to a set of highlights. The sole thing consumerism wants you to watch is the climactic act, the goal, the touchdown, the slam dunk, the home run. The rest of the time, multinationals want you to pay attention to their advertising while engaging in mindless consumption.

Why bother to watch a three-hour game when you can watch the highlights on ESPN? Because a highlight is not a game. It is not even the most important aspect of the game. A game is a complete event from beginning to end. Its beauty, intricacy and fascination will not be conveyed in the highlight that you catch between the beers and pizza. Sport highlights detract from your understanding and appreciation of sport by undermining your patience, desire and mental discipline to watch a complete game.

To those of you who are highlight reel people, the time has come to discover the true beauty of sport. Here's how:

First, watch the game. The whole game from beginning to end, and the game as a whole, not just the star players.

Next, learn the game. Educate yourself in what makes the game tick, what are the stratagems used by the players and coaches, what are the subtleties of each player's role.

Finally, love the game. Only with true understanding will you love the game.

Statistics

An avalanche of statistics has buried the true meaning of sport. Sport is not a summary of numbers. Studying the numbers will not convey to you the true beauty of sport, the drama, the passion, the trickery, the suspense, the conflicts, the effort, the successes, the failures, the ebb and flow of a game. These can only be understood by seeing the spectacle unfold itself in all its majesty and its bathos, its tragedy and its farce. That is sports. Numbers are sterile, numbers are dry, numbers are a method through which the consumer propaganda apparatus operates to control your attention, to fill your mind with useless information. Ignore the statistics and you will understand the sport better.

If you can, watch in person: By attending the game in person you avoid commercials and the irritation of the modern sports commentator, part wannabe stand-up comic, part all-knowing pompous ass. The preeminent role of sports commentators is nothing more than an attempt to manipulate your understanding of the game. By relying on the commentator's interpretation, you are stifling your own creative and intellectual abilities. You do not need hordes of parasitical analysts, many of whom cannot or have not played the game themselves, to tell you what you should extract from an athlete's performance. Figure it out yourself.

Support the amateurs: While amateur sport might not be of the highest caliber, it provides more room for interaction and intimacy. Small crowds and highly accessible players bridge the distance between the spectator and the game, and help diminish the mystical aura that surrounds athletes.

Amateur games tend to be a more intense experience for the spectator. Spectators are often the relatives and friends of the players themselves. It's much easier to cheer for your son or your sister or your best friend than it is to cheer on a millionaire athlete who you do not know and will probably never meet.

Amateur sports maintain the original purpose of spectators in sports, which is to encourage the team to win.[23] Best of all amateur sports, at least at the lowest levels, tend to be free of the consumer trappings that have infected professional sport. If you have to choose between catching a pro game and catching your best friend's softball tournament, choose your friend. It's inexpensive and you can have a beer with your friend afterwards. Can you do the same thing with a pro athlete?

Avoid purchasing team merchandize: There is no need for you to bankroll the outrageous profits of the multinationals. Give your pocketbook a rest, and spend your hard-earned money on things that will bring a tangible benefit to the self.

Multinationals own pro sports and will continue to own it until you chase them away. And the only way to do that is to hit them on the bottom line until they bleed red ink all over the books. Refuse buying into the sports merchandize craze and you will destroy a principal moneymaking source for the multinationals. Help chase the multinationals out of sport altogether. Only then will there still be a chance for professional sport to regain some of its former glory, and evolve beyond the cynical business transaction it has become.[24]

Be a true fan: You do not have to be a consumer to be a fan. You do not have to be a consumer to support your team. The concept of fandom, of attachment to what used to be the local team,[25] has been perverted by multinationals eager to establish merchandising empires. Purchasing team merchandize has become inextricably linked with fandom.

---

23. As opposed to the contemporary purpose of sports, putting money in the multinationals' pockets.
24. The glory days existed when a club was family-owned, or else was the property of a group of fans or players.
25. Although globalization has made loyalties much more wide-ranging; many sneer that none of the Manchester United's fans are from Manchester.

The association is illogical. You can parade in your team colours without lining the pockets of multinationals. If your teams sports red shirts, wear one of your red shirts when you go to the game. There is no need to wear one of the team's red shirts, whose production has been licensed out to a multinational, in order to demonstrate your allegiance. Similarly, you can support the team using home-made placards rather than buying the flags or pennants of the multinationals.

True fandom is more than shelling out some cash on a replica shirt and catching a game on the tube. True fans are those who live or hail from the city of their team.

Teams are extensions and manifestations of the city and region where they are located, the source of civic pride. It is the locals that form the fan base, the true core team supporters. It is they who interact with the players, who console and cajole them, who criticize and applaud. The team is part of their identity just as much as they are part of the team's identity. These are the fans who know the team songs, cherish the memories, meet in bars before and after games to discuss their team's exploits. These are the true fans. Are you one of those? If you are not, then rest assured you can't buy your fandom through merchandize. All you are buying into is the further destruction of the team you claim to support. All you are buying into are the lies of the multinationals.

Don't buy into the hype: Many will say that multinationals have been a great addition to professional sports. Aside from the suddenly wealthy athletes and management, few others have benefited from the addition. Moreover, while the athletes have benefited financially, they have suffered as human beings.

Before the multinationals distorted professional sports, athletes themselves were better persons. Since sport's salaries were insufficient, athletes often worked jobs on the side. Knowing that their sports career was brief and that they needed a job to support themselves afterwards, they either had a trade or educated themselves. They were often productive, conscientious citizens. Now what we've got is a crop of barely literate millionaires, most of which, in their supremely unmerited arrogance, fancy themselves above the law and basic rules of conduct.

Sport was competitive, intense and passionate when athletes were paid a fraction of what they earn today. It will lose none of its luster if the multinationals are kicked out. Do not be afraid of taking down the whole house of cards.

It's just a game: Step back for a moment. What do you win or lose regardless of how well your team performs? How will it affect you? Like my mother said when I was watching an "important" game and she wanted to go grocery shopping: "Are these guys gonna buy you potatoes?" If I was going to eat that evening, I had to leave the game and buy groceries. Win or lose, it does not matter in your personal life and will not or should not affect it one iota.

Furthermore, the whole structure of consumer sports is so repetitive, so unchanging that it ultimately becomes tedious. Game after game, until the games themselves become meaningless, the obsession with statistics, the endless analysis of every conceivable aspect, the self-appointed pundits, the buckets of ink spilled, the television roundtables, and all for what? How much joy does it truly bring to your life? How much pride and personal satisfaction can you derive from the triumph of your consumer team? How much respect will you be afforded, how much will you have gained as a human being if your team wins? It can be an excuse for a good party but nobody that I know of introduces himself like this: "Hi, my name is Bob and I'm a fan of the World Champion L.A. Lakers…." Somehow I do not think that the girls will be swooning over that pronouncement, nor will the men turn green with envy.

Without being facetious, the fact remains that consumer sports are only a pastime and a particularly unwholesome and unhealthy pastime at that. This is not what sport is or was meant to be. Reclaim the true nature of sport the way it was meant to be: do it yourself.

Chapter 11

Travel

Getting away means getting away from the multinationals. This chapter is focuses on the purpose of travel as antithetical to that of consumerism.

Travel is a voyage of self-discovery. In discovering nature, or in discovering other people and cultures, you are fulfilling the potential of the self.

One of the basic purposes of travel is to experience something different. Even when travelling to a place you have visited before, you travel to change your daily routine, to vary your mundane ritual of work and chores. Since travel means stepping outside the comforts of home and routine, there is a certain anxiety associated with it. Too often we make up for that anxiety by seeking to recapture a bit of home while abroad. Unfortunately, the familiar experiences you tend to find abroad are the consumer offerings of the multinationals. Whether it's the Golden Arches of McDonald's or the latest Hollywood movie, the consumer experience is everywhere. If you are tempted by these "slices of home," don't indulge. Travelling is not designed to replicate consumer experience in foreign places. If travelling means stepping outside your daily work routine shouldn't you step outside any consumer routine as well?

Whether you travel within the country or internationally, the why's and how's of holidaying are crucial to developing the self. There are certain steps you must take to ensure the trip will provide the maximum amount of personal reward.

Destinations

The great outdoors

This is the optimal destination. Canoe trips, fishing, hiking and camping not only make for great vacations but they also make for healthy ones.

However, if you truly wish to experience the great outdoors, do not bring the consumerist cavalcade in tow. Make sure the great outdoors are genuinely experienced, rather than having the typical consumer lifestyle reproduced atop a mountain.

There are two types of outdoors experiences:

Hotels/motels/inns

Avoid the consumer tourist industry, the ubiquitous hotel chains, the large garish resorts and the multinational-owned cruise ships. If you choose your experience of nature to be mediated through the safety and comfort of a hotel room, choose a hotel that will provide safety and comfort. Ideally, this should be a small business run by an on-site proprietor dedicated to maximizing the pleasure of your stay. It should provide clean rooms, good food and drink, and information about exploring your surroundings. But it should be devoid of consumer products. That means no television, no video games and no consumer brand name products.

An excellent reason for avoiding multinational hotel chains is they are fast becoming shopping malls. The lobby of most multinational hotel chains is full of shops that will sell you anything from clothes to perfumes to electronics. You could end up spending more time and money shopping rather than sleeping. That is not the way it's supposed to be. Beyond any local artisan's creations, your hotel should have nothing to sell you. Shopping is not the reason you are travelling.

The ideal hotel will integrate seamlessly within your experience of nature. It will serve as the base camp from which to explore and enjoy your natural surroundings. The atmosphere, the food, and the sleeping conditions of the hotel will be designed to enhance your ability to explore nature. The hotel is the place where your body recovers after the exertions of the day, whether hiking or swimming. The hotel is not a place to tire or weaken you with consumerist distractions. The hotel is not a place to trap you with consumer temptations so you will have no interest in the great outdoors. If the hotel detracts from your outdoor experience by recreating a consumer paradise within its walls, then it is not the place for you.

Camping

Camping means the temptations found in hotels and resorts are gone. Make sure you do not bring them with you. Do not equip your RV with the tools of consumer entertainment. Do not haul your portable laptop into the wilderness. Do not bring every single wireless gadget invented by man into the forest. Once again, all you are doing is attempting to reconstruct within nature the Consumer-world you supposedly sought to escape.

Most of all, do not bring consumer food. The whole point of camping is to prepare food by the campfire (and I don't mean marshmallows), not to heat some pre-cooked ready-to-go burgers or stuff your self on Doritos. Bring only the ingredients needed to prepare holistic meals. Even better, wild it out and earn your ingredients by fishing and gathering forest fruit, nuts and mushrooms.

The courage to let go

Consumer tourism has thoroughly deformed the experience of the great outdoors. By reproducing Consumer-world within their hotels and resorts, multinationals have ensured there is no purpose for nature itself. People now travel to the great outdoors for shopping, consumer food and consumer entertainment. In places such as Aspen, Cancun, and St. Tropez, many visitors don't go outside their consumer hotels unless it's to show off their new sports car. Why go outside if you have satellite TV, luxury boutiques and video games for the kids? If that is your mentality, maybe it's time to remember what the great outdoors is all about.

The great outdoors is about fresh air, unpolluted water and wonderful natural scenery. The great outdoors is about sun, sea and surf. It's about having your body and mind relax from the day-to-day toils of work, from the stresses of your suburban existence, and the pollution of cities. Nature is a vast spa filled with healing qualities. And it's free. Take advantage of the bounty it has to offer. Enjoy its gifts. Do not travel to the great outdoors to watch nature through the windows of a consumerist prison, even if it is a five-star prison.

The question of experiencing the great outdoors turns on how authentic you wish that experience to be. How much are you willing to immerse your self within the surrounding environment? While it is up to you to decide the intimacy and degree of that relationship, make sure that some form of genuine interaction is possible in the first place. Do not render it meaningless through a refusal to engage in the purpose of the trip.

For many, nature and the outdoor experience have been so utterly dissociated from their genuine significance as to be utterly meaningless. Due to a suburban existence, nature has become alien. The familiar comforts of the consumer lifestyles overwhelm. Very soon, you forget you are a part of nature altogether.

If you do step into nature, you are not always free of the consumer experience. Consumerism has invaded nature itself. You used go to the beach it is because you liked to swim. You practically lived in the water. You loved to feel the breeze brushing your cheek, delighted in the heat of the sun drying your wet skin and exulted in the sand cushioning your every step. Remember those days? The days when you were a child, the days when there was only sea and sun and sky? I remember those days. They are long gone.

Consumerism has polluted the seaside. In the large resorts, nature is losing out to the multinationals. The cries of the seagulls are drowned out by indistinguishable blasts of consumer music. The beach is awash with consumer symbols from Coke cans to brand name sun umbrellas. Multinational garbage, from soft drink bottles to chocolate bar wrappers, floats on the waves. Speedboats crisscross the waters, while above, the blue sky is scarred by small airplanes trailing ad banners for the latest consumer products.

Most disappointingly, there are plenty of people who don't come to the beach to enjoy nature. In Margarita Island, the beach was lined with Internet cafes so people could play video games or send e-mails. In St. Martin, I met one man who stayed on the beach the whole week without ever entering the water, without ever taking off his shirt or shoes. He stood fully dressed in the shade of his umbrella for brief periods of time, then went to his room to watch television. His room had the air conditioner at full blast. He managed to catch a nasty cold and was sick for the whole week. He was on his honeymoon. To this day I do not understand why he went there. If this is how you plan to experience the great outdoors I have two words of advice for you: STAY HOME.

The student experience

Visits to the great outdoors are more harmful than helpful for today's students. Popular holiday destinations for students have become centres of alcoholic excess and all-night club-hopping. From Daytona Beach to Fort Lauderdale to Cancun, students see holidaying as a drunken orgy. Consumer multinationals preside over these bacchanalian feasts by sponsoring endless numbers of parties and other events where college students can be exposed to their products, often offered up as "prizes."

These consumer parties are the ultimate perversion of the outdoor experience. Instead of finding healing and rest in nature, you find inebriation, exhaustion, vomiting, and violence. Not only do you subject your body to stresses and torments that can end in fatal accidents or alcoholic comas, you are ignoring the nature that surrounds you in the first place. You end up spending most of your holidays indoors: the night in bars and discos, the day sleeping off the hangover.

Saving the Self

If you must experience nightlife on the mountaintop or the beachside, do it reasonably. Remember the nightlife, no matter how good, must always play a secondary part to the main purpose of the trip, which is the enjoyment of the great outdoors. How do you achieve that balance?

First of all, control your alcohol. Drink moderately. The purpose of alcohol is to make you feel good, so drink just enough to warm up your conversation and your dancing and not to leave you prostrate before the porcelain throne.

Second, control your partying. You do not need to go out every single night. You don't need to see every nightclub in Cancun. Take a break, help your body out.

Third, control your time. If you do go out, don't stay up until dawn. Go to the club, dance away a couple of hours, have a drink or two, then go home. If you're looking for a temporary mate, act early and fast. Don't wait until five in the morning, when either you or your intended partner are too drunk to make your moves.

Finally, do not bring the nightlife to the outdoors. You are not going to the beach or lakeside to sit around all day drinking consumer alcohol and blasting consumer music. You are there to get catch some rays and swim.

Sightseeing 1: The cultural experience

Many tourists deny themselves the pleasure of exploring the culture and traditions of the place they are visiting by choosing to live in Consumer-world. To ensure that such consumer travelling is possible multinationals have consumerized top cultural tourist destinations. In Paris, McDonald's and other staples of consumerism are present on the Champs Elysee. Disney has opened one of its theme parks on the outskirts of the French capital. The message from the multinationals is that wherever you go we will be there, we will be with you. Our food, our music, our entertainment will accompany you no matter the destination. If you subscribe to their message then you have never really travelled in the first place. Why fly 5,000 miles to the world capital of *haute cuisine* to eat the same Big Mac you find around the corner from your house? Why go to the global centre for fashion and culture to visit a theme park?

Saving the Self

The multinationals' goal is to create a consumer travelling experience. Your travelling goal must be to assert your individuality through experiencing otherness. You must fight consumer uniformity with experience, the experience gained through exploring different cultures.

When you next visit another cultural destination, remember why you are going there. Your goal is to experience the cultural wealth of that place and not to indulge in the consumer lifestyle. That means you need to know what the cultural attractions are, and that you have to research your destination. Preparation is key and it is a three-step process:

Know your places: Paris boasts an enormous number of tourist attractions, from famous architecture to renowned artwork. It is also the host of numerous cultural events. While you cannot possibly experience everything Paris has to offer, both in terms of its past and its present, you must at least know what there is to see in the fabled City of Lights. That means knowing the museums, the churches, the famous cemeteries, and other landmarks. Instructing yourself on Paris' points of interest is the first step in planning your vacation.

Know what they mean: The key to appreciating the sights and sounds of Paris is understanding them in their context. If you go to Notre-Dame Cathedral read a little bit about the history of this venerable structure, its place and importance in religion, history, architecture and literature. Go armed with at least a superficial knowledge of this wondrous building and you will derive much more satisfaction and pleasure from it than the hordes of gawking tourists who fail to absorb any of its significance.

Indeed, there is no need in going to Paris if you are not properly prepared for the visit. Why bother traipsing through the cavernous halls of the Louvre to see a bunch of paintings whose creators you do not know, whose significance you cannot guess? Without a basic prior knowledge, the works of the Louvre will be disembodied phenomena deprived of any meaning beyond proof of your attendance in the form of photographs or videocassettes. Failing to understand its cultural significance, you will quickly erase the Louvre from memory. The self can benefit only if you comprehend and value what you are experiencing.

Pick only what interests you: The greatest cultural treasure in the world will only have value for the self if you wish to experience and comprehend it. Never visit a place "because that's what it said in the guide book." In planning your tourist itinerary for Paris, make sure you plan on going to sites for which you have a genuine interest and avoid making the visit an empty ritual. If the Eiffel Tower presents no interest to you, leave it out. No need to go there just so you could say you were at the Eiffel Tower. The indifferent tourist is not a tourist at all, but a pre-programmed robot going through the motions. Never sacrifice your time and money for meaningless pilgrimages.

Sightseeing 2: The social experience

The benefit of travelling is equal to what you wish to contribute in terms of interest, education and preparation. The value of the travelling experience is proportional to your willingness to open the self to your surroundings.

Enriching the self by absorbing the artistic and architectural creations of the places you are visiting is only half of the travelling equation. Although cultural artifacts provide texture to the trip, mere sightseeing will make it colourless. Even the most extraordinary art is still an inanimate object. There is something else you need to complete your travelling experience: the people.

Human beings are what will ultimately make the trip memorable. Human beings give life and meaning to the culture that surrounds them and provide you with a living, breathing culture in terms of language, behaviour, dress, food and beliefs. People will throw wide open the portals of experience and allow your self to step into other worlds, to see other approaches to living and understanding the universe. People will help the self prosper by enriching it with the jewels of their knowledge, experience, emotions and spirituality.

A change in your social sphere can catalyze great changes in the self if you have the courage to allow it. In foreign countries you might be able to feel and express your self in ways you did not dare dream of back home. You can learn more about the self's unique ability to fulfill its potential among strangers than among your own countrymen.

Say you are British and you travel to Brazil. In British culture, reticence and self-control are highly prized qualities. People are unwilling to interfere with each other's private space. Approaching strangers on the street will not always yield a positive response.

In Brazil social mores are different. People are more emotional, more whimsical, more comfortable with sharing their private space. They are also more approachable. If you are willing to step into their world, you will experience music, food, dance and love. Plunge deep within their society, and you can experience the Brazilian soul, the fiery essence of the Latin spirit. It will ignite within your self a fire, a fire you never knew you had. It will allow the self to manifest in ways it did not dare back home. Set a barrier between your self and the locals and you will never know what they can give to you, you will never learn what your self is capable of achieving. The choice is yours to make.

Saving the Self

How are you to experience the social life of another country, when, as a tourist, you are invariably the outsider? It's easier than you think.

Know the people you are about to visit: Preparation is key. If you are going to Paris, learn something about French habits. What sort of people are they? What do they like to do for entertainment? How do they have their breakfast? What are the latest Parisian fashions? The answers to these questions present a basic picture of the society you are about to encounter.

Learn a few words of their language and make an effort to use them: Regardless of the place, if you make an effort to speak in their language, only the most inconsiderate will fail to appreciate your attempt. In Portugal, despite learning only a few basic phrases, I befriended a number of locals, striking up friendly chats about famous soccer players. Many locals will reciprocate your efforts to speak their language by summoning the best English they have at their disposal.

Stay with the locals: Forget multinational hotel chains like the Hilton. Choose small inns, preferably operated by the owner, where you are more likely to strike up a relationship with the locals. Even better, stay with a local family that rents out rooms. The more intimate the surrounding, the greater the chance of penetrating the local culture. When in Nice with some friends, we stayed at a small hotel (no more than 10 rooms or so) which not only had very reasonable rates, but also offered the chance for wide and free ranging discussions with the proprietor about culture, philosophy, women (we were three guys) and the present state of French society. I can assure you that you are not likely to have such a conversation with the general manger of the Nice Sheraton.

Eat where locals like to eat: Avoid consumer food outlets and tourist-oriented restaurants serving inferior food at inflated prices. Restaurants frequented by the locals will afford you the opportunity of a genuine dining experience and perhaps a chance to meet a few of the regulars. While holidaying in Venice, the proprietors of the small hotel where my family was staying recommended a neighbourhood pizzeria. It was a large locale, full of long trestle tables, where whole Italian families sat down for dinner. We were seated facing such an Italian family. Despite the fact that nobody in the place spoke a word of English, we had a grand old time. The Italians across the table helped us in making our order and recommended a particular type of wine. By the time we left the place we were on fine terms with the Italian family, the waiter and the owner, who accompanied us outside and asked us to visit him the next time we were in Venice.

Make friends with the locals: Nothing is better than having the locals take you into their world. Not only will you gain easier acceptance within that society but you will also get a truer picture of it. Local friends will open your eyes to the true state of their world, letting you know places you should see and places you should avoid. Local friends serve as a bridge from your world to theirs by explaining their mode of thought. In seeking to understand their world, you will get a fairer picture of yours.

Chapter 12

Culture 1: Inherited Culture

One of the ways in which consumerism destroys you is by annihilating your past. You are born with a legacy, the legacy of your culture whatever that may be. Reclaim that cultural legacy and you will reclaim your true self.

Consumerism and the loss of inherited culture

Your uniqueness is not defined solely by your genetic blueprint. Individuality is also delineated by communal characteristics such as race, religion, tradition, language and nationality. This cultural blueprint is transmitted to you just as surely as the genetic one.

The culture of your society helps shape the self. Within your surrounding cultural context, your identity takes shape. Consumerism seeks to erase these cultural characteristics from your identity so that they do not interfere with the multinationals' control over you. It is often successful.

As a medical student at the University of Grenada, I was surrounded by colleagues from every imaginable cultural background. Despite the astounding variety of races, nationalities and languages, I was appalled at the lack of differentiation between most of these students. They appeared to be consumer clones, whose conversations and interests denoted their subservience to consumer culture. I did not see any manifestations of their inherited culture in their words, their manners or their topics of discussion. Vietnamese, Bangladeshi or Iranian, they seemed to have sprung from the same consumer test tube.

An american tragedy

In America in particular, the loss of inherited culture has been most severe. The tragic thing about being an American is that you are the most unlikely person to have an accurate sense of American identity. Your whole concept of America and Americanism has been twisted into the vision of the consumer giants. What you think is America is a consumerist distortion, a tawdry illusion, the emperor's new clothes. Suburbs, electronics, fast food, brand name clothes and mass entertainment have most likely contoured the edges of your identity as an American. You were raised on consumer culture rather than American culture. As an American, your culture is most removed from the self.

What America is, historically, artistically, geographically, spiritually, culturally, and socially, has been replaced by Consumer-world. Slowly, imperceptibly, consumerism has discarded the genuine framework of American identity and replaced it with its own artificial construct. Where once dwelt Washington and Yellowstone, Emerson and democratic principles, now thrive Disney theme parks, McDonald's and Hollywood. The things that define America and Americana are nothing more than the creations of a few giant corporations. The things that you as an American see as defining your identity are consumerist artifices. The irony is that the main reasons for which Americans are hated abroad, the things which symbolize America, the influences which shape American policy, are in fact direct opposites of what America stands for and what it represents in history.

Consumerism and immigration

If you are an immigrant, your understanding of American culture is even more distorted. The melting pot doctrine was supposed to imbue every immigrant with American culture, to recast the self within an American identity. However, the melting pot approach, like much else in America, has been subverted to the aims of multinationals. They have used the intense assimilative pressure generated by the melting pot doctrine to consumerize new arrivals.

It used to be that each new immigrant was strongly encouraged to adopt the American culture and way of life. Today, the pressure on each new arrival to America is to assimilate within the consumer culture that dominates the land. Instead of becoming Americans, immigrants are transformed into consumer clones which must sacrifice every last scrap of personal identity and serve as automatons to the corporate giants. Today, when you arrive in this promised land, the first lesson you are taught is that being an American means being a consumer. You demonstrate your American identity not by adhering to the noble principles upon which the country was founded but by trumpeting your love for Big Macs and reality TV.

Indeed, as an immigrant you have little chance of discovering the true American identity. You do not have the time or money to educate yourself in American culture, art and history. The sole readily available "knowledge" of America is consumer information. Your perception of America is formed by consumer propaganda, which uses the television as its bully pulpit.

First generation immigrants strive to preserve a part of their former identity within the privacy of their own homes. Nevertheless, as the years roll by, they are hard-pressed to retain this identity, for the constant consumerist pressure saps their cultural strength. With time, it becomes harder and harder to affirm their inherited identity. Children are almost sure to disregard their cultural heritage, mesmerized by the consumer spell. In the end, young and old alike surrender and tumble into the waiting arms of consumerism and its synthetic existence. If this is the trajectory of your immigrant experience, then know that in sacrificing your inherited cultural identity you are sacrificing the potential of the self.

How culture helps the self

In reclaiming your inherited culture, you can help the self in a number of ways.

Escaping Consumer-world: You exit Consumer-world when you enter your cultural sphere. Your culture acts as a shield against the consumer intruder. In searching for your cultural identity, you will step outside the consumer universe, and give your self an infinitely better chance to fulfil its potential.

Embracing consumer culture as a means of developing personal identity is highly malignant to the self. To understand the destructive effects of consumerism upon individual identity it is best to look at the consumerist gods who form the pinnacle of consumerist culture. They are the idols produced by consumer entertainment (actors, musicians, athletes). Worshipped my millions around the globe, their own ersatz lifestyle often plunges them into a world of drug and alcohol abuse, depression, violence and suicide.

For pampered consumer idols, the pressure to surrender their identity is infinitely greater than on consumers. Aside from their consumerist status, many of them have nothing of any worth. Since it is imperative for them to embody the vacuity of consumerism to stay at the top, they are the most empty of vessels. Their personal identity is manipulated and shaped by the industry that created them.

Moreover, since modern consumerist heroes have neither the intellectual rigor, the experience or the mental fortitude of the heroes of old, they are even less likely to cope with the pressures of their status. They fall prey to the various psychoses that afflict their disordered minds, the vanities and insecurities gnawing at a soul wrapped in ersatz glitz and superficial adulation. Fearful they will lose the spotlight, or tormented by the meaninglessness of an existence defined by the consumer spotlight, many of these envied 'sex symbols' and 'stars' are pitiful creatures. Their troubled lives, glamorized and overexposed by the consumerist propaganda machine, are no different from those they led in the trailer parks and ghettoes of America, even as they unravel within mansions, yachts and five-star hotels.[26]

The same cultural vacuity gnaws at all of us to a lesser extent. The lack of a cultural framework destabilizes all of our identities. Building cultural identity on the offering of consumer culture is like building your house on sand. The ground will shift beneath you and your foundation will be blown away.

Reclaiming your people: The process of rediscovering your culture necessitates interacting with others who preserve their cultural identity. In reclaiming your traditions, your dress, your language and your food, you also end up reclaiming your people. It is your people who serve as the cultural context within which you can fulfil your self. They are the people who can best understand your needs, your thoughts, your desires, and your mannerisms. They are the people who hold the knowledge that is key to your success as a fulfilled being.

Communicating through culture: Your culture has something to contribute to humanity that is worth preserving. When you reclaim your cultural identity not only do you catalyze individual expression but, through this process of self-affirmation, you are also offering your culture as a gift to all of humanity. Show the world what that culture is, and those who hate you or are taught to hate you will no longer seek to harm you for your cultural background. Share the beauty of your culture and you advance the global peace and harmony necessary for self-achievement.

Seeking to understand others through ideology or politics is a recipe for misunderstanding and animosity. Understand others through the prism of consumerism and you will have understood nothing but the empty artifice of its products. Only by revealing and explaining your own culture will you be able to communicate with others and profit from the experience.

---

26. A further postscript to the sad story of many of today's consumerist heroes is that they waste the opportunity given to them by their position to help others. For every Bono there are 100 Britney Spears.

Profiting from Cosmopolitanism: By reclaiming your own cultural identity you can step forth into others, embracing philosophies, languages, races and religions, absorbing without being absorbed, experiencing without being consumed by the experience.

You benefit from a society that is increasingly diverse. Large urban centres hold representatives of most of the world's nations. Whether as individuals or as a community, these representatives express their cultures in manifold ways. Profit from this ethnic wealth. Take advantage of this vast storehouse of cultures. Visit an ethnic neighbourhood. Check out some of their small businesses. Try one of their restaurants. If you like the cooking, visit one of their specialty food stores and buy the needed ingredients to make that dish at home. Attend one of their festivals or cultural shows. Purchase their art or traditional products.

Immersing yourself in different cultures might seem a strange way of expressing the individual self, but through these foreign experiences you will expand the self and gain greater insight into your own needs. Each culture possesses its own traditions, its own worldviews and philosophies of life. Mine that knowledge and incorporate it into your own life philosophy. Use the accumulated wisdom of many nations to shape and expand your own unique worldview.

It is not a matter of blindly emulating another ethnicity but of employing its cultural nuggets in terms of food, clothes, sports, books or sex, for your own benefit. Allow the people of the world to share their gifts with you and they will help you on the road towards self-realization. They will enrich your knowledge of the world and open new vistas towards self-knowledge. Sampling other cultures is really an exercise in self-discovery. The only way of finding out who you are and what you like is through experiencing as much as you can.

Forays into other cultures not only benefit you but serve as encouragement and support for ethnic individuals manifesting their culture. Your actions can ensure colourful neighbourhoods and preserve variety to counter monolithic consumer suburbs. Your boldness in exploring a community's ethnic riches will in turn preserve the variety that is the spice of life. The courage to try new things, to diversify your experiences, might also convince would-be businessmen that there is a clientele for ethnic-based products or services they were thinking to sell.

A truly cosmopolitan society is not merely a collection of nationalities. Those nationalities must be free to express themselves rather than forced to subscribe to the same consumerist message. Let's not melt everyone in the consumer pot.

Preventing Cultural Drift: The seas of life are choppy, and without the anchor of your inherited culture, you could be lost amidst its storms. You need the stability of knowing who you are, of having the weight of a language, a tradition, a dress, a music, an art and a literature to define your identity. If your sense of inherited culture is weak, you are liable to submerge yourself in other cultural identities in an attempt to find personal relevance and a community. This phenomenon, called cultural drift, is quite common nowadays.

One widespread example of cultural drift involves Caucasian individuals infatuated with what they see as a "black lifestyle." Hordes of white teenage suburbanites seek to emulate consumer-produced images of African-American "ghetto culture." The incongruity of such behaviour is well noted and often critiqued and derided but not treated for what it is: a misguided search for cultural identity.

Artificially constructed cultural identities mask and hinder the development of the true self. Furthermore, the appropriation of another's culture often disturbs the cultural integrity of individuals within that group, and can result in charges of exploitation or disrespect towards the offended group. Many African-Americans resent the attempted Caucasian intrusion into their cultural and racial identity. Native North Americans are also less than happy about the cultural appropriation of shamanism, totemic representations, dress, tradition, and other aspects of their identity by Caucasians.

Saving the Self

Reviving your cultural inheritance involves four aspects:

Make culture part of your daily routine: There are three simple ways of incorporating your cultural heritage in your daily life. First, eat foods that are part of your culture. Celebrate the richness of your ethnic or regional cuisine. Second, wear a traditional type of dress or the fashions that are in style within your ethnic culture. Third, speak using the accent or words that express the self within your cultural context. Avoid Consumer-speak at all costs.

Observe cultural events: Attend cultural events such as religious observances, festivals, picnics and games related to your culture. If you are a nominal Christian, see what the inside of a church looks like. Celebrate Easter and Christmas by attending a church rather than by purchasing consumer gifts.

Speak with your elders: Many people are unaware of their cultural heritage. One of the prime methods of discovering your culture is by asking your elders. Draw on the living past, your parents or grandparents, and ask them about your cultural heritage. What did they eat before there were fast-food franchises and junk food filled convenience stores? How did they entertain themselves before there was television?

The aged are living repositories of information to help you understand your cultural identity. They hold knowledge of another world, of a world that was not one vast, indistinguishable suburb. Find the culture living in them, so that it may be reborn in you.

Find others who maintain their identity: Communicating with others who maintain their cultural identity will help you reclaim yours. There are two places where you can find people who preserve cultural identity:

The ethnic community centre

The purpose of ethnic community centres is to keep a particular culture alive. Polish, Jewish, Chinese or Hindu, community centres hold the key to your cultural revival. The people running these centres not only are immersed within and dedicated to maintaining their cultural identity, but they are also the hub of a network of individuals and businesses that help promote cultural identity. In the community centre you can find the links to your cultural heritage. Check their calendar of events. See if they offer classes or seminars to educate you about your culture. Draw on their list of businesses offering ethnic products and services. It is through these centres that you may re-enter your inherited culture. Think of them as sanctuaries from Consumer-world.

The rural world

In the countryside, pockets of culture survive. Culture lives in fairs, games, crafts and foods offered by rural people who still celebrate their culture in the face of a consumerist onslaught. Discover these places and you will discover what you have lost.

The rural milieu has always been the bedrock of inherited culture. Although it is getting harder to find rural residents who prefer inherited culture over consumerism, they may still be found. It is just a matter of searching them out. There are still secluded villages of fishermen or farmers, villages that favour old recipes and older traditions. There are still those who live off the land and not out of consumer outlets. Find them, and they will teach you about your own forgotten cultural heritage.

Chapter 13

Culture 2: The Creative Self. You Are an Artist.

Neglecting your artistic self means neglecting an integral part of what it means to be human. Artistic self-expression is a form of self-fulfillment, as this chapter will reveal.

How many of you ever wrote or desired to write your thoughts down on a page? How many of you dabbled in poetry, drawing or painting? How many of you learned a craft like woodworking, pottery or sewing? How many of you learned how to play a musical instrument in high school? How many of you still do any of these things? How many watch television instead?

Regardless of artistic talents, you have an innate appreciation of art and a creative need. These qualities have shrunken under the life-long consumerist barrage. In acquiescing to the consumer lifestyle you neglect one of your most precious gifts, one of the special qualities that differentiate you from the myriad of species that share the globe. It's time to stop denying the creative self. It's time to break out of the consumer trance.

Reclaiming your creative imagination and artistic sensibility is key to reclaiming your stolen identity and fulfilling your potential as a human being. Since we understand so little of this universe the best we can do is seek to understand our self. Our artistic gifts are crucial to the process of self-discovery.

Consumerism seeks to prevent the artistic voyage of self-discovery since it would be fatal to your needs for their products. The satisfaction derived from artistic creation makes consumer pleasures pale by comparison. Just as men have used their artistic creativity to free themselves from the oppression of brutal totalitarian regimes, so you must employ it to escape the thrall of global corporate giants.

Even the most humbly-gifted among us is capable of artistic expression. Our family kitchen business has employed a certain loader for 15 years or so. I shall call him Jean. Jean is a man with minimal education. His social background is rural and working class. A severe myopia has further limited his choices in terms of his activities and career. His professional life consists of carrying heavy objects and doing menial chores for various businesses. To all outward appearances he seems the typical, unskilled labourer, spending his hard-earned money on beer and junk food. But, just like the hero of Hardy's *Jude the Obscure*, Jean's seemingly mundane existence is deceptive, for Jean has discovered an outlet for his artistic self.

Dancing is in some ways the perfect creative release for Jean, considering his lack of education and his myopia. With dancing, it was only a question of concentrating on his partner and memorizing a few steps and he was well on his way. By entering the dancing world not only did he find an excellent method for developing his creative self, but this artistic efflorescence tore him away from the bars and the television that had previously monopolized his existence.

Jean's ascent on the ladder of self-fulfillment has been gathering pace with this discovery. Jean practices daily and is now proficient in various dances such as the tango, the waltz, and the fox trot. He travels to dance competitions with his partner, even winning a competition against other dancing pairs. His dancing partner is a white collar professional, very much taken with his qualities and abilities, who has conquered any initial prejudices about Jean's lower income or "inferior" social status.

If Jean, considering his limited education and disadvantaged background, has achieved so much, what of those of us who benefit from superior education, who have attended colleges and universities? Think about the enormous amount of artistic potential that lies dormant within you, waiting to be awakened.

The expression of artistic impulses catalyzes an unparalleled process of personal growth and self-development. The very act of expression reveals the unexplored territory of your being. It is perhaps the most authentic process of self-discovery available to human beings.

The creative act is an intensely private one, free from the deceptions of Consumer-world. When immersed in the process of creation as an artist or a craftsman, regardless of the influences or inspirations that drive your creation, the ineluctable fact remains that the creation is yours. There is an intertwining between your self and your creation, an inseparable link. Whatever you produce will forever be your legacy, the manifestation of your self in this plane of existence. It is irrelevant whether the finished product is durable or evanescent, whether it has any artistic value or is worthless, whether it is the product of a genius or a simpleton: it is an outward extension of you within the universe.

The act of creation demands that you summon up and impose your self upon the artistic material. It is the process of taking an art and imbuing it with your voice, your touch, your meaning. It is the transposition of your intangible spiritual beauty into a form that can be appreciated by others. In creating, you are nearest to the divine, you are manifesting that infinitesimal fraction of godliness that was given to each of us.

The value of artistic creation does not rest in the finished product but in the act of creation itself. Reared on a diet of finished consumer products, often expertly packaged and marketed, you have lost the value of the process of creation. Underestimating the value of the creative process is an essential obstacle to many an individual's failure to recognize and nurture his creative self.

Too many have either abandoned or are afraid to pursue artistic inclinations because they feel their talents are not up to par with the leading lights in these artistic fields. Some have actively tried to gain recognition for their creations but were discouraged by repeated rejections.

If you have stopped practicing artistic activities due to the modesty of your talents you are not alone. Writers, poets, painters, singers, dancers, sculptors and craftsmen of all sorts have forsaken their calling, convinced that their battered egos could no longer take the pounding. Most have disregarded their creative selves altogether, their self-esteem overwhelmed by the "perfect" creations of consumerism.

The obsession with perfection propagated by consumerism is the principal culprit in destroying the artistic impulse. Consumerism has undermined your self-esteem by constantly telling you that unless you do something extremely well – with the bar being set by the multinationals – you should not do it. The torrent of idealized images and objects produced and mass-marketed by the multinationals has poisoned your mind and has made you reticent to explore the possibilities of your artistic self. Better to fall back in the comforting arms of mass entertainment, brand names and junk food, better to satisfy all of your artistic needs at the shopping mall than struggle to satisfy them yourself.

Saving the Self

Art is for the Self:

To combat this fallacy, remember there is no such thing as failure. Success lies in the attempt. In a Consumer-world where tangible results are the sole mark of success, individual artistic achievement lies in the act of participation. Art is for your benefit alone.[27]

As a child, I instinctively knew my creative self needed to be expressed so I was never self-conscious about my talents. Always a lover of music and art, during my childhood and adolescence I practiced both. In music I took the flute as my instrument of choice and in art, aside from writing, I was particularly attracted to drawing and painting.

I was also atrocious. Both in terms of my music and drawings I was the pinnacle of ineptitude. I nonetheless persisted in exercising my non-existent talents for a good number of years. I had no illusions as to my lack of talent. I was perfectly aware and often frustrated at my inability to render my creative impulses in a more pleasing form.[28] But whether it was the jarring squeals of my flute or the awkward squiggles of my drawings, the act of creation gave me pleasure. Through my rough and awkward attempts I was expressing my own love for these arts, I was manifesting my self's interpretation of them. Lost in a world of my own creation, I was removed from the mesmerizing charms of consumerism, free from any influences but the free play of my own mind.

Music: the interpretation of art

The artistic self does not only exist in your creations. Artistic abilities are expressed in interpreting the creations of others.

Famous classical pieces such as Beethoven's Symphony No. 9 have been interpreted by thousands of orchestras throughout the centuries since their composition. What draws people to classical concerts is not hearing the actual symphony itself. Most classical concert attendees are perfectly familiar with the music and its nuances, and probably own one or more recordings of the piece. They come to the concert to

---

27. If others benefit from it, good for them. But art is not a search for recognition; that is vanity.
28. Although my family was even more frustrated by my incompetence as one day my flute disappeared in mysterious circumstances. It was never seen or heard of again. Strangely, my parents did not seem to mind this unfortunate turn of events.

see that piece interpreted by a particularly accomplished musician or a renowned conductor.

Nor is this confined to classical music. People attend all sorts of musical events to see a "live" rendition of their performer's favourite hits. What attracts them? It is the originality. Each live performance is an original. Your CD recording will always repeat the same performance. That is the beauty of humanity. We are not robots, we are not automatons, we are not perfect. Each of our actions will not, cannot, be a perfect replication of a previous action. No matter how closely we might try to mimic it, there will always be a difference. Musicians celebrate this difference by constantly varying their interpretation of a particular piece. Each version is a new creation. Each version adds to their development as artists and human beings.

It is not only the great performers who delight in interpreting musical compositions. Who among us does not like to whistle along to a favourite tune? Who does not find himself singing a favourite song in the shower? In doing this, you are no different from the original artist or the accomplished musician in one essential respect: just like them, you are expressing your creative self. Your mind and soul's need for art finds expression in your rendering of a musical piece.[29] The same hunger that drives tenor Andrea Bocelli drives you as well. Regardless of what set of pipes nature has given you, you sing for your needs, you sing because it gives you pleasure. The pleasure lies in the fact that it is your performance, your unique and signature performance. The self relishes its own creative expression. Never deny it the joy of manifesting its potential.

The act of artistic creation is also a meditative one. It is a communion of a mind and body, separated from the totality of existence by the concentration required for the generative act. Focused on the task at hand, the creator loses track of time. The stresses and cares of day-to-day life are obliterated. Vanities, fears and frustrations fall by the wayside. Artistic creation provides a sanctuary for the battered ego and assaulted senses, victims of consumer over-stimulation.

Unlike television, artistic creation soothes the mind without numbing or indoctrinating. Through the unadulterated expression of the self which marks the creative act you achieve a greater sense of inner peace and balance. Artistic creation reassures the ego because it knows itself to be in complete control, free from any external menaces. There is no ultimate

---

29. There is actual benefit to derive from the experience of art. Tests have shown that listening to certain types of classical music improves the mind's reasoning faculties.

goal, no barriers to overcome, no deadlines to meet. Artistic creation relishes only the act of creation. The product itself, no matter how satisfying, can never compare to the sheer joy of the process.

Engaging the artistic self inevitably leads to a progression of your art. Once your creativity is stirred it will demand ever more from you. You will seek new avenues to express your artistic abilities, to test their limits. From keeping a daily journal you might dabble in poetry, then try short stories, perhaps even a novella. If you work in embroidery you will attempt ever more complicated and difficult patterns. The canvas for your creation will expand as far as your imagination and ability will take you, from fashioning a crude wooden spoon to single-handedly building your own massive oak library. The artistic impulse becomes a testing ground for the self, where you are constantly trying to better and expand upon your previous work. This is what I term the "progressive pull" of the imagination, and it usually works in tandem with the intellect to help fulfil your potential. In exercising your artistic self you are progressing as a human being.

Work as art: the artistic laborer

Work is usually thought of as a necessary evil. People work to provide for their families and themselves. Work is set in opposition to play, to relaxation and to enjoyment. This opposition is underscored by an essential aspect of the definition of work, namely, that it requires "a considerable expenditure of effort." Work is thus something difficult, something which, if it cannot be avoided, must be endured.

The negative connotations associated with work derive from the dichotomy between labour and creative needs. Correcting this dysfunction means harmonizing the two objectives so they are not at cross-purposes. Ideally, there should be a seamless union between the purpose of work and the purpose of existence, the latter being the achievement of our potential.

Too often, however, work is separate from your needs, tied in with artificial economic necessities. Too often, people seek in a job nothing else but financial rewards, the means through which they can achieve their perceived consumer needs. As such, too many people are unhappy or at least dissatisfied with their professional lives.

The multinationals sustain and benefit from the dichotomy between the purpose of your work and the purpose of your being. Portraying work as a struggle, multinationals claim you can be "rewarded" by consuming their products. Ironically, the people toiling the hardest are the employees of the multinationals themselves, who end up consuming the "rewards" they have helped manufacture.

To bridge the divide between your work and your needs, work must become an extension of your artistic self. In order to transform work into art, a two-step process is required.

First, you must determine how you can achieve your artistic potential. This is a highly personal decision. You must decide how best to develop your innate talents. Childhood and adolescence helped uncover your artistic talents. Adulthood means harnessing them to the chariot of the unrealized self to pull it towards fulfillment. Only you know your artistic talents and only you know how they may be used towards self-fulfillment. Have the courage to use what nature has given you. Choose a path for exploring and manifesting the artistic self.

Second, once you have found your path, the question becomes how and what type of work will help you along the path. Make your work an integral part of the process of self-achievement. Work is an act of creation. When you work, regardless of your job, you create something. Is the something that you create aiding your journey towards fullfillment? When you have found the means of creation that best helps you towards artistic self-realization, work ceases to be a curse and becomes a blessing.

Do not look at superficial pleasures in assessing the value of your work. Look instead to the work's underlying purpose. Self-fulfillment is not merely a matter of liking what you do. Perhaps you have become accustomed to your daily work routine. Perhaps you even enjoy it. That, in itself, means nothing. Habit and routine have taught you to enjoy consumption, although it harms your mind, body and soul. Superficial pleasures are not an adequate guide in determining the value of your work life.

Work ceases to become work not when it is artificially enjoyed, but when it improves the self. Just because you have a nice office and a cushy job does not mean that your work is ideal. On the contrary, it probably means that you are wasting your precious talents instead of fulfilling your potential. Until work serves your purposes, until work is intimately tied in with your genuine needs, it will forever seem a meaningless chore, even if a pleasant one.

In perverting the concept of work by separating it from your artistic needs and transforming it into a chore, consumerism also has engendered the second "evil," sloth. Since work tires you, both through its meaninglessness to the self and through its utter inability to engage the artistic self, you seek "rest" when the workday ends. That "rest" is usually in the form of consumption, especially of consumer entertainment.

Modern-day sloth is an evil of the self, since it is expressed through your subjugation to consumer interests. On one hand you work at cross-purposes to your needs, on the other hand you ignore your needs altogether for consumer sloth.

Saving the Self

Find a job/profession/business that allows for your creative expression

This in itself involves two possibilities:

Direct creative expression: Determine your artistic inclinations and then use them to make a living. If you can draw or paint, become an illustrator or a designer. If you sew, open a shop and offer the world custom-made clothing. No matter what your artistic abilities are, there is a job, profession or business wherein they can be expressed.

Indirect creative expression: Even if you do not have a particularly developed artistic talent, you can still work within the artistic field. If you cannot be a musician you can be a music producer or agent, or a musical technician in a recording studio. Your artistic self will find expression through helping others create the music.

Express the artistic self within your existing job. Personalize your work. If you cannot or will not leave the comfort of your existing job, then use the artistic self within your daily routine. Are you a landscaper? The grass and the greenery is your canvas. Cut the grass in a unique pattern of your own creation, trim the bushes as no one else does. Similarly, if you are a tradesperson, employ personal flourishes, whether you are setting tiles or being a stonemason. The artistic self may be expressed in any profession as long as you allow it to shine through.

Discover the art within the artifice. This is a question of self-education. Perhaps you are not aware of the intrinsic artistic potential of your labour. Perhaps you were taught to do your job in a perfunctory or uniform manner. Perhaps there are other ways of doing that same job, ways that engage your artistic self. You will not be sure unless you investigate further. Ask a co-worker. Find how others employed in the field work by talking to the competition. Read the literature on your profession for suggestions.

Import art within the artless profession. If you cannot think of an artistic means of doing your work then add an artistic expression to your work routine. Sing while you are driving the delivery truck. Write poems as well as memos at the office. Always thread the artistic self into your labour. I once met a Brazilian waiter in Barcelona who danced between serving drinks. Art can form part of the artless job. It is up to you to integrate it within your profession.

The expression of your artistic self during the job is an excellent means of relaxing from the stresses of work and for chasing away boredom. Artistic expression is also eminently superior to your present means of taking a work break, which is consumer entertainment. The next time you want to take a breather, forget playing video games or surfing the Net for celebrity gossip. Do something to express the artist within you. Hum a song. Doodle on a piece of paper. Scribble a few verses. Practice your dance steps in the washroom. Romance your co-worker with outrageous declarations of love. It will make you feel much better than anything you could consume.

Chapter 14

Culture 3: Developing a Personal Culture.

In Consumer-world, taste and manners are a forgotten thing. This final chapter of culture deals with the importance of culture in daily life, from the way you eat to the clothes you wear.

Webster's Dictionary's first two definitions of culture are "the training and development of the mind" and "the refinement of taste and manners acquired by such training". This chapter is concerned with the refinement of taste and manners.

Refinement is not a word with much currency in modern society. For that matter, neither are taste or manners. Social graces, sophistication, elegance, punctilio, decorum are concepts whose time has passed. Far from developing or refining our selves, we are reverting to an ever more primitive status. We are approaching the level of medieval serfs in terms of our regressive social behaviour. Humanity is becoming a race of ill-mannered boors.

You need personal culture in order to differentiate your self from the animals. Personal culture elevates the self by recasting your bestial needs into pleasing artistic forms. Personal culture is the art of everyday living. It transforms basic functions such as eating, walking and keeping warm into events possessed of elegance and artistic beauty. The self may be fulfilled through the simple everyday things all of us must do.

Personal culture is a means through which the basic requirement of communicating with your fellow beings is lifted into another realm. It is a realm the other creatures that share the world with us cannot enter, a realm of beauty and art. Personal culture is a method or transforming the banal into the sublime, of taking your intellectual and spiritual gifts and using them to refine the process of fulfilling your physical needs.

Consumer dining

Personal culture begins with that basic and necessary act which you perform about three times a day: eating. Unfortunately, even the act of eating has been consumerized.

Consumer dining undermines your personal culture in a number of ways:

No utensils or plates: One of the principal characteristics of consumer food is the lack of utensils. If you dine at McDonald's you use your hands to hold your Big Mac and to pick out your fries. Instead of a plate, you have a paper wrapper or a box. If you dine at a more formal restaurant you will have to use forks, spoons, knives and plates.

Convenience store junk food is even further removed from the need for utensils. At least fast-food franchises have plastic cutlery in the unlikely case you will use it. With junk food, there is no chance you will need cutlery. It's just a matter of opening the chip bag or unwrapping the candy bar.

Consumer food is purposely designed to discourage the use of utensils in order to save on costs. If you eat pizza from a fast-food outlet you are much more likely to eat the pizza from the box. If you go to an Italian restaurant, you will eat pizza from the plate, using utensils. Non-consumer restaurants respect the formalities of dining, one of the main reasons why they charge more.

Take-out: The take-out craze, commenced and popularized by consumer food multinationals, has also encouraged eating without utensils or plates. Take-out, which has now become part of modern life, usually means eating from a box or a paper bag.

Take-out has helped destroyed the formality of the dining room by allowing food to travel. Now food is eaten on the go, whenever you have a moment to open the take-out box. Since food now travels with you, you often eat when you are in a hurry, when you are concentrating on other tasks. This means you are deprived of eating at a dining table, where you are free from other distractions.

The dining setting is important in structuring the meal and maximizing the enjoyment of the eating experience. At the dining table you may concentrate on the food, you can use utensils, and you can benefit from the company of your family and friends.

The chaos of 24-hour eating: Non-consumer restaurants have limited opening hours and are busy during the three eating periods of the day, breakfast, lunch and dinner. The restaurant owner respects the three daily meals and seeks to satisfy the needs of those meals. Consumer food can be eaten anytime, any place. There are no more hours to eat, no defined meals. You can eat the same menus 24 hours a day, or very nearly so. McDonald's does have some items they will only sell for breakfast, but in general, junk food items are available for consumption on a 24-hour basis. This perpetual availability is highly unhealthy, and a prime reason for the obesity epidemic.

The constant availability of consumer food also destroys personal culture. First of all, the three meals a day are out the window. The knowledge of constant availability means you will eat when you will have the time. That means breakfast at noon, lunch at six and dinner at midnight. That also means snacks are consumed throughout the day. Nonstop consumer food means you eat to fulfil needs imposed by consumer propaganda rather than your own body. Consumer propaganda-induced 3 a.m. donut urges can now be satisfied with just a short drive. The process of eating has been reduced from a formal, orderly dining setting into a mindless, chaotic mess.

The consequences

By eating consumer food in hurried conditions and informal settings, and by dispensing with utensils, you will have lost the knowledge of eating properly. When such uncultured behaviour seeps into more formal dining situations, it can have devastating consequences for both your professional and personal life:

Employment: If you seek employment, you must pass through the dreaded job interview. Often, the interview will take the form of a luncheon. The luncheon is a method for an employer to assess your skills and personality in the more relaxed setting of a dining establishment. Employers will also look at your manners, as demonstrated in the way you eat. Do you speak with your mouth full? Do you use utensils and do you know how to use them properly? Eating your meal in an elegant and sophisticated manner will show the employer what type of individual you are: the type they want to hire.[30]

Business: When doing business, appropriate eating manners are even more important. Business deals might involve companies, but they are made by individuals. The difference between signing a lucrative deal and going home empty-handed rests in making the right connection with

30. I speak from personal experience. While interviewing for a position with a law firm, I was specifically told by the employer that the purpose of the cocktail and the luncheon was to see if prospective employees "could eat and talk at the same time" and "whether they knew how to hold a spoon."

your prospective business partner. If you cannot demonstrate the ability to eat in an appropriate manner you will have little chance to secure the deal. Businesspersons look at personality as much as the actual deal when making decisions. Even if the product or deal you offer is good, your behaviour at the table could turn off your potential partner. They might believe your poor table manners are symptomatic of a deeper malaise. After all, how can you be trusted to deliver on your end of the bargain if you cannot even eat properly? You might be a great businessperson, but your uncultured behaviour has detracted from and obscured both your qualities and your products/services.

Even if you do secure a deal, it is unlikely to be on such good terms as it would have been had you truly impressed the other person with your dining elegance. Your partner might sign on, but they will be more professional about the situation, driving a harder bargain.

Social functions: Nobody wants to hang around a slob. If you want to have an active social life, having a mastery over the dining experience will ensure repeated invitations at dinner parties.

More importantly, a person who eats in an elegant manner is likely to make a good first impression at the dinner date. It is not only a question of the way you treat the food on your plate and the way you use your utensils – it is also a question of how you treat your dates. They are watching and assessing you while you eat. The dining experience can make or break you. It can serve as a romantic catalyst or as a romantic turn-off.

Saving the Self

The dining experience is more than just an agglomeration of rules. It is an expression of the artistic self and the self as a whole. Through your dining habits you are revealing the self. Great men are seen in simple things. Something as basic as the act of eating can go a long way towards fulfilling and revealing the greatness of the self.

Learn the art of dining

Eating is an event. It extends beyond the food. Putting food in your stomach is like a rough gem just sifted from the ore. It is valuable but unfinished and lacking true beauty. A cultured dining experience is like a polished diamond. It has a myriad of facets.

It is beyond the scope of this book to determine your eating manners. Indeed, it would be presumptuous. Your cultural background will play a large parting crafting your personal eating manners. The following outline of Western dining's salient aspects serves as a guideline to discover the art of dining.

Dress: No baseball caps.

Preparation: Setting the table. Tablecloth. Utensils. Plates. Glasses. Napkins.

Posture: Using utensils. Placement and use of napkins.

Drinking preliminaries: Proper use of glasses depending on the beverage. Pouring drinks. Holding the glass.

Eating: Portions. Size of food morsels. Pace. Menu and order choices.

Drinking: How to drink various beverages.

Dining companions: Seating. Serving. Cutting portions. Pouring drinks.

Post-eating: Appropriate drinks. Leaving the dining table. Thanking the host/cook.

Restaurant etiquette: Waiters and other employees. Fellow patrons. Fellow diners.

Accidents: The proper way of dealing with them.

Keep regular dining practices

Forget the chaos and excesses of 24-hour eating. Listen to your body's needs. Follow your natural body cycles and your Circadian rhythms. Regular dining practices involve the following:

Regular meals: Do not skip breakfast or any other meal in the day.

Regular times: Do not eat too late and go to bed full and bloated. The stomach does its best digestion when you are awake.

Commensurate dining: If you are eating lunch, eat lunch, not your breakfast for lunch. Each meal of the day is supposed to account for the needs of your body at that time and until the next meal.

Cultured dining and freedom

The "freedom" from manners that is espoused by consumer food multinationals is really a form of enslavement. The reason you are encouraged to eat fast, on the go, 24-hours a day, without regard to the food, is to enslave you to consumer food. Consumer food is the only type of food that offers these dining conditions on a consistent basis. You are being trapped within the consumer manner of eating by indulging in your "freedom" from the formalities of dining.

A cultured eating experience counteracts that deadliest of all combinations, the simultaneous consumption of consumer food and consumer entertainment. A cultured dining experience cannot be combined with other forms of consumption. The art of eating means eating is the extent of your experience. There is no eating and watching TV, eating and playing video games or eating and surfing the Net. Most of all, a cultured dining experience is more than mere affectation. It provides tangible benefits for your mind and your body.

Cultured dining and well-being

Cultured dining promotes the well-being of body and mind:

Body: If one half of the health equation is eating good food, then the other half is eating it in a good way. Cultured dining is the best way of avoiding heartburn, stomach pain, bloating and ulcers. Rather than resort to consumer drugs such as Tums, Rolaids or Pepto-Bismol to alleviate these symptoms, you can avoid them altogether by dining in a cultured manner. The secret to a truly satisfying meal is feeling satisfied after the meal.

Cultured dining is a healthy habit for the following reasons:

Smaller morsels: Cutting your food into bite sized pieces is a primary requirement of the fine art of dining. Bite-sized pieces make it easier for your body to break down the food.

More chewing: Wolfing down platefuls of food is not an acceptable dining practice. Cultured dining requires eating in a deliberate manner. This will aid in the digestive process and help your body absorb food better.

Longer meal times: Cultured dining has no concern with time. The focus is on enjoying the experience and to ensure this, you eat at a leisurely pace. Your body thus has ample time to digest the incoming food rather than being overwhelmed with a five-minute food avalanche.

Less stress: Stress increases the stomach's acidity, making heartburn a foregone conclusion of the meal. Consumer food is usually eaten under conditions of stress, whether of time, of work, or of being in a car. Cultured dining focuses you solely on the food and lowers external stresses, preventing the onset of stomach acidity.

Mind: Cultured dining is also the key to gastronomic pleasure. By focusing your mind on the food, you can truly savour your meal. Cultured dining is about appreciating food and the act of eating. Consumer dining is just about filling your stomach. Cultured dining is a ritual that treats the body as a temple and the food as a sacrifice to the joy of bodily fulfillment. Consumer dining treats your body like a bucket to be filled with shovels of slop.

Consumer entertainment

If consumer food has ruined the proprieties of dining, consumer entertainment has undermined cultured language, dress, and etiquette. Consumer entertainment has degraded your personal culture by promoting anti-cultural, anti-civilized and anti-social behaviour. The more repulsive or outrageous the behaviour, the more it is glamourized.

It is consumer idols who are popularizing disgraceful behaviour. Their massive egos, combined with their enormous wealth has led them to believe that they can behave in any way they see fit, and dispense with decorum. Many pop stars, actors and athletes are not only intellectually limited, they are also uncouth to the point of barbarity. Pathologically undereducated, constantly spoiled by virtue their so-called "star" status, they fail to acknowledge the social conventions that contour human interactions. But that in itself is not the main problem.

The main problem is the reason they do it. The reason they do it is to serve their masters who have taught them that beyond God, beyond even money, there is PUBLICITY.

Whenever stars trample over the last shred of common decency they are glorified and rewarded by their consumerist masters who ensure that their every transgression is overexposed in the mass media. Every athlete who gets into a brawling match at a bar, every actor who trashes his hotel room and verbally abuses the staff, every singer who exposes himself and spits banal profanities at authority figures will make front page headlines. The effect of their rudeness upon people is inverse. The more outrageous the behaviour, the more likely it will be emulated by hordes of fans eager to be as uncouth and impolite as their heroes, hungering for their fifteen minutes of fame.

The renunciation of manners and taste forms part of the consumerist-controlled concept of "rebelliousness." You have been brainwashed into thinking you are engaging in a process of individualization and self-expression through body piercing, tattoos, and multi-coloured hair. This rebellion is actually *en masse* imitation of consumer heroes, who are the most tattooed, body-pierced and multicoloured-haired of the lot.

Shoddy dress and an impertinent mouth do not make you a rebel. Being different does not mean looking and acting like some sort of modern day barbarian. Originality and self-expression are far more likely to be found in proper manners and an unfailing punctiliousness. You are more likely to be anti-social and misanthrophic, more likely to be removed from your fellow human beings by virtue of being polite and properly behaved than all the hordes of coarse, vulgar and obnoxious "rebels" who trumpet their alienation from contemporary society.

Even if not directly influenced by the antics of consumer idols, you are nonetheless affected by the predomination of consumer culture. The embrace of rude behaviour in today's consumer society serves as an unrelenting pressure on your own sense of personal culture. In order to keep pace with consumer society, in order to fit in with the new mores, you begin to behave the same way. Certainly not to the extreme extent of consumer idols but you may have become a little less reticent in using vulgar language, a little less careful about your dress, a little less concerned with minding your manners. The change is gradual, and probably unnoticeable in a Consumer-world where most of these things are a given but there is an impact, a disastrous impact on that most important thing of all: your self. Under the consumer influence, you have allowed your personal culture to slip. Unless you re-establish the civilizing influence of a personal culture, the self will be forever denied the possibility of fulfillment.

Recapturing your personal culture involves the following three aspects: Language, Dress and Personal Etiquette.

Language

Refinement begins with the way you express yourself and that means communicating with the necessary propriety. In an earlier chapter, I have referred to the contraction of the English language and its replacement with Consumer-speak. Not only is that process well advanced, but of the English vocabulary that you possess, choice of expression is often ineffective.

Profanity: From Quentin Tarantino movies to rap artists, consumer entertainment has made profanity an integral part of the language. Profanity has reached the status of a punctuation mark in the everyday conversations of a large and growing segment of the population. The recourse to swearing is excessive and gratuitous. The "f" word used to be reserved for expressions of utmost anger and served as an insult of utmost power. Now, through consumer entertainment, the "f" word has become part and parcel of the language. The use of the word is so common, so prevalent, that it has lost its power. The "f" word has become a highly versatile, omnipresent term to be used in all situations. It can be a verb, a noun or an adjective. It is a method for most people to emphasize their intentions. You do not say "that's great;" you say "that's f'…ng great." You signify your disbelief, your pain, your excitement, in short, the whole gamut of emotion through the use of the "f" word.

Gratuitous words and phrases: Beyond the profanity, your speech is replete with gratuitous words and phrases such as "like" and "oh, my god." Again these superfluous terms have infected and degraded the beauty of your expression. The constant repetition of such terms is not only annoying for the listener, but also has a number of negative effects upon the self.

First, you are unlikely to be taken seriously when using such language. Many people, rightly or wrongly, associate the constant use of these stock phrases and terms with a lower intelligence quotient. It will be much harder for you to achieve your goals, and fulfil the self, if you create an obstacle towards self-fulfillment through this type of language.

Second, the repeated use of gratuitous words limits the self by reducing your vocabulary. There is no need to think of alternative ways of self-expression, but merely spew forth a stock phrase. The resort to these words and phrases becomes instinctive and unthinking, a conditioned reflex. You are behaving more like a lab rat than a human being.

Impoliteness: Rudeness has become a way of life. This is not a question of profanity. It is a question of abandoning terms of politeness such as the very basic "please" and "thank you." You are encouraged to demand rather than ask politely. Consumerism has taught you that if you have the money everything you have been trained to want is rightfully yours. Consumer-world is a society of takers, where no consideration is spared for your fellow human beings.

The lessons of consumerism extend into daily life. You fail to use polite terms in all of your social interactions. You might ask someone for the time or directions and still adopt the same rude manners.

Impoliteness harms the self not only by erasing your personal culture but also by undermining the self within society. Politeness will gain you respect and co-operation in achieving fulfillment of the self. Rudeness will serve as an obstacle, causing others to resist fulfilling your desires.

Aggression: Language has also become more aggressive. Consumer entertainment has dispensed with modesty and reason, preferring mindless emotion and violence. This approach has seeped into social behaviour. Every little dispute is likely to culminate in threats of bodily injury and even death. While in many cases only heated words are exchanged, in many others language serves as a prelude to violence.

Part of your gift as a human being is the ability of self-control. The aggressive impulse is a primal one, but civilization has smoothed it out and muted it, so all of society can prosper. Violence creates poverty, anarchy, chaos and injustice within society and within the self. Self-fulfillment requires that you master your emotions, and to do that you must master your language. The cultured person resists provocation and does not fall prey to the heat of passion but responds using reason. The uncultured person uses language to further bestial impulses and shows itself to be wanting as a human being.

Demeaning approaches towards the opposite sex: Language is also used to disparage the opposite sex. Consumer entertainment has popularized the denigration of women as "whores" and "bitches" to be used as sexual playthings. Females in the consumer entertainment industry have responded by encouraging women to mistreat men as a way of fighting back. Language has become a weapon for belittling the opposite sex. The language of scorn towards the opposite sex not only makes relationships more difficult to establish but also more difficult to maintain. If you do not respect the opposite sex, you will use language as a repellent to chase potential or existing mates away. The soaring divorce rates in the Western world are partially due to the gender disrespect prevalent in consumer language.

Saving the Self

Language is an instrument of self-refinement

Purify your language of incivilities and you will purify the self. In order to adopt cultured language and use it to advance the self's interests, the following steps must be taken:

Listen to yourself: Monitor your language to weed out profanity and gratuitous terms. Oftentimes, you use these terms subconsciously as a matter of habit and conditioning. By consciously seeking to expunge these Consumer-speak staples from your vernacular, you will be much more sensitized to their presence. Many people are surprised as to how often they swear or use stock phrases once made aware of it. The heightened awareness also means you will be better positioned to correct your self.

A good method of raising your sensitivity is by taping yourself while engaged in a normal conversation. If you cannot do that without feeling self-conscious, dig through the home video vault and watch the show. You will instantly become painfully aware of the constant recourse to gratuitous or profane language.

Speak slowly: Once sensitized to your language faults, you can begin the cleansing process. By slowing down when you are speaking, you have more time to avoid the trap of gratuitous or profane language, you have more chance to measure your words. The key to expunging unwanted Consumer-speak malignancies from your vocabulary is nipping them in the bud, before they have a chance to leave your mouth.

Think before you speak: This old adage is rarely followed today. Cultured language is the product of deliberate thought, not verbal diarrhea. Too often, modern conversations are a sort of time-filler. As such, they revolve around uncontroversial subjects, namely consumer entertainment. Stop acting as a propaganda mouthpiece for the entertainment multinationals. Do not open your mouth until you have something worthwhile to say.

Use the language of reason not of emotion: The language of consumerism is a language of violence, derived from the uncontrolled aggressive impulses celebrated in action films, rap songs and video games. The language of reason is the language of culture. Reason settles passions and prevents physical violence. React to a provocation with measured language. Ask someone who feels wronged and bellicose to explain themselves. Offer an explanation, even an apology for any slight, perceived or real. You will demonstrate your superiority as a human being.

Be polite: Power is found in respect, not in disrespect. The cultured individual will have greater influence by speaking in a polite manner. The old canard of good guys finishing last is another consumer concoction designed to reduce the self to a bestial and hateful creature. A well-spoken individual whose words show respect will find their needs respected and fulfilled. Despite consumerism's propagation of rudeness, respect impresses and attracts. Vulgar and demeaning posturing is the language of fools.

The language of respect is the language of love. A healthy relationship is based on a cultured language. As mentioned above, one of the reasons for the soaring divorce rates in consumerized societies is that consumerism has undermined respect within the relationship. Partners no longer respect each other through the language. If familiarity breeds contempt, that contempt is generally expressed in verbal communication. Polite language serves the self best when directed towards your partner. Saying "I love you" is important, but treating your partner like a lady or a gentleman will make or break a relationship. Cultured language is a very important facet of this treatment.

Consumer wear: the tyranny of blandness

Consumer-wear has four principal characteristics:

Consumer-wear is produced and/or sold by multinationals: There are two types of multinationals dealing in consumer wear: Brand-namers, such as the Gap, Nike, Ralph Lauren and Tommy Hilfiger and

Mega-sellers, such as Wal-Mart, K-mart, and Sears. Mega-sellers will often produce their own line of clothes, as well as selling brand-name products.

Consumer-wear is predominantly casual wear: Although many brand names will offer a line of formal wear, the emphasis is clearly on the casual. Aside from the omnipresent baseball cap, Consumer-wear fashion staples include sneakers (preferably of brand name and highly expensive) t-shirts and shorts.

Consumer-wear is made by factory workers: As a result, it is mass-produced and possesses a limited number of styles.

Consumer-wear is bland and/or tasteless. This comes as a natural result of its economy of scale production methods that preclude costly individual touches, as well as the necessity to make boring and inoffensive clothes for mass appeal.

The deceptions of Consumer-wear

The natural response to Consumer-wear is that you like to be comfortable and to wear what you please; that you wear your freedom in your choice of dress. You will argue that dispensing with the snobbery of formal wear has nourished the self's ability for individual expression. Why be held back by antiquated customs or rigid dress codes? Being comfortable and doing what you please is the ultimate freedom, even if that entails adopting Consumer-wear. If that is what you believe, you have fallen prey to the deceptions of the Consumer-wear multinationals.

Consumer-wear promotes self-expression, formal wear is constrictive

Since Consumer-wear is predominantly casual wear, it is advertised in stark contrast to formal wear. Multinationals present their clothes as the choice of self-expression. Formal wear is portrayed as symbolic of rigid social convention, as clothes with an identity-stifling uniformity.

If you think that formal wear is identity-constrictive, it is nothing compared to Consumer-wear. Consumer-wear is designed to eliminate the individual self. It seeks to reconfigure the self in the image propagated by the multinationals, which is a paradigm based on the lowest common denominator, the consumer.

Consumer-wear is merely an expression of your slavery to the brands. You are not indulging in a genuine expression of your identity by wearing the creations offered by Wal-mart, the Gap, Nike, Sears or JC Penney.

You are allowing multinational clothing stores to define your identity through their sartorial hold over you. Turning your back on fashion culture is an act of self-entrapment, of chaining your self to the uniformity of the multinationals "fashion."

Consumer-wear's uniformity bears a frightening resemblance to the dress codes of totalitarian regimes. There is little difference between the uniformity of dress imposed by totalitarian regimes such as North Korea's and the uniformity imposed by the global giants. What does it matter if the Great Leader Kim Il Jong orders everyone to wear bland, tasteless clothes through his propaganda machine, or the Gap commands you to wear its bland, tasteless offerings via their propaganda machine?

Consumer-wear fights class snobbery

Consumer-wear is not an act of social emancipation. The comparison posited by consumerist giants makes you choose between upper-class, aristocratic formal wear and democratic, middle and working-class casual clothes. The true question in choosing your clothes is a matter of taste, elegance and refinement. Formal dress can be just as tasteless and bland as its casual counterpart. Non-consumer casual clothing can be tasteful, elegant and sophisticated. Casual clothes are not demonstrative of greater social flexibility or a higher degree of social tolerance.

Taste is not a matter of class or wealth. It is a matter of personal development. The fundamental question regarding clothes is whether or not they are civilized. Your dress should reflect a corresponding sophistication and refinement befitting the advancement of the self. However, that will not happen as long as consumerist giants dress you.

Consumer-wear frees you from traditional clothing

Consumer-wear claims to promote self-expression by making traditional clothing a way of the past. In fact, the opposite is true, as Consumer-wear destroys your inherited culture and replaces it with meaningless clothes. You cannot be yourself if you forsake the clothes of your people, the clothes that define an integral part of your being, for the offerings of a corporation.

Saving the Self

The choice is simple: either you dress your self, or the multinationals will dress you. If you choose to benefit your self rather than the multinationals, here are the necessary steps you must take to develop and maintain your unique fashion culture.

Control your clothes

Learn how to sew or have someone in the family who does. Unlike agriculture, sewing only requires a machine and can be easily accomplished within an apartment.

Purchase only natural fabrics. Choose cotton, wool, silk, hemp, leather (at your option) and satin over polyesters, nylons and other artificial fibres.

Purchase your fabrics from privately-owned specialty stores rather than multinational outlets.

Have clothes tailor-made rather than purchased from stores. Independent tailors and couturiers are rapidly becoming extinct. Unless they benefit from your support and patronage, you will be doomed to purchasing from the multinationals. Tailors and couturiers do more than just custom-fit your clothes. Tailors and couturiers deal in dreams. Your dreams. Only the tailor will make that which you always wanted to wear but could never find on a store rack. These people are to be valued both for their own innate sartorial creativity and for the ability to bring your own fashion artistry to life.

If purchasing your clothes, again purchase from family-owned stores rather than large department stores. Profit from the superior service and the ability to negotiate on price with the proprietor.

Wear your own creations

Expressing the self through dress is both a means of engaging the artist within you and an affirmation of a personal fashion culture. Whether you are capable of fashioning your own wear or can do no better than a rough sketch for a tailor, there is no greater fashion satisfaction than knowing that your clothes precisely reflect your unique personal culture. Rather than employ another's vision, use your own imagination in bringing your sartorial dreams to life. The process will be more time-consuming and undoubtedly more expensive, but ultimately it will be more rewarding as well. By creating your own clothes, they will become an extension of the self, buttressing your individuality, rather than masking it within the multinational style. When the clothes on your back are your own creation, they are a part of the self's identity; when they are the inventions of multinationals they impose a consumer identity upon you.

Taking control of your dress involves six steps.

Imagine: Sit back and let the self roam. Discover the clothes that ideally express you.

Draw: To the best of your ability put your imagination on paper. If you can't draw, or your drawings do not fully reflect your vision, supplement them with words. Describe your vision in as much detail as possible.

Find a tailor: Get a reputable and skilled tailor and tell them what you want.

Get measured: The tailor will do that for you.

Pick your fabrics: Even if you know the general fabric you want to use i.e. silk, you can choose among a variety of silks.

Pick your colours: Again, find the sample closest to your vision.

Revert to traditional dress

Far from being quaint and outmoded, wearing national, ethnic or religious dress denotes a cultural background and non-adherence to consumer propaganda. It is an affirmation of the individual's desire to pursue self-expression and social refinement within their own cultural context, rather than subscribing to multinational offerings. Traditional dress is often associated with a host of proprieties guiding daily social interactions. In societies where traditional clothing predominates, dress is a form of ritual. By putting it on each morning, you are accepting a cultural heritage and a civic responsibility. In effect, you are clothing yourself with a mark of your civilization. As such, traditional dress maintains and strengthens your connection to an essential pylon of the self, your inherited culture. But what associations are derived from wearing consumer clothes? What civilizing responsibilities do they impose upon you? Utterly decontextualized, the clothes of the multinationals are as devoid of meaning as they are of taste.

Traditional dress is often accompanied by a host of other civilizing requirements. They range the gamut from fashion accessories such as jewelry and sashes, to tattoos and body paint. However these accessories, unlike pale consumer imitations, serve to complete and enforce the representation of the self within its inherited culture. A Hindu woman's nose ring or a Maori man's tattoos are part of their respective cultures and traditions. Along with traditional clothing, they form a complete portrait of the civilized self within the context of their respective civilizations. The consumer tattoos, piercing and accessories that you might wear do not have any cultural significance. They are not expressions of your self, but slavish imitations of the whims of your consumer idols.

Appropriate wear

The self progresses when it embraces civilization rather than savagery. From the earliest days of human civilization, primitive tribes marked significant dates or events by adopting a particular dress or a certain accessory. These customs persisted and have been refined until modern times. However, the onslaught of Consumer-wear has brought about a regression from civilized behaviour. Dress requirements for occasions such as weddings and graduations, as well as for certain professions, are increasingly ignored. Sartorial customs for social events have fallen by the wayside.

Appropriate wear recognizes the dual cultural purpose of dress. First and foremost it is a means of individual self-expression, a reflection of one's personal culture. But dress is also a method of communal affirmation. Appropriate wear respects the community both in terms of people and events.

Your clothes must acknowledge an awareness of the public dimension of your life. In the privacy of the home, almost any dress, or lack thereof, is acceptable. When appearing in public your dress should reflect a commensurate appreciation for the society you live in. Attend to the requirements of civility. Do not wear clothes that spurn the social mores and cultural norms of your society.

Appropriate wear goes beyond mere technical formality. Whether the dress requirement is formal, semi-formal or casual, you can still be uncultured by wearing something inappropriate for the occasion. If you go to a funeral wearing a neon pink suit, your choice of suit denotes a failure of personal culture. A cultured individual will ensure that the dress is in tone with the occasion and the fellow attendees.

Following civilization's norms is to your advantage. Appropriate wear offers the occasion to develop and refine your personal culture. Clothes reflect an understanding and an ability to function within the greater social order that is necessary for your development. A rejection of this social order through the adoption of inappropriate dress is a rejection of the self, of one's inherited culture. Far from displaying your freedom, inappropriate wear is a form of self-isolation. By heeding consumerism's call to reject social mores in terms of dress you are imprisoning the self within the meaninglessness of a consumer existence.

The elements of taste

Taste, like beauty, is in the eye of the beholder. Your fashion elegance is another's fashion disaster. However, the question is not what clothes are tasteful, or what clothes are elegant, or what clothes denote refinement and personal culture. Indeed the question lies even deeper than discovering your own unique taste. The true question is whether you make taste and elegance a consideration of your dress choice in the first place.

Dress with a conscious design. Strive to determine not only your particular taste, but to develop a sense for clothing that denotes personal culture. Taste and elegance have an objective and a subjective component. The subjective component is what you must discover by studying fashion and by relying on your artistic self. But the basis of the subjective component is the objective one: whether the clothes reflect a personal culture in terms of a holistic ensemble. Tasteful clothes must reflect an intelligent design by being coordinated.

Co-ordination, both in terms of colour and assortment, is really the establishment of order. Culture, civilization itself, is premised on order. Coordinated clothes define the self as an ordered individual. This order is necessary for the self to have meaning.

Although you might favour anarchy or chaos, fundamentally you are an ordered individual. If the trillions of cells in your body did not function in an orderly fashion, you would instantly cease to exist. Your garb is a method of extending the order of the self beyond the body. Tasteful, elegant clothes are a stamp of the self upon reality. They impose the order of your personal culture upon the universe, and as such signify a superior state of being.

Consumer etiquette

Consumerism's rule in terms of etiquette is simple: Anything goes. The example set by the world of consumer entertainment is one of utter scorn for the "the rules of behaviour standard in polite society."[31] In Consumer-world, adopting a personal etiquette is considered stuffy, rigid and old-fashioned. Why walk with an erect posture when you can slouch or swagger like your favourite hip-hop artist? Why open the door for a woman when she can open it herself? Why not spit on the sidewalk or belch at the mall food court? You're free, says consumerism, free to do as you wish.

31. Webster's Dictionary definition of "etiquette".

Not quite. Your choice does not lie between a formal rigidity of manners and behavioural freedom but between consumerism and culture. Consumer etiquette is not freedom, but anarchy and chaos within the self. Far from giving the self an opportunity to develop, this so-called freedom hinders the self by leaving it without direction and meaning. The chaos of consumer etiquette reflects the chaotic madness of consumerism itself, an out-of-control beast that predicates infinite consumption in the face of the Earth's finite resources. Conversely, the madness of consumerist theory is replicated in the behaviour it encourages. What consumerism really offers under the guise of freedom from social niceties is self-abandonment. Consumerism's "anything goes" theory preaches the abandonment of your self to the chaos of rudeness, vulgarity and an unworthy arrogance.

The type of anarchy consumerism proposes is very restricted, well within the control of the multinationals. This outlet of social freedom is being given to you to mask the control exerted upon you by the multinationals. By acting without consideration for the self and for the rules governing polite behaviour, you are made to feel you are above social norms, you are given a false sense of independence. In fact, many of these acts of "freedom" have been inculcated into your mind by repeatedly watching the behaviour of consumer idols. Consumer idols have programmed your walk, your gestures, your public display of physical needs. Your actions do not originate from the self, they are acts manipulated by consumer propaganda. Even if, by chance, these acts are of your own provenance, they are encouraged by the multinationals to obscure the fact that in every other act in your life, from what you eat to what you wear, you are a slave to consumerism.

A personal etiquette, on the other hand, betokens an ordered, self-controlled individual whose gestures and mien reflect the fulfillment of his potential. Controlling gestures does not restrict the self but merely guides it towards a more felicitous expression of your potential. Freedom is maintaining control over your actions and guiding your body towards the goal of self-achievement.

Saving the self

There are three aspects to social etiquette:

Posture/carriage

Etiquette implies a certain demeanor, a certain way of carrying yourself. It is the art of controlling the movement and positioning of your body. It can be further broken down into three sub-components:

Walking: Walk is an advertisement of the self. Make sure your walk reveals the inherent nobility of the self. Measure your gait. Too fast and you are likely to be thought of as hurried. Too slow and you will appear indolent.

Walk with purpose. When you step, step with confidence. A firm step denotes a self that is in charge and knows the goals it seeks to achieve.

Keep the body straight. Do not slouch, swagger or hunch.

Keep the head up. Your eyes should be facing straight ahead, not up or down. The self emanates through the eyes. Looking straight ahead means eye contact with your fellow human beings, means engaging within the social sphere. Avoid other people's gazes and you avoid exposing the self; you retreat into a cowardly solipsism.

Do not bring any encumbrances. Do not eat, drink, read or listen to music while walking. All such activities are exclusive within themselves. Furthermore, they tend only to ruin your posture and detract from your carriage.

Sitting: Poor sitting postures can result in long-term health problems such as lumbar pain. So, do not sprawl. Do not dangle. Do not spread your legs and hang over the furniture. Do not bend forward or lean to one side.

Uncontrolled postures also denote a displaced self that has allowed the body to act in contravention of social mores. Dictate to your body. Assert the primacy of the self in configuring a sitting position.

Gestures: Avoid all vulgar gestures such as giving the finger. Expressing your disapproval or anger can take more elegant forms such as a well-chosen sarcastic remark.

Control movements at all times. Master the art of flawless navigation among your fellow human beings. Do not be a human wrecking ball. Be aware of your body's placement so that you will not inadvertently bump into people, step on their toes, or elbow them. Needless to say, be sure to apologize if you do hit someone inadvertently.

Do not surrender control and allow emotion to dictate your movements. Emotions tend to promote chaotic movements, flailing limbs and contorting bodies.[32]

---

32. The greater the emotion, the greater the temptation to surrender your body to it. Unless it is a controlled and ritualized cultural display of emotion, such as the distinctive lamentations of Muslim women at funerals, self-control in extreme emotional situations does not imply heartlessness but rather shows the true strength of the self. Those who sit by the grave in impassive silence shedding quiet tears but not losing their minds are those who gain the admiration of their fellow man. In pain or in joy, always exercise restraint and moderation. Otherwise, the self will be subject to emotional vacillations that act as significant obstacles on the road of fulfillment.

Refrain from inappropriate but non-vulgar gestures. One such familiar and common faux-pas is pointing with your finger. However, the vast majority of gestures are inappropriate because of the occasion. Grabbing your partner's behind in public or nuzzling on your partner's ear when you have dinner guests are just two examples of behaviours that are appropriate in private but should not be a cause for public exposure. If you are among your fellow humans, your gestures should mark you as a civilized member of society. The self must constantly be alive to respecting others so that, in turn, its presence may also be respected.

Controlling physical needs

One of the principal methods of distinguishing your self from the animals is by controlling the manifestation of needs that you share with them. Some foods make us flatulent. Fizzy drinks provoke belching. Sometimes we itch in private places, sometimes we sneeze or cough, sometimes we need to clean our nose or clear our throat. All perfectly normal, but the self must demonstrate its superiority in satisfying these urges.

This is done in four ways:

Apologize: Best to do it ahead of time, or else immediately after. An apology demonstrates a genuine awareness that your bestial instincts might cause some minor discomfort or give offense to your fellow human beings. Prefacing such gestures with the appropriate "excuse me" is a mark of personal culture.

Use the appropriate accessory: Use tissue or a napkin for expectorating, clearing your nose, or sneezing. Cover your mouth when you cough.

Retreat from the public eye: Avoid performing these actions in public. Contain your self until you find a private space to satisfy these urges.

Minimize the event: Be as discreet as possible when carrying out these necessary actions. Do not make a big show of it, or be overly loud. On the contrary, aim to reduce their effect especially if they overtake you in the public arena.

Deferral to the vulnerable

Personal culture is reflected in deferring to those who are weaker. Unlike in nature, where the strongest survive, human compassion has recognized the value of those who are, due to age or a particular condition, in a physically disadvantageous position. In respecting and aiding these disadvantaged people, you are affirming the compassion that elevates you above the rest of the animal kingdom. The self that acts in furtherance of its superior qualities, such as compassion, will be a more enlightened self. Be alert for the opportunity to give your seat on a crowded bus to a more vulnerable person. Help them cross a street. Carry their groceries. It is not a question of doing a good act, it a question of affirming your civilized self.

A second, more controversial aspect of social etiquette, involves a man's chivalrous attitude towards a woman. Some would argue that such politeness is demeaning to women. In approaching the debate, I want to point out that the flip side of the coin, "consumer etiquette", is even more demeaning. Consumer culture such as rap music suggests that women are to be treated as whores, and condones abusive, even violent behaviour towards the fairer sex.

Chivalrous behaviour is not a measure of disrespect but of respect. Politeness does not imply that women are inferior to men. Opening a door or holding the chair for a woman merely shows that the self appreciates the other and seeks to facilitate its existence. Similarly, a woman is not submissive in politely accepting the man's help. It merely shows that her self is attuned to the civilizing norms of society and appreciates the offer of help.

Conclusion

A personal culture makes living an art, your movements, a dance. It is the epitome of controlled self-expression, of using your body to denote cultural refinement and a surpassing civility. A personal etiquette implies a certain behavioural matrix to be sure, but how you act within that matrix can denote your own individual style, your unique elegance. If this sounds artificial, well then, so is human civilization.

Do not think of a personal culture as a façade to be used solely in social encounters. If you dine by yourself, at home, there is no reason to forsake the basics of civility. Can you act like a brute just because there is no one to observe your behaviour? The answer is, of course, no. It would be abnormal, schizophrenic, a Dr. Jekyll and Mr. Hyde existence. A personal culture must form a permanent part of your existence.

A personal etiquette is a means of affirming your civility, not for the sake of others, but for the upkeep and development of your own personal culture. Since the process of self-refinement is perpetual, the lack of a public setting is no reason for abandoning a personal etiquette. The art of living, the everyday dance executed by your body's movements must not cease in the absence of an audience. The performance is necessary to the self.

Chapter 15

Business/Finances

If it's your money, how come the multinationals control it?
Find out how your money should benefit you
and not consumerism.

Making your money

What better way to express the self than by pressing the offence on consumerism's home field? By starting your own business and competing in the marketplace, you are advancing the self in a number of important ways.

Stop being an employee

As an entrepreneur, you do not have to be anybody's employee. That includes working for the benefit of the global giants. You have removed your self (and possibly others, such as dependent family members) from the pool of available labour that the multinationals can exploit.

Although employment has its advantages, such as a relatively secure salary and a number of side benefits, it also comes with a hefty price tag. That price is paid by your individuality.

The cost of employment

As an employee, your opportunities for self-expression are circumscribed within the narrow bounds of your assigned task. Your employer's primary concern is that you execute orders, not that you interpret them in accordance with your intellectual and creative needs. In general, employers will frown on any departure from their instructions. Bland personalities are favoured. Anybody too colourful is deemed a disturbance.

In the social milieu of the workplace, with its gossip, invidiousness, petty ambitions, cliques and rivalries, the best way to survive and prosper is by submerging your genuine personality. By assuming a neutral, colourless work persona, you will not risk making any enemies and endangering your position in the company. Maintaining cordial relations with your fellow employees often means hiding your true self behind bland platitudes and trite prattle.

Working for the multinationals

Becoming a clone: The problem of self-expression is even more acute when employed by the corporate giants. The corporate giants have a rigid, hierarchical structure that does not allow for individual expression. The key to their efficient functioning rests on economic models that will not permit individual variations. Multinationals depend on economies of scale, where profit margins are razor thin and generally determined by the sheer quantity of goods sold. Consequently their production, distribution and transportation networks have been organized and perfected to the smallest detail, leaving small room for error or chance.

When employed by the multinationals you will be assigned a task and expected to perform it without any deviation from the established norm. Anything else is seen as upsetting the delicate balance of the company's "ecosystem." A personal touch, a different interpretation or a novel approach to fulfilling that task is unacceptable and will be sanctioned. You are the proverbial cog in the machine. The sole function of people in a multinational's work environment is to maintain smooth operations by performing the necessary tasks. Everything is routinized, automated, and dehumanized.

The lack of opportunity for individual expression is not only limited to low-paying multinational jobs. The blue-collar worker on the factory floor, the teenager in the fast food industry and the Third World child making Nike shoes are prime candidates for this type of self-annihilation. But well-paid, highly educated, white-collar computer engineers are no better off.[33] Working for the hi-tech multinationals promotes the same monotony and is just as deleterious to individualism. As for the multinational management and executive ranks, they are the most indoctrinated and automated of the lot, since it is their responsibility to ensure the multinational runs like a well-oiled machine.

---

33. There is a reason why supposedly pampered Microsoft employees have been renamed "microserfs."

To ensure that you perform your assigned tasks with robotic precision multinationals have developed detailed training programs. These programs promote the corporate culture, philosophy and code of conduct deemed necessary to make you a good employee. By redesigning intellectual and behavioural patterns through training, multinationals such as McDonald's hope to assure uniformity of service around the globe. In seeking to make you as predictable as a math equation, multinational training functions as an assembly line for producing model employees.

Becoming the product: It is more than just clones or programmed automatons that the multinationals seek to create. One of the aims of their training programs is to transform you into their product. For the multinationals you are more than just an employee; you form part and parcel of their product. A McDonalds' or Disney employee is just as much a part of the multinational product as a Big Mac or a Disneyland ride. If you wish to be employed by multinationals you are expected to become their product through your dress, actions and speech.

In order to transform you into their product, multinationals interfere in your private life more than any other employer. While businesses great and small seek to maintain good employer-employee relations with group events such as company parties or barbeques, few can match the multinational corporations in terms of their influence over your personal life. Multinationals expect you to embrace their corporate culture and mentality as a paradigm for life. They expect nothing less than a complete change in your personality.

Success and advancement within the multinational hierarchy depends on how closely you align your self with their needs. The change has both mental and physical components. The mental aspect is a profound shift in your thinking patterns to put you in a multinational state of being. You are also expected to change your physical appearance to conform with the multinational's needs. Disney, for example, will not permit facial hair on its male employees. No other employment opportunity is so invasive in terms of your private life.

To ensure complete domination, some multinationals act like mini-states. They provide you with numerous benefits, seeking to care for all of your needs. However, this caring is merely a form of control, for every benefit comes with a host of attendant obligations upon you. The sum total of these obligations means sacrificing your freedom and remaking your self in the image they desire.

The opportunity for self-expression

Ownership challenges and engages the potential of the self. Starting and running your own business is a testing ground for your abilities.

Starting the business: Whether you are starting up your own restaurant or your own web page, you must formulate a business plan or at least have a concept of how the business will look like and function. Even if you subcontract interior decorators, tradespersons, architects or web designers to help you, in the end you must make the decisions. All of these people will inevitably demand your creative input as the source for their inspiration.

Running the business: Once the doors open, the business owner must constantly fight to attract clients and increase revenue while always on the lookout for cost reduction measures. There are no strategies from above to be implemented. It is up to you to devise your own marketing strategy, to choose the means and methods whereby you advertise, to fight the daily fight for the survival of your entrepreneurial creation. You are forced to employ your talents, your imagination and your intellect in order to keep the business afloat.

Business owners are invariably identified with their creation. When customers walk into McDonald's, they care little for who serves them. The human aspect is not important to the multinational experience. When dining at a privately-owned restaurant, the personal touch of the restaurateur keeps them coming back. The owner's personal relationships with business partners and clientele are essential to promoting the image of the business. Establishing such a network of relationships is an excellent method of self-expression. The entrepreneur uses all of his social skills to gain the confidence of those with whom he has business dealings.

The constant demands of ownership, the anxieties, problems, potential deals and available opportunities that preoccupy the entrepreneur's mind act as a form of mental calisthenics for the self. As an owner, you are always exercising your critical and creative faculties in the service of your business. Business ownership is like a perpetual pencil sharpener for your mind. The crank is constantly turning to ensure the tip is kept in optimum condition.

Ownership protects against consumerism

The rigorous mental and temporal demands of entrepreneurship protect you from the mental atrophy produced by consumerism. Simply put, you have neither the inclination nor the time to sit in a consumerist-induced stupor. The flame of ownership burns within you, constantly propelling you to devise new methods for improving the business or for starting a new venture.

Owner, fighter

Engaged in the cutthroat competition of the market, you must become an active person, a fighter. You are more than just wily, intelligent or creative. You are a warrior, battling to protect your creation. This aggressive spirit, this entrepreneurial bellicosity is exactly what will enable you to resist the temptations of consumerism. Since businesspeople are self-motivated, they are less likely to accept being motivated or controlled by others, including the multinationals. In challenging the competition, you are likely to challenge the lies of the consumer universe.

Broaden the self's professional abilities

If you own a business, you quickly become a jack-of-all-trades. The business owner often subsumes within himself a myriad of professions, from accounting to human resources. You learn about incorporating a business, leasing commercial space and the various trades that will prepare your space for the business. You control your finances, hire and fire your own employees, develop marketing campaigns, deal with suppliers, in short, a million things which you most likely never had to deal with in your previous profession. The self benefits enormously from gaining knowledge in many fields to which it was not previously exposed.

Problem solving

Problem solving is one of your most underused qualities. In the multinational workplace, where tasks are compartmentalized and there are precise instructions for dealing with every possible glitch in the system, the necessity of using your own creativity to fashion solutions to a problem is minimal. For intractable problems, multinationals can always outsource to various specialists and consultants or just absorb the financial costs and move on. For the business owner, necessity is the mother of invention. Due to relatively modest financial resources, business owners must rely on their own inventiveness to cobble together a solution to their problems.

The holistic self

As an employee, you lead a dual life. You have your work and you have your leisure time. They are separate, self-contained worlds. As a business owner your business is a vehicle of the self. It is not a separate sphere of your life, but forms part of a holistic whole.

The holistic self promoted by business ownership must be carefully distinguished from the multinationals' attempt to establish absolute control over their employees. In the former case, business ownership unifies your fractured self, in the latter, multinationals seek to usurp it altogether by branding it as one of their products. Ownership promotes individual self-expression; multinationals annihilate it.

Creating your universe

The business owner operates within his own microcosm. Businesspeople exist and rule absolutely within the self-created structure of the business rather than being part of someone else's. No longer will you be a cog in another's machine; you are now free to express yourself in a professional setting.

Personal responsibility and self-sufficiency

Freedom means responsibility. The business is an extension of you. You do not respond to anyone in choosing how to operate it. Conversely, there can be no passing of the buck. There is no other higher decision-maker, no other superior authority to be held accountable or to shoulder the blame. You must account for all your actions.

The incessant demands of the business make it a permanent companion. It is inextricably linked to you and always lurking beneath your surface thoughts. You can forget work after five p.m., but you cannot leave your business behind any more than you can leave any other part of your self.

Personal responsibility is tough. It is also the best thing that can happen to you. Acquiring the means to live has now become exclusively dependent on the self. You are now self-sufficient. You no longer depend upon the whims of others. There is no chance of being laid off. There is no chance of being told off by the boss. There is no need for ladder-climbing obsequiousness, no need to watch out for back-stabbing co-workers. You are the apex of the pyramid. You are free. And once you get a taste of freedom, you will never want to go back.[34]

Controlling your money

You have your own business up and running. You control your income. You are self-sufficient. Everything is perfect, right? Not quite.

Owning your business forms but one-half of the financial independence equation. The other half involves managing, investing and spending that hard-earned business income for your benefit, rather than the benefit of the multinationals. It will not be easy. Multinationals depend upon accessing and controlling your money, and they have a number of ways of getting their hands on it:

Taxes/mandatory contributions; They appear beyond your control as an individual. Taxes have acquired the status of a necessary evil in modern societies. Governments are addicted to them. Unfortunately, some of the money the government collects from you is made available to the multinationals. Take the example of the pension fund.[35] Pension contributions force you to give your cash to pension funds that plough the money into the coffers of the multinationals so they may consumerize you the better.

Through financial institutions: Banks are the prime example. Not only do they take your money and use it to fund the globalization strategies of other multinationals, but as multinationals themselves, they exert significant financial control upon you. Few among us are not involved in a long-term relationship of dependency with banks through various instruments such as mortgages, loans and leases. Bank financing for your big ticket purchases, which comes along with the signing of personal guarantees or putting up significant collateral, ensures that your personal finances will be constantly in the bank's shadow.

The bank is your taskmaster, indirectly enforcing your subjugation to the consumerist economic system via the monthly mortgage payment.

---

34. A former business partner of my father had a cushy bureaucratic job for many years. Then, he went into business. Before long he had a double mortgage on the house, the business was in trouble and he was facing financial ruin. Despite it all, he never regretted leaving his government post. Why? Because the tedium and boredom of a job could never replace the satisfaction of being in charge of your own destiny, for better or worse. And if the government is tedious, wait until you see what the multinationals have in store for you.
35. My definition of taxes includes any contributions the government encourages or forces you to make.

The threat of foreclosure hangs over your head like a sword of Damocles. Your fate is sealed the day you sign your mortgage papers. When you sign off on your mortgage you have signed on to thirty years of hard work to repay it. When you sign off on a mortgage you have mortgaged your future to an implacable multinational. Regardless of your interests and desires for self-fulfillment, you must henceforth produce the monthly tribute or risk being thrown out of your suburban castle.

Banks control your finances as the keepers of your money. Although most people have bank accounts, few of them know or even care about the relationship between their money and the banks. While it is not the purpose of this book to examine these legal complexities, suffice it to say that despite outward appearances, once you deposit money into the bank, that money is no longer exclusively yours. The bank gains certain legal rights in regards to your money, rights that can be triggered by specific events, so that the bank may for example freeze your accounts, or even disburse their contents to someone else. Keeping your money in a bank is not the same thing as keeping your money in your back pocket.

The credit card: Banks work in concert with other multinationals to help underpin this consumer staple. Without doubt, the credit card is the most iniquitous drain on your personal finances. It serves as a primary means of consumer enslavement by giving you the illusion that you have more purchasing power than you actually have. When using a credit card even expensive items don't really cost that much because of a comparatively low monthly payment rate and therefore you can indulge in consumer excess.

The credit card is a debt machine that functions like a leech, steadily draining your economic lifeblood until you are financially exhausted. It is tailored specifically towards advancing global consumerism. Buy more than you need, it coos. Buy what you do not need, it whispers. How much does it cost? Don't worry, you don't have to pay for it. You can just put it on the card. That's why they call it the "plastic fantastic."

By structuring your debt into monthly installments, the credit card is specifically designed to make you lose track of, and therefore control over, your finances. You are encouraged to surrender control to the consumer impulse and the all-obliterating glint of that plastic strip. The result is only too well known. Credit card debt is damaging your financial health and destroying your financial freedom. Usurious interest rates ensure that you will be paying for items bought years ago, without actually ever paying them off. The credit card road leads to personal bankruptcy and financial ruin.

The Markets: If you do not wish to keep your life savings in the bank, investment companies are only too happy to 'manage' that money for you. Don't make that mistake. The markets are one of the greatest sources of financing for the multinationals. For you, however, they are a great risk. While the multinationals are guaranteed to receive your investment money, you are not guaranteed any profits on those investments. Indeed, you should be happy if you don't end up with a loss.

The only people who truly profit from the markets are the owners. In the case of the markets, the owners are the multinationals. There are two kinds of multinationals that profit from the markets:

a. The middlemen: These are the investment banks, mutual fund companies, stockbrokers and traders that maintain, administer and work the markets.
b. The listed companies. The giants of consumerism, from food to entertainment and beyond, are all listed on the stock exchanges, hungering to access your much-needed cash.

The market is a casino

The performance of the stock market over the last few years and the high-tech bubble points to the hidden truth of the stock market: It is nothing more than a glorified casino. You can win and lose in the markets, just as you can at the casino. Before investing, ask yourself if you would want to risk your life savings in Vegas. Is the poker table a good place to improve your financial situation? If it is, then you might as well go to the casinos and cut out the financial middlemen that "manage" your stock portfolios. But if you won't let your nest egg slide on the roulette table why gamble it away on the stock market?

You must assume fiscal responsibility over your money. Only you and you alone can secure your financial independence. It is time to use the cash you've earned to benefit the self, and not the multinationals.

Saving the Self

Smart tax planning

Although taxes, like death, are unavoidable, you can nonetheless preserve your financial freedom by following a few simple guidelines:

Plan for the self: Tax planning usually involves investing in various government-approved funds controlled by and for the benefit of multinationals. But governments also give tax breaks for a number of initiatives that are designed to profit individuals. Farmers and fishermen generally benefit from tax-breaks in relation to their profession. Businesses that invest in upgrading, modernizing or hiring new employees can similarly benefit. Search out and apply for tax breaks designed to improve or maintain your income source.

Plan with the family: Income-splitting with spouses and other family members can be a perfectly legitimate method of lowering your tax burden. Our family business was just that, with all working-age members drawing salaries and reducing the overall tax burden.

Choose charity over taxes: Help the self by giving to those who wish to help you. Whether giving to charities who work to eliminate a physical ailment that affects you or a loved one, or giving to a charity that fights for your right to clean water or clean air, control the ultimate destination of your money. Do not allow a multinational or even the government to make that determination for you.

Never spend more than you have

Live on what you have and you will live free. Debt is slavery. But how do you cut debts?

Cutting your credit cards means cutting your debts. No need to spend the rest of your life paying usurious interest rates to Visa and Mastercard. No need to achieve a good credit rating, which is only a euphemism for saying you are a docile consumer slave, and as a reward the multinationals shall give you the opportunity to further enslave yourself by borrowing even more money from them. By keeping your spending within your income level, you will never have to resort to the credit card to finance your needs.

Imposing control on your finances also means reining in your consumer habits. Live within your means. Once you willingly limit your consumption to the available monthly income, choices will have to be made. Purchasing enormous amounts of unnecessary consumer products will no longer be an option. You will become more focused on what your actual needs are, and you will learn to direct your spending to satisfy those needs. The artificial lures consumerism dangles before your eyes will lose some of their lustre. The constant barrage of commercials will not be as effective in indoctrinating you when you are living on a budget.

Controlling your debts means peace of mind. No longer the dread of the monthly credit card bills; no longer the possibility of interest accumulating on that interest. Once your finances are tamed, your stress levels will see a corresponding decline and you will be a happier and healthier individual.

Return to the cash society

Forget credit cards, debit cards, cheques and electronic transactions. Keep all the money necessary for your living expenses in cash. By using cash wherever possible[36], you will be constantly aware of how much you are spending. Non-cash transactions are designed to make you lose track of spending and run into debt. Losing track of spending also facilitates excessive consumption. Cash in hand will breed restraint and perhaps even a modicum of frugality, further buttressing your resistance towards consumer products.

Cash also means no bank fees. You can avoid wasting your money on the hidden and not-so-hidden fees banks charge for their services. Despite offering interest rates bordering on the non-existent, banks charge you for the privilege of accessing your account, either on the basis of a set fee, a transaction fee, or both. These fees make keeping your money in the bank a useless or even losing proposition. If you compare bank fees with bank interest, you will quickly learn that you end up paying a steep price for having banks "keep" your money. Far from benefiting you, banks steal from your accounts. They take a few dollars at a time, so you don't feel the pinch, but theft by any other name is just the same. Stop the theft! No need to diminish your financial resources by bleeding fees all over your monthly bank statement. Keep as much as you can in your pocket or in your house, and invest the rest.

Invest it yourself

Why depend upon the promises of others, why be lulled by economic system that you cannot control, whose intricacies and complexities completely defy your knowledge? Why let investment companies remove the money from your control and invest it as they see fit? Take responsibility for managing your funds and engage in economic self-expression. Nurture your own nest egg and ignore the markets. Use the same abilities that have allowed you to earn your money in order to preserve and grow it. Remember, for every activity you surrender to others, you are curtailing a form of self-fulfillment.

But how do you invest? The difference between being an investor and a businessman is a hazy one, and indeed in law, differentiating between

36. Unfortunately, it is becoming increasingly difficult to use cash in modern society. Banks and multinationals are actively pushing payment methods involving the use of credit or reliance on their services. Mandating the use of credit cards for renting vehicles or equipment is one method of doing this.

an investment and a business is often a vexing question. However, the investor is generally in a more passive role when it comes to managing wealth. This often means purchasing real property, or perhaps investing in art, precious metals and jewels, objects that tend to maintain or increase their value through time.

There are two basic principles that should govern your investment activities:

Invest in the people you know

Always look towards people you know when giving your money to someone else as an investment. If you know and trust any entrepreneurs planning to open a business, ask to be a silent partner. Better still if those entrepreneurs are members of your family or close friends. Investing in people you know has a host of advantages:

More control, greater influence: You will have more control over your investment in terms of how you want the money spent, and indeed the direction of the venture as a whole. Investing a few thousand of dollars into your friend's restaurant will carry more weight than placing the same amount in the shares of a multinational. A friend or relative you've helped out will at least listen politely to your opinions, glad to have benefited from your investment. Buy one hundred shares in Pepsico and try to tell them how to run their business. No one in charge will know you from a hole in the ground.

Greater access: Due to a personal relationship with your investee and the greater weight attached to your investment, you will gain unparalleled access into the business' intricacies. As a silent partner, friend or family member you can request information that multinationals would never even conceive to share.

Investment flexibility: You can negotiate the structure and amount of your contribution with well-known business partners. The other choice is having some anonymous fund manager whom you have never met and will never meet shape your financial future for you.

Dealing with the boss: Finally, whenever you have questions, you know you will always be getting your answers from the person in charge. Getting the attention of a multinational's CEO will not be quite as easy.

Create your own investment portfolio

You don't need investment advisors to create a diversified investment portfolio. You can create your unique investment portfolio by choosing to invest in real estate, buy precious metals, art or collectibles, as well as investing in various small business ventures as a silent partner. Structure your portfolio as you want, rather than having someone else do it for you.

Finally, if you do wish to gamble in the markets, avoid the investment firms. Make the investments yourself. Whether you adopt a long-term strategy or seek your profits as a day-trader, ensure that it is you who holds the reins.

Ploughing your money into the markets should be your least desirable option. By entering the markets you are inevitably forced to enter and work within the financial structure upholding the multinationals and will inevitably provide them with some benefits, if only through the commissions they make off your trades.

Use alternative financing

When starting your own business or buying a home, money could very well be a problem. If you cannot finance the venture or purchase yourself, find alternative ways of raising capital.

Use the family and the community: Rely on close relations within family and community to raise capital for any new venture or investment. An extended family can pool its finances to help a segment of the family group purchase a home without resort to the banks. Members of an ethnic or religious community can work together to help one of their own renovate a building or commercial space and make it ready for a business venture.

If you have such options available to you, make the best of the opportunity and avoid the banks. Not only will you get better interest rates from your family or the community, any interest they might charge you will be profiting your family or ethnic/religious kin rather than the multinationals. Family or communal lenders will also be more co-operative, flexible and proactive in order to prevent the failure of your initiative. They will give you a break if you are struggling by suspending a monthly payment, or allowing your debt to fall in arrears. You are much more likely to alter or even completely restructure the nature of the transaction with close associates. The monolithic, impersonal bank is solely interested in getting its pound of flesh and is backed by an army of lawyers to ensure it will have it.

Partner up: Partnerships are another means of avoiding the banks. If you lack the necessary funds to start up your own business, find a partner who can help bring your dreams to fruition. By a partner, I mean another individual or group of individuals, not a multinational financial institution. While family members can be partners, partnership structures provide more financing options than family relations, since they are based on self-interest rather than bloodlines. You can pair up with virtually anyone you trust in order to achieve your goals, whereas your choice of relatives and even community members is more finite. Partnerships are an effective and mutually beneficial method of finding the money when you do not have close family or ethnic groupings to rely on, and you do not want to resort to the banks.

There are two types of partnerships:

Active partners: Active partners are a group of individuals who pool their financial resources to start and run a business. All of the partners are personally involved in the day-to-day business operations and the decision-making.

Silent partners: This second type of partnerships involves an incipient business venture started by an individual or group that seeks financial help from other individuals or groups to bring the venture to fruition. Silent partners contribute start-up capital and share in the profits, but are not involved in the operation of the business.

Whether your partners are long-time associates or silent partners, they are preferable to multinational financial institutions. With partnerships, you can choose who you are dealing with, and decide whether you want to give that individual a stake in your business. You know who is profiting from your business venture. You are working at the human level. You establish an actual relationship with your fellow investor.

If you borrow money from a bank you will be dealing only with the agent of the corporate investor. However well you get along with the bank's agent is irrelevant. You are working at the institutional level, where policy guidelines decide your fate. The bank's agent is only the servant of your institutional partner. The agent will not personally profit or lose from your investment. The agent does not care. Even if the agent does care, there is nothing that they can do in contravention of the contract you signed with the bank.

The partnership of the bank is an utterly impersonal one, motivated solely by economic figures. If you do not meet the bank's criteria, the bank will not hesitate to terminate that relationship regardless of the personal cost to you. Human partners involve relationships. You don't go for drinks with the bank manager but you do with your human partners. You don't invite the bank manager to your barbecues, but your human partners will be there. You can't argue with or challenge the bank as you can human partners. Human partnership broadens your possibility for self-expression. The human factor injects understanding, compassion and forgiveness into the business relationship. Just like family members, human partners are more likely to give you a break in situations where the bank pulls the plug.

Support people-owned businesses

Entrepreneurs build community

Family-owned businesses are the vertebrae that form the backbone of the community. It is upon their sturdy frame that your self builds a sense of community. For unlike the multinationals, with whom you engage in purely consumerist transactions, family-owned businesses are built on personal relationships.

In the seven years that I have shopped at the nearby multinational supermarket, I have never had a glimmer of recognition from any of its myriad of employees. This is not surprising considering the enormous amount of clients that pass daily through the doors of this giant store. It is also to be expected considering the rapid employee turnover experienced at these large operations. When I purchase Italian delicacies at La Bottega Nicastro, a family-run Italian deli in downtown Ottawa, I am always greeted by the reassuring faces of the owners, the Nicastro family. Not only do these people recognize me as an individual, but they also know my family. They ask about the family business. They tell me things going on in their lives and I tell them about mine. It's like shopping from a good friend. You feel comfortable in their environment. You feel at home. Yet I am no different than many other of the customers with whom the various Nicastro family members have established a rapport.[37] These non-business interactions, these friendly conversations that occur between the patrons and owners at the Bottega are woefully absent in the multinational supermakets. There, the faces that greet you are indifferent and bored, or at best have a glazed smile attached to them. In the consumerist temples there is no friendly banter, no warm hellos of recognition, no one who already knows your preferences and purchasing habits. You do not feel part of the community, you do not feel any social links, however tenuous, to the store employees. You are merely an assembly line consumer, utterly undifferentiated from the next, and forgotten just as soon as you have been served.

---

37. Recently, a former Nicastro customer who moved away to Washington D.C.'s suburbs wrote an article in Ottawa's local newspaper complaining about the lack of food choices when it comes to grocery shopping in her new city. She told Ottawans to count their blessings for having Nicastro in their midst.

Business diversity strengthens the self

By patronizing family-owned businesses, you are increasing the variety of choices available in your particular business sector. In their attempt to monopolize you, multinationals have bankrupted or bought out many family-owned competitors. The dearth of competitors limits you to choosing one multinational over the other. In directly competing with the multinationals, family-owned businesses offer you a means of escaping the consumer trap.

The consequences of a lack of choice are evident whenever you wish to eat on a road trip. Unless you have packed your own food or plan to drive into a city, you are likely to eat at a highway food stop. Each food stop consists of either an individual or a collection of fast-food outlets.

Such situations are not only limited to highway food stops. The absence of family-owned businesses is prevalent in other industries, from gas stations to convenience store products, to convenience stores themselves.

The lack of choice is even more pronounced in the entertainment industry, where multinationals control the means of distribution. If you are an independent filmmaker, publisher or record producer, you will only be able to reach a mass audience through the Cineplexes, music stores, television networks and mega-bookstores controlled by the multinationals. Only the multinationals have the necessary means of marketing and distributing your product to a wide audience. This vicious cycle whereby multinationals are necessary to your success, a success which only strengthens their grip on the industry, can be broken only through your support of family-owned distributors and marketers. Give them the means to distribute and market your product.

Supporting family-owned businesses is not easy. Consumer propaganda has instilled such an utter fear of the new and the different that you are reluctant to attempt new products or services unless they have the multinational stamp of approval.[38] Your sense of adventurousness, even at the very modest level of trying a new restaurant or a new product, has been atrophied by consumer propaganda. Family-owned businesses, which cannot afford huge marketing campaigns to overcome the public's reluctance, are very likely to perish for daring to be different and innovative. Indeed family-owned businesses are likely to perish solely by virtue of NOT being a multinational. For even if the product they are

---

38. A new product will only be sampled if offered by a multinational, which, in people's brainwashed minds, guarantees its "safety."

selling is a well-known one, like a hamburger, most people will still stream to McDonald's rather than try the hamburgers at their food joint.

If you have experienced this type of frustration as a business-owner do not succumb to consumer fear. Remember, if you wish others to patronize your business then you must repay the favour by patronizing theirs.[39] The next time you are faced with a new product offered by a family-owned business, give it a chance. Don't refuse things outright. Remember Frost, and take the less-travelled road. It will make all the difference.

---

39. For one brief summer a dozen years ago, our family owned a store selling innovative meat pies of my father's invention. People saw our pies and asked whether they were either a) pizza or b) dessert pies. When told they were neither, they would look skeptical and walk away. Worse, people were so afraid of trying the pies that they would refuse free samples. We would walk out in the middle of the crowded downtown street where our store was situated, trying to entice passersby with slices of free meat pies, hot and fresh from the oven. People would run away from us as if we were carrying the plague. There was nothing that we could do to break through the fear. In the end the business was sold, victim of consumer conditioning at its worst.

Chapter 16

The Environment

If the environment you live in serves consumerism, then it is harming your self. Changing your environment to suit your needs is a gigantic step towards freedom.

Consumer propaganda: why you don't care about the environment

Consumerism has developed three principal tactics to ensure that you will not care for your surroundings:

The Environment is "out there": A tragic thing about the environment is that you don't realize that you live inside it. The environment is presented as something far away, a thing removed from your life. It is the jungles of the Amazon, the snow-capped Rockies, the Saharan desert. The environment is a tourist destination, a nature preserve for plants and animals, but NOT a place for humans. You can visit the environment in national parks such as Yellowstone or Banff, but you do not live there. Separated from your life, you do not give the environment much thought or importance.

Blinded by the economy: The economy is an artificial creation. Your environment is the most real of all things you can know. It is the womb in which you are protected and nourished. It is the giver of life. It is the defender of your existence. It is the place where all of your hopes and dreams are realized, where your existence finds meaning. And yet, you consistently hold economic interests above your environmental needs.

Consumerism has taught you to place economic interests above all by presenting the economy as your problem. You fear tax hikes, shrinking investment portfolios, disappearing retirement funds or losing your job. You worry about money and not global warming. Global warming is a problem, habitat loss is a problem, the extinction of species is a problem, but having the money to consume is **your** problem.

Creating and sustaining stereotypes: Consumerism has also identified caring for the environment with a particular way of life, with making particular social choices and, most importantly, with adhering to a well-defined political viewpoint and ideology. Consumerism has portrayed environmentalists as kooky socialists at best, eco-terrorists at worst. Multinationals have gone to extreme lengths in order to destroy the validity of the environmentalist movement, knowing that if you will care about your surroundings you will invariably reduce your consumption.

Understanding environmentalism

Let me dispel some common myths about being an environmentalist. To care about the environment does not mean you have to be a tree-hugger. You do not have to like the great outdoors, or think it is great. You do not have to have a special spiritual kinship with animals. You do not even have to like dogs, cats, parrots or any other critter that catches people's fancy. You do not have to be a vegetarian, dress in rags, refuse to wash for months or live in a tree house perched on a giant redwood like some forlorn Ewok. All you have to do is care for your environment.

The environment is not something out there. The environment is the space where you exist. The environment is **your** environment. Your house. Your lawn. Your workplace. Your favourite fishing spot. The highway you take to get to work. It's all the environment. If you care about any of the above, you are an environmentalist.

The multinationals have perverted the true meaning of environmentalism by popularizing environmentalist stereotypes. In order to combat this consumer propaganda, distinguish between the meaning of environmentalism and the form in which the multinationals present it. This means you can be a right-wing, anti-abortion, pro-death penalty, sexist, religious fundamentalist, and still be an environmentalist. Or you can be a Paris Hilton clone, preoccupied only with fashions and cosmetics and still be an environmentalist. Your mode of expression might be different, but you can still show your environmentalist colours by the type of cosmetics you choose (non-chemical based), or the kind of clothes you wear (natural fabrics).

Be as different and unique as possible in expressing your environmentalism. Set a new standard that breaks with the consumer stereotypes. Let the self determine how you express your concern for your surroundings. For environmentalism is not about trees and animals, but about creating the conditions necessary for the fulfillment of the self.

Consumer "improvements" can harm the self

You often manifest concern for your surroundings by attempting to improve them. If your efforts take the form of consumer improvements, you will end up making things worse. Consumer improvements harm your surroundings and your self, for they are predicated on an antagonistic relationship with the natural environment. The usual effect of consumer improvements is to eliminate all traces of the natural from your surroundings and replace it with chemical substitutes. There are two principal types of consumer improvements that cause more harm than good:

Improving the house

Chemical cleaning: You could clean the house with a natural mixture of water, lemon juice and vinegar. Unfortunately, consumerism has taught you to desire more than mere cleanliness. You are not satisfied if the floor is clean. You want to make it shine. In making the floor shine, you use chemicals. So it is with the furniture. You don't just want it clean, you want it to have that glossy polished look. Well that gloss comes at a price, and the price means inhaling the fumes emanated by the wood-polishing cream or spray.

By using chemical cleaning agents, you poison your house with a toxic chemical soup. In trying to get rid of dirt and dust, you end up filling the house with chemicals that have adverse health effects, from allergies to cancer.

Renovating: Renovating involves further exposure to dangerous chemicals. Whether it's painting the house or refinishing the kitchen, the amounts of harmful chemicals in your environment will increase exponentially. Paints, glues and lacquers contain a laundry list of unsavoury chemicals. Unless you use natural-based alternatives, a renovated house will result in a dilapidated body.

The controlled climate: By enclosing yourself in an artificial, air-conditioned environment, you are more likely to catch colds as you alternate between the outside heat and the inside cool. You are also decreasing the quality of air you breathe.

A controlled climate is really a form of self-pollution. In closing the windows, you have deprived yourself of fresh air and substituted a stale and artificial replacement. More importantly, the accumulated indoor pollutants floating about your house have no chance of leaving your hermetically sealed environment.

The lawn: Never in the history of mankind has there been a more useless, unnecessary and wasteful occupation than lawn maintenance. The obsession with the perfect lawn is an exercise in self–destruction.

Keeping the lawn green and short hurts you in many ways. Lawns take the place of trees, which not only provide shade, stabilize soil and serve as barriers against the fury of Mother Nature, but are also nature's best and most effective air cleaners.

Second, lawns tend to waste a lot of water to be kept green. One reason why water reservoirs are drying up across North America is that everybody is watering their lawns.[40] Watering the lawn is like keeping a comatose patient on life support. If you pull the plug, you know it will die. Yet, we keep millions of blades of grass on life support. Last time I checked, natural grass never needed human help to grow and survive. Let nature care for itself. Save the water for yourself, not for keeping some rent-a-grass alive.

The lawn is also polluting. First, indirectly, via the greenhouse gasses emitted by the lawn-cutting machinery used to keep it closely cropped (and thus requiring even more water to be kept artificially green). Second, by the fertilizers, many of them chemical, dumped on the lawn so it can grow faster.

Finally, the lawn is a weakling that cannot defend itself. The artificially modified turf that landscapers use to cover your property has little resistance towards natural predators such as mites or beetles, not to mention hardy natural competitors such as weeds. Consequently, tons of insecticides, pesticides, herbicides and other such wholesome products are needed to protect it. Too bad that in protecting the lawn, these same products hurt you, aggravating your allergies and setting you up as the world's next cancer victim.

Improving the self

Self-"sterilization": While it is important to stop sterilizing your environment with cleaning chemicals, it is even more important to stop sterilizing your body with such chemicals.

The obsession with eliminating germs and bacteria has crossed the line of reason. Consumerism taught you to eliminate germs at all costs

---

40. Water, and especially access to clean water, which 20 per cent of the world's population does not presently enjoy, will become the most precious resource of the 21st century unless drastic steps are taken to alter the present course of humanity. From wasteful North America to the drought-stricken Middle-East, water will be at the root of many human conflicts.

by using its chemical-based products. What consumerism does not tell you is that living in a germ-free environment is unhealthy.

Coming in contact with bacteria is actually good for your body. Exposure to germs helps your immune system build a resistance towards them. Children who play outside and come into contact with germs on a regular basis are usually healthier than those who live in a sterilized house and are kept clean with tons of antibacterial soap and shampoos. Unfortunately, as adults, regardless of your childhood, you tend to lessen your contact with germs, and consequently are ever more vulnerable to being sick.

Practicing good hygiene is commendable. Sterilizing the self with chemicals is harmful. Throw away your antibacterial soaps and shampoos. Do not allow the multinational-propagated obsession with cleanliness destroy your immune system. Stop chemically cleansing your self.

Chemical Beauty: Improving the self via perfumes, fragrances, deodorants and cosmetics is as old as human civilization. Unfortunately, the products we use to achieve the desired aesthetic and olfactory effects have changed greatly over the years.

In older times, fragrances and perfumes were made of plant and flower extracts. Since multinationals produce vast quantities of these products, they cannot afford or depend on using natural ingredients. As such they have resorted to readily available chemical substitutes. Consumer scents might smell like roses, but all you are sniffing are chemical concoctions.

Stop this chemical assault on your body. Spraying chemicals on your self is extremely dangerous. They will provoke your allergies and play havoc with your immune system. Your skin will absorb them and they will enter your bloodstream. That's when they really start hurting you. Chemicals found in cosmetics have been found responsible for cancerous tumors, lower fertility and an increase in the chance of birth defects. Chemical cosmetics do not improve the self. They only harm it.

Saving the Self

A good environmentalist does nothing

Caring for your surroundings does not mean you have to be proactive in terms of participating in protests or any such stereotypical "environmentalist" activity. You can be a great environmentalist if you are aware of your surroundings and do not act in a self-destructive manner. Environmentalism, at its most basic, means leaving things be. It is an exercise in passivity. It is about things you should not do, rather than things you should.

Doing nothing is often better because you cannot improve on nature. Your body was created to function best within natural surroundings. You cannot, by artificial means or actions, improve natural surroundings for the self. The best you can do is to work within your self's needs, and that means working with nature, not against it. Even culture, that most human of inventions, is valuable when it functions organically and holistically within the surrounding natural environment. Culture is the artistry of life and that life is led within natural surroundings.

Three reasons you need to care

1. Eating

One crucial reason has to do with the quality of your food. I have already discussed the perils of eating consumer food. Unfortunately even a healthy diet of vegetables, fruits, grains and milk can harm you when these foods are produced by multinational farms.

The bedrock of the consumer food industry is formed by multinational farms. These agribusiness giants are making the family farm, your best hope for holistic ingredients, an endangered species. Multinationals directly or indirectly control most of the world's food supply, and almost all of the food that ends up on your table. That means your food is shaped through the prism of economic models that do not treat agricultural products as creations of nature, but of corporations.

Corporate farms maximize production and profit by any means necessary. No amount of chemical fertilizer and genetic modification is spared to fatten the bottom line. No destructive practice is forsaken if it can raise shareholder value.

Farmers care about the land. CEO's care about the numbers. As long as CEO's make the decisions about your food, your body will suffer the consequences.

Consumer produce: the price of perfection

Vegetables, fruits and grains

Consumer farm produce looks perfect, but this unnatural perfection comes at a heavy price. The most obvious price is measured by your senses. Bite into a fruit or vegetable from a consumer farm and you will have tasted the lie. Or better yet, you will not have tasted the lie.

Consumer produce is esthetically perfect, but devoid of any aroma or taste. You recognize consumer fruits and vegetables by their shape rather than their smell or taste.

Go to a local supermarket and smell the tomatoes. Not much to smell, is there? Taste the apricots. Or better put, taste those bland reminiscences of apricots. Of course, that's assuming you've tasted real tomatoes and real apricots in the first place. If you have not, bland consumerist confections are all you know. I would suggest that you try and taste some real fruits and vegetables, organically pure and freshly picked. Only then will you discover how poorly consumer produce compares in terms of taste, perfume and texture with the bounty of organic farmers.

Chemical perfection

There is a more important aspect to consumer produce than its blandness. When you bite into an apple, not only are you biting into a poor facsimile of a genuine apple, a pale imitation of true apple taste, but you are also biting into all of the pesticides, herbicides, insecticides and chemicals fertilizers that went into producing that perfect apple. That is the true price of perfection.

Do you think those chemicals are good for you? Do you know what effects these sort of chemicals are having on your body? On you, not on some lab rats at Harvard or the Beluga whales in the St. Lawrence River. Do you know that these chemicals are responsible for a host of medical problems, from sterility to cancer? Do you want to take that risk?

Let's assume that nothing is proven, that we do not know what the effects of these chemicals are. Let's assume that all the scientific tests showing the links between these chemicals and various human ailments are wrong. Let's give the corporate farmers and the chemical-producing multinationals the benefit of the doubt. Even if this is so, you know two things for sure: First, whatever your diet consists of, the human body does not need any of these chemicals. Pesticides, herbicides, insecticides and chemical fertilizers are NOT the four basic food groups. Second, you deserve the freedom to eat what you want. If you want to eat an apple that is precisely what you should get. An apple. Nothing more, nothing less.

Meat and dairy products

Hormones and medicines

You also deserve to eat meat and dairy products free from the antibiotics and the hormones pumped into the animals at the factory farms run by the corporate giants.[41] Recently, governmental health departments have begun to investigate the effects of such hormones and antibiotics on humans.[42] Hormones are believed to be responsible for the ever-decreasing age at which girls reach puberty. They also contribute to our ever-increasing size and mass. As for the antibiotics, the last thing your body needs is veterinary medicines.

The prevalence of antibiotics hastens the appearance of antibiotic-resistant bacteria. A vicious cycle arises where new, more powerful antibiotics must be developed to overcome the resistant bacterial strains until the bacteria develop resistance against these new antibiotics, starting the whole process all over again.

The Brave New World of GM foods: When is an apple no longer an apple?

There are three basic reasons why you should worry about genetically modified foods:

What is it?

When you eat a genetically engineered product the question becomes just how different is this from the original? What exactly did they do with it? If you want to eat an apple then you should be getting an apple that looks taste and feels like an apple, not some artificial concoction that is purple, triangular and produces its own insect repellent. Yet that is the future if genetic engineering is allowed to run rampant.

What's in it?

Perhaps you are one of the millions who are watching their diet in some way or another, whether eating multigrain breakfast cereals or trying to fulfil the guidelines for suggested servings of fruits and vegetables. Well, the benefits of such foods are calculated on a regular apple, or

41. Corporate farming practices impact traditional family farming in two ways. First, large-scale agriculture displaces many small farmers from their land (which is often bought out by corporate farms). Second, the remaining small farmers, to survive, find themselves constrained to follow the 'if you can't beat them, join them,' policy. Family farmers are thus increasingly corporatizing their practices.
42. Indeed, a recent test in Canada has found traces of antibiotics and other medicines in our water.

regular oats, or a regular tomato. Who knows what benefits, if any, will genetic food bring to you? Who knows what possible side-effects they might have?

With GM foods, multinationals rather than nature decide what you eat. That means they can decide to grow foods laced with addictive chemicals or foods designed to make you happy or hungry or anything else that the mind can conceive. They can already grow foods with antibiotics and various other pharmaceutical properties. You could be medicated or chemically controlled without ever knowing it. Think about it. Food is the ultimate tool of control since you need it every single day. When you eat a GM product, you could be getting a lot more than you bargained for.

GM food infects non-genetically-modified foods

GM seeds have proven to be a type of Pandora's Box, like so many other human inventions. They tend to spread far and wide beyond the place of their seeding, beyond their so-called controlled environment, infecting the fields of organic farmers as well as wild varieties of the plant species. GM corn has been found among the wild mountain corn of Mexico, which is the most genetically diverse type of corn in the world. Canadian organic farmers have already begun suing the agribusiness giants for spoiling their crops with these uncontrollable and unwelcome invaders. You have a right to be able to eat an apple free from genetic modification. But as genetically modified seeds taint the fields of organic farmers, will you still have that choice? Protect your food rights. Make sure you never touch GM foods.

Don't miss the forest for the trees

The terrible and unknown qualities of consumer produce makes for rich irony. At a time when many people are seeking alternative means of treating their body through natural healing processes, they eat and drink consumer produce laced with unnatural hormones and medicines. The shelves are full of healthy foods, the books full of low-fat recipes, but the basic ingredients are all laced with chemical and biological poisons.

Do you fear terrorism and weapons of mass destruction? Fear instead the agribusiness giants. They are practicing a brand of food terrorism on your internal organs, slipping chemical and biological weapons into your bloodstream. Nature's bounty has been polluted and the pollution is stealthily accumulating in your body.

Again, the fundamental question is one of personal freedom. It is your basic right to eat a steak and cheese sandwich without worrying what else you're getting in the bargain. While growing your own food is the optimal solution, if this is not possible, then at least all the so called "natural" products should state exactly what they contain, just like processed foods. In other words, apples, milk and beef better have a list of all the chemicals, medicines and hormones that the agribusiness giants employed in producing these "marvels of nature." If the hamburger meat in your grocer's freezer had a label listing all of the ingredients besides the ground beef, namely the hormones and antibiotics, would you not think twice before buying it?

Few people do not care about what they put into their bodies. If you are one of those few, remember this. Discounting your body's needs is not only the ultimate self-disrespect, since your body is your temple, but it is also the final surrender of your freedom. Instead of eating to fulfil your body's needs, you are now offering your body to the corporate farmers. For as long as you patronize consumer produce, you ingest, digest and excrete just so some multinational can have a better profit margin.

2. Drinking

The importance of water cannot be overestimated considering that 55-60 per cent of our body mass is composed of the stuff. Water is part of our intrinsic nature. We need it to drink, to function and to exist. Unfortunately, the water we depend on is increasingly poisoned.

The lack of pure water

Swimming in the waterways that pass through the world's large cities is generally not a good proposition. Who swims in the Thames? Or the Seine? Or the mighty Mississippi? Once they were rivers of life. Now, they are filthy and polluted rivers of sickness.

The same water you dare not even bathe in flows through your tap. It is the water you are supposed to drink. Of course, in order to make it drinkable and bathable, it has been treated. Chemically. So it's not just plain H2O. There's also chlorine, fluorine and various other chemicals. But this "chemical solution" to the problem of dirty water has an unexpected and paradoxical result: you will not drink tap water precisely because of the chemical treatment designed to make it potable.

The danger of living with dirty water

Although you might not drink it, you still probably use tap water for cooking and tea. The quality of that tap water is dependent upon the water-treatment plant. But what happens if something should go wrong at the water-treatment plant?

Walkerton: The dangers of depending on chemicals to clean your water have been revealed to the Canadian public by the Walkerton case. Walkerton is a small town in southern Ontario that has risen to unfortunate prominence in the Canadian mind. Six people died and hundreds became sick by drinking tainted water after staff at the water treatment plant failed to properly monitor and control the quality of the town's tap water. Although a government inquiry apportioned blame and recommended changes, and although a class-action lawsuit brought some financial recompense to the town's residents, nobody saw fit to comment, in print or on television, about the underlying problem. Water has become so dangerously poisoned that the smallest error or failure in a treatment plant can cause death.

Purified/Natural water: the wrong solution

Preference for filtered and natural spring water attests to your fear of drinking tap water. Perhaps you have gone so far as to get a purifier for the shower, unwilling to bathe in the chemically-laced waters that come from the tap. However, such solutions cannot solve the underlying problem. By relying upon artificial means to clean your water, you are placed in a highly vulnerable position.

Water Filters: Water filters do not filter out all impurities. While they may reduce the numbers of chemicals in your drinking water, they cannot eliminate them altogether. Furthermore, most water filters eliminate only certain types of impurities, leaving others to pass through, unimpeded.

Water purifiers often use chemical filters to remove impurities. The filtration process might remove impurities, but can often result in the filter chemicals leaking into the water. You end up trading one type of chemical for another.

Finally, water filters, as a general rule, do not filter out bacteria such as *e.coli*, and it is these bacteria that caused all the sickness and death in the Walkerton case.

Spring Water: Spring water depends on natural filtration for its purity. However, as more pollutants accumulate within the environment, spreading from pole to pole, from ocean depth to mountain peak, it becomes harder and harder for nature to filter them out. Man-made pollutants mean pure spring water is rapidly losing its purity. Soon, even Evian and Perrier water will have to be chemically filtered.

You can't always control your water: Even if you think yourself safe by using water purifiers and drinking only bottled water can you guarantee that the restaurant takes the same precautions? How pure is the water served at the beginning of your meals? What about the ice cubes in your Perrier or Coke? Do you know that soda fountains use tap water and concentrated syrup to create your favourite soft drinks? How about the soup or tea at the cafeteria? You guessed it. Tap water.

3. Breathing

Every time you draw a breath, you're getting a lot more than you bargained for. Smog is tainting the air and filling your lungs with poison. Man-made pollutants have shaded the blue sky with a sickly brown in many of the world's cities. Air used to be colourless and odourless; now it carries the colour and odour of death. In Toronto, 1,700 annual premature deaths have been blamed on poor air quality. The asthmatic and others suffering from respiratory illnesses are usually its primary victims. It also kills the most vulnerable, children and the elderly.

There are two sources of air pollution:

Consumer products: The consumer products you buy are partly responsible for the poor quality of your air. From your car to your appliances, to the fireplace, the multinationals sell you the means of self-destruction.

Consumer product manufacturing: The factories that make your favourite consumer products spew pollutants into the air.

Finding a solution for dirty air is difficult because of the nature of air and its relationship to you. Air has three qualities:

a) It's everywhere. Wherever you go, short of leaving the atmosphere, there is no escape from the pollution.
b) It's inseparable. You cannot take bad air and leave the good air behind.
c) It's constantly taken in. Every single moment you live, you breathe. As such, it is the body's greatest necessity and the most urgent. You can survive weeks without food, days without water, but only minutes without air.

The wrong solutions

Air Conditioning: Do you think air conditioning can save you? Fat chance. Studies have shown that indoor air pollution is a greater threat to your health than outdoor pollution by the sheer concentration of pollutants. Keeping outdoor air out will do more harm than good to the self.

Air Purifiers: Air purifiers might help (the jury is out among the scientific community), but they only work partially at best, and remove only a limited type of pollutants.

The Countryside: Ahh, but at least you can escape to the cottage. Or can you? There is no respite from poisonous air even in the countryside. In fact, recent studies have shown that air quality in rural settings is often worse than in the city.

Saving the Self

Nature is the only solution

Since consumer life has distanced you from nature, you no longer feel the need for natural environment. You are content with stale, man-made environments, with plastic, metal and cement. You are content with a chemical existence, with chemical water, chemical food and chemical air. Even if you are not content with it, your solutions are consumerist ones, such as filtered water, purified air and irradiated food.

The answers to your food, water and air problems are found in nature. Only nature can provide you with these three necessities. Only nature can give your body what it needs without chemicals or preservatives. Only nature can provide the right solutions. If you are to benefit from good food, clean water and fresh air, it is time to reconcile the self with nature.

Wilding the Self: Establishing your personal wilderness

The deterioration of food, water and air are the result of global problems. The solution is a personal one. In order to improve the qualities of these three basic necessities you must focus on improving them for the self. In other words, you must concentrate on your food, your water and your air. There are a myriad of actions you can take to help your environment and these have been well documented. They are summarized in the environmental credo of "reduce, reuse and recycle." While these actions are commendable and indeed encouraged, your priority must be re-establishing a connection with the natural world. It is time to "wild the self."

Wilding the self means acknowledging you need natural systems to flourish, to achieve your potential as a human being. Wilding the self means embracing your physical self rather than ignoring or dismissing it. It does not mean living in a forest or abnegating civilization. It means accepting nature as part of civilization, as the ultimate foundation of your culture.

Wilding the self involves altering your environment so that it is closer to nature. Surround yourself with natural living systems rather than dead, artificial or sterile ones. Resurrect the wildness of your environment and remember how to live within it.

Above all, wilding the self means rediscovering the wildness of your body. The more needs you fulfill through nature, the more you will fulfil your self.

Wilding the self has three principal aspects:

Wild the body

Wilding the body means taking the following steps to increase the contact between your body and nature:

Maintain your body with natural products: Beyond organic food and spring water, use natural cleansing products for your body. Avoid cleansing and beautifying your self with consumer chemicals. Use bath and cosmetic products made of natural oils, containing plant, flower and algae extracts.

Maintain your environment with natural products: The test for cleaning products is a simple one: if you can't drink it, don't use it. Water, lemon juice, baking soda and vinegar can act as powerful cleaners, and have none of the harmful effects associated with consumer chemical cleaners.

Engage in natural recreational activities: Swim in lake or a river, not in a swimming pool. Play soccer on a meadow not on artificial turf. Jog on a nature path, not on a treadmill. You care for the body by paying a high premium to the multinationals to "care" for your body. You pay for the privilege of using their products and services. You pay for the privilege of shutting your self off in artificial enclosures. Nature allows you to engage in the same activities for free, without the glare of artificial light or the pungent air of sweaty bodies found at your local fitness center. Most of all, the beauty of natural scenery lessens the need for consumer distractions. Working out in the gym means you are either watching the walls or you are watching the television, you are either listening to the squeak of metal and the grunts of effort, or you are listening to consumer music.

Fulfil your body's needs in nature: Getting your food from nature is ideal. Preparing and consuming your food within nature is also great.

Barbequing is one way of doing this. Cooking by a campfire is another. Even if you prepare a simple cold dish that does not require cooking, consume it within nature. Learn to eat within the environment.

Sleeping within the natural world is also a great way of reconciling your self with nature. If weather conditions permit, sleep in the fresh air, sleep among the grass or the trees or on the sand. Let nature's breeze caress you to slumber with its windy lullaby.

Eliminate the intermediary from the natural experience: Get out of the car. Remove your shoes. Walk barefoot on the grass. Touch the natural world, feel its living essence in all its wonder. Walking on nature is walking on the carpet of life. Walking on anything made by man is walking on inanimate objects. The surfaces created by men are built upon death, and murdered nature lies beneath. Feel what it's like to walk upon a living pulsating world, a world of greenery and foliage. It will stir the life within you, and bring feeling to your stone soul, petrified by consumerism. Only by touching life will you learn that you were meant to exist in the living world, not in a Consumer Hades populated by virtual ghosts and inanimate objects.

Make your green space a wilderness

Use native plants: Transforming the lawn into a wilderness involves understanding your local environment. Educate yourself on the plant species native to your personal environment. Seed with natural grasses, local plants and wild flowers. They are sturdier and hardier, better positioned to resist the various mites and beetles that feast on consumer greenery.

Do not design: Do not create geometric patterns or arrange the plants in an ordered design. A precisely manicured garden is an exercise in artifice. Let nature take its course. Wherever plants and flowers take root, let them flourish. The apparent chaos of nature belies a much deeper natural order than humankind may comprehend.

Do not interfere: Once you've created wildspace, and it is flourishing, leave it alone. Be a good environmentalist and do nothing. Do not try to help nature. Resist the all too human temptation to meddle by remembering two things:

a) Weeds are good. If weeds start to make inroads into your wildspace, don't rip them out to "protect" flower species. Weeds are part of the environment; they should be part of your environment as well.

b) Overgrown is healthy: Left to its own devices, your wildspace will thrive. Your property will soon look like a long-haired hippie among the crew-cut soldier lawns of your neighbours. Good. That's the way you want it to be. Overgrown wildspace is working overtime to preserve the quality of your environment.

Don't forget the trees: Surround yourself with your own patch of forest. Trees are the world's best air purifiers. They work 24 hours a day and they last for centuries without breaking down. Plant native species that protect your own personal air and ensure it is the freshest air possible.

Create an internal wilderness

An internal wilderness is highly important, especially if you do not have any external green space to begin with. If you live in an apartment building, then your apartment will have to be "naturalized."[43]

Decorate with nature: Many of the natural plants and flowers of your region will survive indoors. It is just a question of taking them into your environment. Decorate the house with living things instead of consumer products. Plants, flowers, shrubs and small trees can bring colour and beauty to the house, more so than any man-made object. They also bring fresh air, sweet smells and a healthier self by acting as both air purifiers and air fresheners.

Develop a natural space: Balconies are especially good for this. A natural space is more than just potted plants and flower vases. A natural space is your own personal ecosystem. It is a chunk of nature imported into your home. There are two types of ecosystems you can import into your living space:

The box of life. Transform a part of your house into a self-contained ecosystem. Take a large box or a wooden crate, fill it with earth, and seed various wild plants and flowers. Let nature take its course without your interference aside from the occasional watering.

The living wall. Living walls are another example of wildspace. Let creeping ivy grow either on the inside or outside of your walls. This living wall will attract more nature in the form of insects and birds. Nature will grow and thrive around you and you will thrive as a consequence.

Open your self to nature: Try to break down the separation between your home and the outdoors as much as possible. Keep your windows and doors open whenever weather conditions permit. Let butterflies flit among your flowers, let bees enter your home and pollinate your living wall or your box of life. Above all, let fresh air circulate. Your body will thank you for it.

---

43. That is, given to nature.

In opening your home to nature you will get unwanted visitors, wasps, flies and mosquitoes. This is a small price to pay in exchange for the benefits of existing in a living world rather than a consumer one. Moreover, some unwelcome visitors can prove useful. By allowing a spider to set up web in a house corner, you can end up with a natural method of resolving your fly and mosquito problem.

Conclusion

The environment is a question of health. Your health. Nature exists for your advantage. The natural world provides you with the basic necessities of life and nurtures your body so that you may concentrate on the all-important task of self-achievement.

Caring for the self is not a question of bottled water and air purifiers. These things may seem to help your body but in the greater balance they ultimately do more harm, through their plastic components and environmentally destructive manufacturing processes. Nature alone provides you with life's necessities without harming the self in the process. Nature alone is the guarantor of the physical self. Live within a natural environment and you are living for your self. Live within a consumer environment, and you are living for a multinational corporation.

Chapter 17

Sexuality

Discover how consumerism is manipulating your most intimate and basic instinct and what you can do to make sure sex is based on self-attraction, rather than consumer lust.

Why multinationals hate sex

The sexual act, at its most basic, is the union of two human beings. This union is one of the most natural, pure and unchanged expressions of human behaviour. Leaving aside the infinite variations, innovations and accessories, the basic mechanics of coitus have not changed significantly from the act performed by our ancestors 1,000, 10,000 or even 100,000 years ago. The biological impulse that unites two humans in a sexual act has also seen no significant evolution over the millenia.

As long as you are engaging in sexual acts, you are doing so to the detriment of the corporate giants. Since the biological act remains unchanged, and indeed cannot change short of genetic manipulations of our bodies, the multinationals cannot participate in it. Consumer products have no role in sex. You do not need McDonald's, Hollywood movies or Gap clothing to have coitus; suitably aroused genitals will do. Multinationals are completely irrelevant to the successful functioning of this biological imperative. Unlike eating or drinking, natural processes which can be mediated through consumer products, multinationals cannot profit from sex. Sex is completely self-contained. Multinationals cannot fashion themselves even an artificial role in the sexual act. Sex and consumerism do not mix well. Sex tends to be a private, all-exclusive act. A satisfying sexual experience requires a comparatively high degree of concentration. The intimacy of the act, the closeness of joined and entwined bodies, the pleasure and sweat of it all leaves little room for other pursuits. When people have sex that's usually all they're doing. Although it is possible to engage in consumer activities while copulating, that's usually a sign of a troubled sexual relationship. Munching on pizza and watching the tube is a common activity. Making love while watching the tube is not in the cards for most couples.

Beyond the sexual act itself, the predominance of the sexual impulse vies with the consumerist impulse for your attention. Sexual thoughts play at the surface of consciousness more than any other type of thoughts. Instead of thinking about consumer products all the time, your mind is detoured by biological impulses that are beyond the pale of multinational influence. Sexual desires can obliterate virtually all other contending stimuli, aside from the basic survival needs of water and food. The infatuated youth, male or female, thinks of little else but the object of their infatuation. The kindled passion of two new lovers compresses the universe and swallows time itself. When your mind is taken with carnal desire, the consumer within you, like everything else in the cosmos, is forgotten.

Global consumerism's attack on sexuality

When the product is held above the human, the multinationals win.

A basic strategy of consumerism is trying to mediate human seduction via consumer goods. Unable to interfere with the act, multinationals have attempted to co-opt the process that leads to it by consumerizing the human mating ritual. The focus is shifted away from pheromones and biology. Intellect and spirituality are also discarded. The interplay of looks and gestures, the touches and whispers that constitute the human mating dance are transformed into a ghastly parade of manufactured goods and glitzy products.

Consumer courtship 1

Destroying female sexuality

Unable to subvert the brief glorious union whereby two beings are intertwined as one, consumerism seeks to demean it instead. Consumerism acts as a global pimp, encouraging women to use their bodies as currency in a disgusting form of barter. Consumer propaganda brainwashes you[44] into thinking that a woman does not seek sexual contact, but rather uses her sexuality as a means of attracting consumer goods. Women are to find sexual satisfaction through the substitute of material goods offered

44. Regardless of whether you are a man or a woman.

by the man. In exchange for these consumer goods, women must then share their bodies, now reduced to receptacles for satisfying male desire. Sadly, many men believe this consumer lie. Tragically, many women believe it as well.

Some might say that this is nothing new. These sorts of things have been going on for ages. Prostitution is the world's oldest profession. There have always been small numbers of women willing to trade their bodies for wealth or power. But the consumer malaise has penetrated much deeper than streetwalkers or the stereotypical pairing of rich old men with young, beautiful wives. It has become a social epidemic. Women of all types and from all walks of life are succumbing to the consumerist brainwashing and enslaving themselves to the multinational pimps. Young girls don't need boys to hold their hand. They need boys that will take them shopping, that will buy them "stuff." Mature singles establish relationships based on the consumer goods the woman needs. Trading your body for consumer goods has become an acceptable social norm for many women. Consumerism's virus is so widespread that it threatens to turn every single woman into a consumer goods prostitute.

Consumer courtship 2

Destroying male sexuality

Consumerism has not made men much better off. The emphasis on consumer goods as a means to sexual gratification automatically denies the importance of male sexuality. The male body becomes irrelevant. The male self, the potency and virility that underpins the gender, is suddenly superfluous. The phallic symbol is deprived of its symbolism. The male ego is obliterated. What you now need to attract a mate are consumer goods or the ability to purchase them. Size does matter, but only when it comes to bank accounts.

By annihilating the male ego, consumerism succeeds in turning you away from sex. Even worse, it promotes misogyny. Regardless of the number of "conquests" you make using consumer goods, there lies an underlying knowledge that you are not a true man, that your successes turned on the multinationals' products. As such you disrespect the woman and her intentions towards you are viewed with suspicion, thinking that she is attracted not to you, but to the consumer goods you can offer.

This line of thinking plays into the hands of the multinationals. You come to prize consumer goods above women. Women become a corollary to achieving consumer Nirvana. The focus is shifted away from sexuality and towards the accumulation of consumer goods. Women are a dime a dozen but a Mercedes…. ahh, that's another thing.

Even if you despise consumer goods, consumerism can transform you into a virulent misogynist. Let's say you wish to find a mate based on instinctive mating rituals alone. You put yourself out there, seeking to attract women with your physical attributes, your intellect, your humour, in short, your self. Instead, you are rejected for some guy with a BMW and a Platinum Visa. What happens to you? You become bitter. Not only is the woman devalued in your eyes, but your wounded ego, emasculated by consumerism, paradoxically despises the object of its desire.

Consumer anti-sex

When a relationship based on consumer goods is consummated, the sexual act is devoid of energy and meaning. The male is exhausted and disgusted by the efforts to purchase the woman's affections. Sex loses its lustre for him. Indeed, many men forsake the effort altogether, preferring to live in Consumer-world rather than enter the trenches of modern relationships. Better to watch Monday Night Football or go shopping than to have your ego trampled by a woman you like.

As for the woman, the act itself is a travesty. She has offered her most intimate physical self for the purpose of acquiring consumer goods. To withstand this violation of her inner self she seeks to minimize the importance of the sexual act. Copulating with her consumerist benefactor is seen as a chore, a routine, or a necessary evil. By draining the meaning from this most intimate act, she ultimately renders her sexuality irrelevant. Indifferent to the pleasures of sex, she views the man as a means to her consumer ends. He can offer consumer goods, but can never substitute for them.

In destroying sexuality, consumerism is distorting the self. As a woman, you become cynical about sex, as a man, you become cynical about women. The result is a deformed society, characterized by animosity between the sexes. On one hand, there is a host of angry men, growing ever angrier as most of their potential partners are seeking consumer goods. On the other hand, the number of women willing to trade their bodies in order to attract consumer goods is on the increase.

Consumerism as sex substitute

Not all is doom and gloom. Despite consumerism's efforts to the contrary, many people still choose their partners without regard to any consumer goods. Indeed, only a certain category of people is swayed by the consumer lie. They are the people with low self-esteem, emotionally shallow people who need the consumer crutch to feel important. What if for you, consumerism plays little, if any part in the choices you make as to your sexual partners? What if you are involved in a meaningful long-term relationship and have a committed sexual partner that you do not need to keep via consumer goods? If you are one of those people, stop smiling: you are not safe. For those of you who are in stable, loving relationships, consumerism has devised another trap: consumerism as a substitute for sexuality.

The multinationals are encouraging you to forget about sex. Sex is boring, sex is something you've done a million times before, they tell you. You can have sex any time you want, they say. We can offer you something more interesting, something better.

What can they offer you? Three things, principally:

Consumer food

Eating consumer food has assumed the role of sexual activity. Gluttony is sexualized by consumer propaganda and transformed into a substitute sin for lust. For overweight couples especially, consumer food has usurped the place of a dormant sexuality, sleeping under folds of fat. Couples now bond through sharing in all-you-can-eat excesses rather than sharing in their bodies. Whereas before they hungered for each other's bodies, now they just feed an artificial hunger with mounds of consumer food. The new sexual Nirvana is the Seven Eleven.

Obesity and sex

Consumer food-induced obesity impacts your sexuality both physically and psychologically:

Physically: Obesity makes the physical act more difficult for a number of reasons, starting with the sheer amount of weight that must be moved around. And if sex becomes more effort than pleasure, why bother? That's exactly the thinking of the multinationals and that's why they want you to be fat.

Sex for the obese can also be downright dangerous. Obesity is often accompanied by heart disease and elevated blood pressure. The exertions of sexual activity could be a recipe for a stroke or a heart attack.

Finally, obesity can lead to a decrease in libido and erectile problems in men, making sex a non-starter to begin with.

Psychologically: Obesity creates image problems for both you and your partner. Many obese people suffer from low self-esteem and are very conscious of their unhealthy bodies, so that they are unwilling to reveal their nakedness. As such, if you are obese you are likely to be more reticent about having sex. Furthermore your partner, whether or not he or she is obese, is likely to find the prospect of sexual intercourse with an obese partner less attractive. It is merely human nature. If one partner is overweight, it is often sufficient to destroy the sexuality of both.

Obesity and sex form a vicious cycle. As increasing weight stunts your sexuality, both you and your partner begin looking for an escape. That escape is through consumer food binges, further increasing your weight and lowering your sex drive.

Consumer entertainment

The attack on sex began in earnest when the multinationals came up with what can only be labeled as a stroke of evil genius: bringing the television into the bedroom. Once the TV enters your bedroom, there is no stopping it. The temptation to turn on the TV and to turn off your sexuality becomes irresistible. Even if one of you is aroused, the TV distracts the other's attention and ruins the experience. The only tension in your bedroom is over who controls the remote. Despite sitting beside each other the couple is separated, interacting only through the medium of the TV.

Consumer porn

Virtual sex and sexual selfishness

Consumer porn is comprised of sexual images manufactured and/or distributed by multinationals. Consumer porn includes softcore movies, television shows and music videos as well as hardcore XXX movies. Regardless of the origin of the actual pornographic images, multinationals control them. Like all other consumer products, consumer porn has its own brand names and peddles the notion of infinite consumption as the ideal state of being. *Playboy*, a multinational listed on the New York Stock Exchange, is an excellent example of the consumer porn brand.

While graphic depictions of sexual acts have a centuries-old tradition, consumer porn has made titillation an end in itself. Historically, sexually explicit images were used to educate and as a form of foreplay, in other words as accessories to the sex act. Consumer porn seeks to replace the sex act altogether.

Consumer porn recasts sexuality as an individual rather than a shared experience. The consumerist message is that real sex with "average" men or women is not quite as interesting as fantasizing over idealized sexual images. By encouraging physical satisfaction via masturbation over consumer porn, consumerism transforms sexuality into a form of escapism. Jaded from the surfeit of virtual sex, you lose interest in having an actual partner. The problem with consumer pornography is therefore not its graphic sexual content but its effect of denying real sexual experiences. Consumer porn neuters the sexual self.

Consumer porn attacks your sexual self through a combination of addiction and overexposure. Addiction condemns you to express and experience your sexuality via technologically mediated masturbation. Overexposure means you are constantly searching for imagery outside the boundaries of all known morality in order to achieve sexual satisfaction.

Addiction

Addiction to consumer porn is maintained in two ways: variety and control.

Variety: Every porn consumer has the possibility of virtually experiencing sexual congress with thousands of partners. The amount of sexual product offered by consumer porn outstrips physical capacity a thousandfold. No human being could go in a lifetime through the sexual catalogue that you can view in a single night of consumer porn. Consumer porn offers nearly infinite partners and couplings to satisfy your fantasies. It is attractive because it defies all spatial and temporal limits and allows you to absorb, if only vicariously, a superhuman amount of sexual experiences.

Ironically, addiction to consumer porn destroys your sexual imagination. Since consumer porn is absorbed only imaginatively, it obviates the need for your own imagination to create sexual fantasies. Consumer porn presents you with ready-made fantasies, sensory stimulation via the sights and sounds emanating from your computer or television screen. As such, consumer porn attacks the greatest sexual organ in your body: your mind.

Control: Porn is safe. It is marketed as safe. Since it is only masturbation in front of a screen, there are no inherent dangers such as sexual diseases, unwanted pregnancies or performance anxiety. Consumed in the comfort of your own home, consumer porn is also reassuringly anonymous. You cannot feel threatened by another.

Best of all, with consumer porn there is no rejection. If you are a porn consumer plagued by a fragile ego and poor socializing skills, this is a welcome release for a frustrated sexuality. No longer do you have to suffer the daily humiliations of a society that rejects you, a society where you have failed to find a partner. In the virtual porn universe there is no denial and nothing out of reach. The object of sexual desire is just an object; you decide how you want to treat it.

To emphasize this idea of control, consumer porn offers interactive web sites, where the consumer can command the porn 'actor/actress'.[45] The consumer is placed in a position of supreme sexual power. In the porn virtual universe, anyone can be made to feel like a sexual god. But the power is a hollow one. Yes, you can give instructions, yes, you can be obeyed, yes, you can humiliate another being, but ultimately you are still alone, in your room, facing a computer screen.

Overexposure

Overexposure results in a constant search for stronger sexual stimuli. This search stems from the failure of consumer porn, like all other consumer products, to provide genuine fulfillment for the self. Consumer porn offers you only snippets of the actual act, as videos or still images. Consumer porn cannot replicate the pleasures of a complete sexual encounter, from the seduction to the foreplay, through the encounter and afterglow. There is no physical satiation, no need for post-coital recovery, none of the after-effects of a genuine physical sexual congress.

The end of consumer porn experience brings only loneliness. Where is the partner to cuddle with after you are both spent? Where is the warmth of another's body to press against your own? Where are the whispers, the giggles, the shared confidences? There is no one but the inanimate computer or television. Consumer porn is a purely subjective experience, a lonesome, cold and sterile parade of images of strangers acting out what you, the consumer, should be doing yourself. Consequently, the images you are absorbing are at best superficially satisfying, flitting through your mind to be quickly forgotten. How unlike genuine sexual experiences, which remain embedded in the memory.

Unfulfilled, the consumer becomes jaded. Porn consumers quickly reach a saturation point where images of the normal sexual act lose their impact to arouse, becoming meaningless and ineffectual. Ever more graphic and shocking images are necessary for your titillation. This slippery moral slope leads to a search for greater degradations and humiliations

---

45. Some porn sites go even further, encouraging its consumers to send in condoms full of semen whose contents will be poured on the "models" staffing their site. Porn merchants profit from the sad desperation of these consumers, driven to near madness by their inability to satisfy that most powerful of biological impulses, the mating instinct.

of other human beings in order to satisfy your desires. Arousal now becomes a matter of seeing abuse, even violence, perpetrated upon another human being. With such a deformed picture of sex, how can one ever activate the sexual self and find a partner?

Consumer porn deforms actual sex

If you view sexuality through the prism of consumer porn, you will expect your partners to behave as in those images, to act as porn actors and actresses. When it comes to actual sex, you will not seek to understand or explore your sexuality, but rather slavishly imitate what you have seen on the screen. Men, as primary consumer porn addicts, are particularly susceptible to the delusion that women exist purely to satisfy their needs and expect the woman to perform according to script. Consumer porn encourages you to treat your partner as a mechanical object, a physical incarnation of a digital image, and not as a human being. In distancing you from your sexuality, consumer porn is taking away a big part of what it means to be human.

Saving the Self

Return to Eden

Remember there are two basic aspects to sexuality: reproduction and pleasure. If you're not doing it for one of these two reasons then you're either in the sex trade, you have serious mental problems, or you have been consumerized. Assuming that, like most people, the principal purpose of your sexual acts is pleasure, remember the basics:

Get a partner

Unless validated by physical experience with another human being, the sexual self can never find fulfillment. Regardless of how much consumer porn might try to convince you otherwise, sex is better with two. Masturbation is fine as an occasional escape valve, but rather than limiting your fantasies to the intellect, start acting them out in flesh. Use the energy you spent in consuming porn to acquire a real sexual partner.

Use the self in courting

Have the courage to rely on the self: When approaching a potential partner, do not rely on consumer goods to achieve your goals. Be confident in your physical, intellectual, emotional and spiritual qualities and use them to achieve your purpose. Conversely, if you are the object of courtship, ensure that your partner is relying on the self and not on consumer goods in order to charm you.

Courtship is the presentation of the self in the search of compatibility, sexual and otherwise. Courtship is not deceit. Using the self does not mean dissimulating in order to get someone in bed or to start a relationship, but presenting the self for what it really is. If you lie to attract prospective partners, and using consumer goods is the worst of all lies, you will not have gained a partner; you will have diminished your self.

There is no greater reward than when a prospective partner agrees to give himself or herself over to you rather than to what you have. There is no greater satisfaction than when a partner accepts your courtship solely based on the self's qualities and not your possessions. The self rejoices when it is acknowledged. The self expands and fulfils when it is appreciated.

Pick your partner based on the self: Ensure the self is what attracts you to a partner. Do not be blinded by consumer goods. On the contrary, avoid consumerized partners. They will only tempt you back into the world of consumerism. Even worse, those who've been consumerized have given their selves over to the multinationals, and cannot give themselves to you.

Conversely, choose your prospective partner based on their response to your self, to the exposure of your qualities and not extraneous things such as consumer goods. If you appreciate someone for their qualities but they fail to appreciate yours, best find another partner.

Discover the self's sexual needs

Do not superimpose consumer sex fantasies over your own sexuality. Do not expect success in attracting or keeping partners by using the consumer porn approach to sex. Sexual satisfaction comes from discovering your body's own sexual identity.

Concentrate on what you feel: When you are having sex, empty the mind of thought, fear, and anxiety. Feel. Open the floodgates of sensation, aim for a preternatural awareness of every tingle, every shudder of pleasure, every throb and every impulse travelling along your neural pathways. Do not allow the mind to interpret or analyze the sensations but experience them instinctively, without conscious thought. Focus only on what gives you maximum pleasure. You have to work at feeling good, although that work generally means relaxing enough to appreciate the event in all its unfolding sensations.

Understand your pleasure: Sexual pleasure is very much about understanding. Seek to comprehend the impact of every impulse that courses through you in order to derive maximum joy. This is not some call for technical analysis but merely an encouragement to note what makes you feel good. A word, a caress, a thrust, or a position, discover what elevates you to the peak of enjoyment. Only through understanding can you hope to repeat and recapture that pleasure. Only through understanding will you find a pathway to deepening pleasure, to a higher state of fulfillment for your sexual being.

Make sure you figure out what your partner wants

Sex is based on mutual pleasure. It's hard to play out your fantasies without the willing and enthusiastic cooperation of your partner. Maximizing your pleasure means maximizing your partner's pleasure. True sexual fulfillment is dependent on and found in your partner's fulfillment. The other's orgasm validates your sexual self and reverberates waves of pleasure and satisfaction into your own mind and body. Until you are ready to commit your self to a true sexual union, one dedicated to the sexual fulfillment of both partners, it is better if you refrain from the sexual act.

Get an education

Exploring your sexual sensations is one method of achieving sexual fulfillment. But there are sensations locked within you that you will never experience, simply because you do not know how to access them or that they even exist. In order to discover and release these unfathomable pathways to sexual pleasure you must draw on the vast storehouse of sexual knowledge that mankind has accumulated. To further advance on the way towards fulfillment, you need a sexual education.

There are three legitimate means of sex education:

Literary erotica: There are two types of literary erotica, fiction and non-fiction. Fictional erotica includes novels and short stories authored by various literary figures. They will inspire your sexual imagination while enabling you to gain a deeper understanding of the opposite sex and thus enhance your ability to both feel and disseminate pleasure. The erotic writings of literary lights such as D. H. Lawrence can reveal more about sexuality than all the consumer porn you could ever absorb.

Non-fiction erotica includes manuals and books detailing and illustrating sexual positions. The *Kama Sutra* as well as writings on Tantric sex are but two such examples of culturally valid sexual non-fiction. The value of these writings is found not so much in the pragmatism of their sexual positions, which, at least in the case of the *Kama Sutra*, is often dubious. Their true value rests in a holistic approach towards sexuality. Literary non-fiction erotica focuses on employing mind, body and soul in achieving sexual fulfillment. These guides deal with the complete individual rather than just the genitals. They acknowledge the impact of your personal character upon the sexual act and show how it modulates your approach towards sexual fulfillment. They are also infinitely superior to the sex advice found in consumer magazines such as *Cosmopolitan.*

Scientific manuals: Read these books to understand the biology of sex, and the mechanics of your sexual impulses. A biological understanding of sex might not be very romantic, but it will be extremely useful in revealing such things as the body's erogenous zones, the best time for having sex, and the most sexually-sensitive parts of your genitals. Sexual fulfillment is that much closer once you comprehend the science behind your sensations.

Mentors: Especially good for beginners and highly underused. A mentor is someone who understands the dynamics of sexuality, who understands that the key to a full exploration of sexuality rests in a person's imagination, adaptability, patience and self-control. A mentor is a willing lover, not a prostitute or a sexual surrogate.

Experience your sexuality away from consumer influences

Sexual freedom is achieved when the sole reason you are engaging in sexual encounters is a natural one, whether reproduction or pleasure. Sexual freedom means knowing nothing about your partner beyond what that individual is, a human body inhabited by a mind and spirit. That sort of freedom is possible solely when sex occurs within nature.

It is no coincidence that natural settings are often portrayed in literature as allegories for uncontrollable sexuality. Nature encourages a surrender to impulse and instinct. Whether it is through the pulsating jungle or the ungovernable sea, the natural world serves to stimulate and liberate sexual desires from the chains you have forged for your self.

Natural settings offer a sexual experience untainted by consumerism. In nature, there are no consumer distractions to interfere with your sexual fulfillment. In nature, you are free. So, whenever the opportunity exists, unleash your desires in parks, beaches and campsites. Let the living world stir your own sexuality to life.

Chapter 18

Spirituality

Uncover your spiritual self, and you will conquer consumerism in the process.

Spirituality is that within you which cannot find expression in the physical world. It is the sum total of desires, yearnings, joys, pains and needs that transcend your material existence. As such, even the least spiritually inclined person has a spiritual dimension that can't be ignored without dire consequences for one's development as a human being.

Spirituality is the first and foremost line of defense against the consumerist assault. It encompasses faith, which deals with OTHER spiritual beings or dimensions, but it is greater than that. You can be an agnostic and embrace spirituality. You can even be an atheist and be a deeply spiritual being.

Spirituality refers to your personal transcendence, which may find expression through faith or belief in divinity, but which is ultimately a personal quality. Spirituality is the manifestation of the self and, as such, it is a subjective rather than an objective experience, perhaps the most intensely private experience felt by humans. Spirituality is the antithesis of consumerism because it shuns the material, especially the idea of consumption as the path towards happiness. You can never be a consumer and a spiritual being. You have to make a choice[46].

---

46. For those of you who experience spirituality through the framework of faith, making the choice is obligatory. Most of the world's major religions eschew materialism and worldly goods and encourage an ascetic lifestyle oriented towards a God or gods. The key to salvation or to eternal life rests in a modest lifestyle. Consumerism is the religion of worldly goods, of eternal materialism. Consumerism is the religion of mindless excess. You must choose between these competing faiths: Will you be a Christian, a Muslim, a Buddhist or will you be a consumer? You cannot be both. They are mutually exclusive. Read the seminal text of your faith and speak to your religious leaders so that you know what is expected of you. Know that a life dedicated to consumerism is a life of sin. Then, decide: faith or consumerism.

Faith

Faith is the most common avenue for expressing the spiritual self. True faith is not found in the rituals and ceremonies of your religion. Nor is it found in regularly attending a house of worship, in religious observances, or in prayer. True faith is found in you. For your spirituality to find expression through faith, you must believe. Unless you believe, all of the prayers, the rituals and the ceremonies are empty, meaningless exercises. Unless you believe, do not go before a priest, a rabbi or an imam to sanctify your marriage, child, or dead relative.

If you do believe, if you do have faith, how will you express it? How can you embark on a spiritual pilgrimage under the guidance of faith?

Faith is expressed through following the example of a revered spiritual figure. Take the example of Jesus. As the Son of God, as a manifestation of the divine, as an avatar, he may be infinite, but that infinity was not and could not have been presented before humankind since it vastly outstrips our comprehensive capabilities. What was presented before mankind was a human being. Jesus of Nazareth might have been the Son of God, but he was also a man. Not only that, but he was not a great man. At least not great in the terms we usually judge men by. He was neither wealthy, nor politically powerful, nor well educated, nor an aristocrat. Yet, look at the stature he has achieved in death. He achieved greatness, greater than a hundred kings, greater than a thousand emperors, by leading a simple life, by being humble and by teaching humility. The humble life of this cherished and worshipped figure underscores the illusory nature of what is today termed human greatness.

Faith for the faithless

The lesson to be drawn from prophets such as Jesus and from the founders of the world's great religions is that they achieved self-realization. Mohammed, Abraham, Buddha, and virtually every other prophetic figure that ever inhabited this planet was self-realized. This was their true "greatness." They were just being themselves. Fully being themselves. They did this in two ways. First, they realized they needed nothing of human construction to reach the pinnacle of individual achievement, although they lived and interacted with the "civilized" world. Second, they understood that self-realization demanded an implication within and improvement of the surrounding world.

Use your faith to do the same for you. Take these two lessons from the prophets and use them in your own life. Do not be awed by their example. They were no different from you in that all persons have potential and are given the means to realize it through their spirituality. Follow their example not as the chosen of God, but as human beings complete in their self-fulfillment. Regardless of your faith, or even if you are faithless, the prophets' lives hold value by demonstrating that absolute self-fulfillment is possible.

The natural world

While faith is the principal method of engaging the spiritual self, the natural world may also cater to your spiritual needs. Nature can provoke the contemplative self, serving as a source of spiritual inspiration. The tranquility of a placid day, a caressing zephyr, the murmur of bees among fields of flowers, all may enact spiritual awakenings and liberate the self on a journey towards a deeper understanding.

Nature need not be experienced with a consciously spiritual purpose. Spirituality through nature means living the moment without needs, with the physical being sated, without thought of time and space. It is a forsaking of consciousness for that which may only be felt. It is absorbing experience without any attempt to assimilate it within the context of the mortal, but rather allowing it to radiate and warm the eternal self. There is no reflection, no meditation and no attempt to direct the feeling. There is only absolute, unmitigated, uncompromised absorption. It is an effortless and thoughtless process, distinguishable from the conscious attempt to commune with nature.

Nature facilitates the manifestation of the spiritual instinct, our equivalent of the animals' physical instinct. While the animal instinct is designed to maintain physical existence, spiritual instinct affords us a momentary transcendence, a respite from the mortal self. Hold on to that moment, seek and cherish those brief interludes of satiation, satisfaction, and infinite ease, before the harsh taskmaster that is your body breaks the reverie and sets about fulfilling its needs.

The spirituality of nature can be as simple and elegant as the pure joy of existence, the simple, uncontrived act of being. Perhaps alone out of all living creatures, human beings are able to perceive the joy of their existence, to bask in its glow. If you can, through your spiritual self, embrace existence as the greatest gift of them all and rejoice in the knowledge that you are able to walk the earth, then the products of the multinationals will pale by comparison.

The joy of existence means celebrating things in which you have no moral, carnal, intellectual or material reason to rejoice in. If you can enjoy things that will bring you no material profit, things that were not designed for consumption, then you can free the self from consumerism. Every day the multinationals tell you that the path towards happiness lies through consumption. Find happiness in the song of a bird or the warmth of the sun and you will have found freedom.

A spirituality of nature imbues you with a radically different perspective on self-fulfillment. Spirituality teaches you that closing a multibillion dollar deal is not as valuable an achievement as petting the family dog. In the former case, the value of your action is measured with an artificial yardstick, money. In the latter case, spirituality gives you a much better measuring yardstick, joy.

A spirituality of nature also broadens your horizons. From a spiritual standpoint, the contemplation of the Mona Lisa is on a par with contemplating the movements of a solitary ant. Both have the same importance in the greater scheme of things. The realization of the complete insignificance of your actions within a universal context is one of the greatest gifts offered by the spiritual self. This realization begets the humility necessary to achieving your potential.

Humility

Humility is not an affectation, a coat worn for the sake of religion, or a false modesty, but the genuine spiritual state of being for the human. What else but utter, abject humility can be your reaction when your own limited existence confronts the infinity of the universe?

Humility shapes and tapers our actions to conform to their actual significance. Too often, we are guilty of imbuing our actions with a false sense of worth, either due to our own self-inflated ego or the flattery of others. In order to achieve a more realistic perspective, actions must be assessed not within the value hierarchies of human civilization but within the universe as a whole. Considered in this light, the objective effect of human actions, be they of a Bangladeshi orphan boy picking through a rubbish heap in Dacca or of America's president charting the course for global action from the White House, are equally close to nil.

But how can acknowledging the humble nature of our existence, be it a cosmic caprice or a divine grant, help in effecting the process of self-fulfillment?

Humility brings freedom, a release from the artificial demands of Consumer-world. Undoubtedly there are tasks you must perform to maintain your physical existence, but too many of your actions are tied in with false consumer needs. Consumerism corrupts life. The humility conferred by a spiritual existence is a return to innocence. Humility leaves you naked as Adam and Eve and shows your potential is best fulfilled through a life of simplicity, through the gifts of earth and sky, and through fellow beings, human and otherwise.

Alas, the simplicity necessary to fulfillment forms only a tiny part of existence. How many have had brief interludes where you experienced this unmitigated joy of the simple life? Lying on a deserted beach, basking in the rays of the sun, listening to the lap of the waves, contemplating the blue expanse of sea and sky? You cherish these interludes, you cherish the memories, but they seem unreal, lost among reality the daily grind of work and bills and grocery shopping. You seek to relive that pure joy through consumption, but consumption only complicates your life. Although you know that the simple life is the true life, you needlessly torment the self with consumer "necessities." Cease placing obstacles in the path to fulfillment. Let spiritual humility guide you back to the life you were meant to live.

While the ultimate meaning of the spiritual may be reserved for another world, here on earth spirituality is cultivated through the love, friendship, charity and joy stemming from interaction with an objective world that is natural, pure and uncommodified. Spirituality is not available in manufactured objects, save possibly for art and religious artifacts, and even their significance fades when compared to the glory of the natural world. In cultivating your spiritual garden you will be able to realize your potential, to manifest the full extent of the self and its beauty. It is a manifestation antithetically removed from the consumer vision the multinationals seek to perpetuate upon the human race.

Spirituality and goods

Spirituality does not necessitate that you surrender all your worldly possessions for a hermit's life. However, the value of goods changes within the spiritual perspective. Viewed in a spiritual light, the sole possible value of human goods rests in fulfilling your potential. Your potential is measured by the maximum possible interaction between your self and the natural world, the world you inhabit. You fulfil yourself by using goods as instruments for unleashing your creativity, your intellect and your physical talents. You fulfil yourself by using goods as instruments for spreading joy, happiness, healing. That is the sole possible "good" of goods. There is no inherent value in possession. Ownership breeds pride, accumulation - greed, and consumption - suffering. No man is great by virtue of his wealth, let alone his consumption. Spirituality shows us that another path must be taken in fulfilling the self.

The fear of love

The greater your spiritual potential, the harder you must strive to achieve it. It is not enough to say I have done as much as my neighbour, for much more is demanded. However, and this is crucial to remember, the striving is not an effort, it is not sweat of the brow work. The striving involves loving more, caring more and befriending more. You strive to maximize the amount of love and joy within and without you. The more selfless the love and joy, the more people you share it with, the closer you will be to realizing the self.

Unfortunately, boundless love is what we fear most, for this is what makes us vulnerable. The reason you avoid displaying love is the fear it will be unrequited. Consumerism exploits this vulnerability by encouraging you to abandon love. Why expose the self to this thorny problem, it asks. Why make the self vulnerable to rejection? Become a consumer.

In consumerism there is no rejection. Consumerism promises no pain, no suffering and no trepidation. All you need is money. In embracing consumerism you forsake love for satisfaction, although it is the empty satisfaction of acquiring things you never needed in the first place. In forsaking love, you forsake the greatest ability and gift of your self, as well as your greatest tool in the quest of self-fulfillment.

The unworthy fear of love and the retreat into consumerism is rooted in your failure to understand the significance of displaying love. You fear love because someone you loved rejected you. But the pain and suffering you feel when your love is spurned or ignored is merely an expression of your selfishness. You are demeaning an act of love by making it conditional on the other person returning that love. In fact, love is most valuable to the self when it is selfless, when it does not expect to be rewarded in kind, but loves merely for the joy of loving.

No one can take from you the significance of an unrequited, selfless act of love. Its beauty cannot be marred by refusal or ingratitude. It will persist like a glowing jewel in time, and perhaps beyond, marking a manifestation of your potential, an elevation towards self-fulfillment. Rejoice and be happy in loving, knowing the more selfless love is, the closer you are to self-fulfillment.

In failing to appreciate the significance of unrequited love, you pervert it. Bitter at being jilted you swear never to love again. Worse, you may seek to exact vengeance upon all those who might give you their love henceforth. You want to punish people for daring to love you. This punishment is a self-inflicted wound that diminishes your glory and buries your spirituality in the grave of cowardly fear and self-pitying pain.

Do not shut your heart to love if others close theirs. Let your love be greater than their indifference or their hate. Love can only be willingly given, never demanded or expected. The true joy of love rests in the giving. Love unconditionally. Look again to the example of Jesus, the man. His story has value not only in its teachings or miracles, but in the question he asks you through his sacrifice, and it is this: could you have loved on the cross? Could you?

Chapter 19

Death

In the make-believe Consumer-world, nobody dies.
You will. If you want to get the most out of life,
learn what death is all about.

The death of death

Consumerism hates death for nothing pops the illusion of perpetual gratification like the Grim Reaper. Faced with the inevitability of death, all consumerist needs pale by comparison. Death is so effective exposing the sheer futility of consumption that it is undoubtedly the greatest enemy of the multinationals.

The multinationals have adopted a number of strategies for dealing with death:

Burying death

Never in the history of mankind has man been as ignorant of death as the average consumer. Consumerism does not want you to have any first hand experience of death. It has hidden death from view, placed it in a dark corner and made it a taboo not to be spoken of or contemplated. As long as you live in Consumer-world you will never be exposed to real death, never attend a funeral or hold the hand of a dying person. The multinational experience has no room for death. There is eating, drinking, entertainment and shopping, but not death. Death is simply not a part of the consumer life.

The Forgotten Death

It is not only human death that has been swept under the rug. The death of living things, in particular the constant butchery of domestic animals to sate our carnivorous instincts, has also been concealed. Every single day, every single hour, every single minute, animals are being slaughtered. But no one, except for those involved in the slaughter, is ever exposed to this death. Have you ever witnessed the process of transformation whereby a cow becomes a burger patty? It's not a pretty thing. But your consumerist masters do not want to ruin the pretty images of their consumer food with the bloody reality. Not many kids would go to McDonald's if they saw how their Big Macs started out.

The other carnivores, the predators of the wild, have earned the right to consume meat. They are the agents of transformation, the takers of life, the killers. They are the ones who down the prey, who tear its life out, who rip open its entrails and feed on its flesh. And theirs is an infinitely more intimate killing than ours, for they do not have tools, non-sentient extensions to achieve their goal, but use their own bodies as weapons to slay their enemy. The spurt of blood that jets from the sliced artery of the prey does not fall on the metal edge of the knife, but gurgles in the predator's mouth and trickles on the killing jaws.

You have eschewed the moral responsibility, the ferocity and the necessary fortitude to commit that ultimate act, the act of killing another living being. You pamper and preen yourself as civilized, you despise killing and violence as barbarous, you look down on other people as primitive, all the while ignoring the fact that somewhere, out of sight and out of mind, someone is wielding the knife that will make a cow into your next Big Mac. You are completely detached from these killing fields. The greatest slaughters are committed in your name and yet every night your sleep is easy and untroubled.

Misunderstanding Death

The multinationals know that no matter how much they seek to deny death, it is unavoidable. As such, they seek to take the sting out of death by manipulating your image of it. The diminution of death is accomplished through consumer entertainment.

Television death

There are two types of television death:

Fictional death: Every day you see death on television. None of it is real. And you know none of it is real. Overexposure to artificial death makes death lose its significance. Through constant repetition, death has been transformed from an inevitable aspect of life to an unreal, intangible product of Hollywood. You see so many people die on-screen that you lose all perspective of the finality of death.

Real Death: Even when faced with real death on newscasts, death cannot assume any meaning within your existence. Since death is relayed through the television, it stunts your ability to appreciate its momentousness. Whether it's a TV show or a fatal accident on the six o'clock news, the medium distances you from the reality. Television does not show us death, but a picture of death. Death becomes a word defined through the pictures we see on television. But a picture is not reality. Death is more than just a visual experience. Death is touching, even for a brief second, the dead person, to ascertain its cold rigidity. Death is something no camera can convey.

Death is more than the sum of your senses. In order to know death you must be in its presence. You must see it in real time and not as a snippet of a newscast. In order to comprehend its finality you must witness its irrevocability, its stillness, its silence. On TV, you can either flip the channel or wait until they go on to the next news story or movie scene. Death is merely a point in time. But when you are in its presence, you will have realized that death is unchangeable. You will have understood the closure of death. In a society that subsists on a rapid sequence of consumer stimuli in a vain attempt towards satisfaction, death stands in stark contrast, changeless and eternal.

By limiting your experience of death to televised images, consumerism has made death remote. You might acknowledge to yourself the existence of death but it is somewhere else, far away, trapped somewhere in the netherworld of the television. Death is out there, death is externalized, death is objective. It does not impinge in your daily life, it does not affect your daily existence. There is no reason to understand it. Indeed, you cannot understand it since it is alien to your consumerist controlled brain patterns, premised on immortality. The consumer mindset prevents understanding of death unless tragedy strikes and a loved one is taken away. Lacking such a tragedy, or worse yet, lacking any loved ones, death remains forever a stranger to the consumer.

By transforming death into a form of consumer entertainment, consumerism also seeks to endow you with an illusory power over death. In Consumer-world, you control death with the click of a button. If you do not like to see the handiwork of a suicide bomber, flip the channel to the reassuring images of Monday Night Football, or some laugh track-heavy sitcom and poof, death has disappeared. The message of consumerism is simple: there is no reason to worry about death since we have given you the means to manipulate it.

Electronic death

If television has distanced you from death, has given you a false sense of control over death, video games have promoted the acceptance and enjoyment of death. Video games allow you to experience death even more remotely than television since the "people" being killed are virtual creations.

Video game addicts subsist on death. Death is delightful, the primary measure of your success. It is to be distributed to all those who oppose you. Advancement of the self, embodied in your video game alter ego, may only be achieved through killing. Killing not only becomes acceptable, it is a basic necessity. Video games infect you with a passion for death.

Violent video games not only promote complete disdain for the value of life, they give a highly distorted picture of death. Whether it's your character or the enemy who perishes, you can always begin again. Death means nothing. Video games destroy the notion of the finality of death, both for adults but especially for the young, who often receive their education in death through this unhappy medium.

Video games go beyond television, where no matter how numb you are to seeing death, the death of an actual human being, whether real or staged, will nonetheless elicit a minimal emotional response. But seeing a video game creation blown to bits is an emotional cipher. The player is completely immunized to the meaning of death. By divorcing death from the emotional response, consumerism creates the conditions wherein vulnerable, ignorant youth are more likely to overstep electronic bounds and enact their killing sprees in schools all across the globe.

Fearing death

Faith, immortality and aging

Ignorance of death has made it a terrible nightmare. Never in the history of mankind have human beings feared death as the consumer slaves of the Western world fear it now. What accounts for this primal fear of the Grim Reaper?

A fading faith

Fear of death is rooted in the dying faith of the Western world. As religion fades from your life, so does faith in an afterworld, faith in an eternal paradise.

Islamic fundamentalists are feared and branded as fanatics because they have no fear of death. Although they come from a world that is viewed as poor, primitive, and weak, their willingness to engage in "martyrdom operations" makes them a formidable foe. Rather than dismissing their actions as the product of lunatic minds, look beneath the surface to understand their behaviour.

Why is it that so many in the Islamic world do not fear death? It is because of their faith. Faith is the source of their power. In faith, they find their strength. September 11 did not occur because of a failure of U.S. intelligence or the meticulous planning of Al-Quaeda. September 11 happened because nineteen young men were convinced that paradise awaited them, and that martyrdom provided the key to opening the Pearly Gates. These notions are completely alien to the Western world, raised on its diet of vapid consumerism.

Not too long ago, many in the West had the same faith in a Christian paradise. However, the age of religion, the age of faith, the age of martyrs, has passed in the West. Having lost your belief in an afterworld, you now fear death.

Immortal consumer, perpetual consumerism

It is not solely to the loss of faith that you can attribute your fear of death. The multinationals have stoked within you the fear of death and for a very simple reason: without consumers there can't be consumerism. Without consumers, they don't exist. If you, the consumer, do not fear death, multinationals do. They want you to be around as long as possible.

Multinationals offer their version of immortality to replace the one you've lost through your dead faith. Although your faith has died, your desire for immortality has not. Consumerism stepped in to fill the gap. Consumerism is now the new faith, the new dogma, the new religion. But consumerism can't sidestep the fact that each and every one of its adherents will die. So consumerism has instilled you with a new desire, the desire for earthly immortality, the desire to avoid the grave altogether. Only then it will be assured of an infinite and ever-growing supply of consumers, only then can its economic models make sense.

Consumerism lurks behind the attempts to vanquish death altogether. Not wanting to die is not enough reason to live. Yet, you are constantly bombarded to strive towards immortality without ever quite knowing why. Perhaps it is time to ask who wants you to live forever.

In fact, the immortality prepared for you is one of eternal consumer slavery. If you realize why multinationals encourage you to aspire towards eternal life on earth, you will fear earthly immortality a lot more than death. If, just for a second, you lose the fear of death and think about the hellish consequences of living on a planet where nobody dies, the consumer myth of earthly immortality will be exploded. Ponder the apocalypse this planet would become as the population surged into the trillions, and you will progress to the maturity level needed to accept death.

Alas, the deeper you are imprisoned within Consumer-world, the more difficult it becomes to maintain a sane perspective. This is why the richest among us, who feel they have the most to lose by leaving the consumer paradise, constantly seek ways to cheat death, sparing no expense in the bargain.

Seeking to vanquish death, consumerism has perverted medicine. Medicine used to accept death. No longer. Not since the pharmaceutical multinationals have stepped in and changed doctors' perspectives. Now death is feared, death is unacceptable, death is a failure. Desperate to stave off a patient's death, doctors have forgotten about the quality of life. As long as the patient has a pulse, the medical treatment is considered a success. This is why there is constant talk of imminent medical breakthroughs that will prolong your life. A growing number of doctors and scientists believe that earthly immortality is just around the corner. Few are those who ask themselves why you would want it, and at what price. Few in the medical field think that the right of every human being is not only to live with dignity, but to die with dignity as well.

Death and aging

Consumerism has encouraged the fear of death through its attitude towards aging. Aging is the child of death. Despite the fact that the populations of the Western world are rapidly aging, the aged are removed from consumerist images. Being old is not cool. Being old is passe. Youth dominates consumer entertainment and consumer music.[47] Youth is the face of consumer advertising, youth is the focus of consumer products. Bombarded by images of perpetual youth, you have become neurotic about the natural process of aging. You are prepared to take whatever steps necessary to reverse the signs of aging. Taking those ultimately vain steps only shows you are under the spell of the multinationals.

---

47. Hollywood, that bastion of consumerism, has embraced youth with a maniacal fervor. Not only are the stars of the screen becoming increasingly younger, but the other branches of the entertainment industry are being ruthlessly cleansed of anybody pushing forty. From writers to producers to directors and executives, either you're young, or you're finished.

To maintain fear and loathing of death, consumerism encourages the isolation, alienation, and marginalization of the old. With Darwinian efficiency, the old are weeded out from Consumer-world. Significant generational rifts have appeared in Western society as the aged are increasingly shunted aside, walled off in retirement homes. We live in a society that seeks to sweep death under the rug by burying the elderly.

As soon as you reach your golden years, you are encouraged to brutally remove yourself from your family, indeed from society at large, and voluntarily imprison yourself within a senior citizen's jail. There, under the watchful supervision of your captors, you will live a preprogrammed life in the company of strangers. Your jailers will ensure you will adhere to their rigid schedule. They will feed, wash and treat you with robotic efficiency, all the while depriving you of what you seek most: the warmth, love and human contact of your family members. Best of all, you will have spent your hard-earned retirement savings to finance this terrible fate.[48]

The treatment of the aged in the Western world is a collective moral crime of our civilization, and a harsh indictment of its much-vaunted values. The individualist philosophy cannot justify this behaviour. Arguments as to the elderly's needs for specialized care are merely a method through which all those who have packed off their parents to retirement homes seek to absolve themselves of the guilt. You do not send the old to retirement homes for their benefit. They are sent there because you, their children and grandchildren, will not commit the time and effort to care for them. The old are carted away to their prisons because you will not drain your emotional resources to deal with them and love them on a daily basis.

You cannot stand the old because they are slow, because they require time and care, in other words because they distract you from consumption. That, in itself, is a reason why the multinationals want the elderly out of the way; the young always consume more if given the time. With age come health problems, deteriorating mental capacities and the inevitability of death; consumption loses its lustre. Multinationals do not want the aged to impart this wisdom, the wisdom of age and the knowledge of death, to their younger relatives. Shutting them up in retirement homes conveniently keeps them out of the way.

---

48. This is why responsibility between parents and children must cut both ways. If your parents cared for you for 18 years or more, you must return the favour and assume responsibility in caring for them during their retirement.

Consumerism does not hate the old solely because they are old. Consumerism hates the old because they are dying. The old stink of death. The old reek of mortality. The scent of death is inescapable when you are around them. The presence of death accompanies them wherever they are. Saggy, blotchy skin, feeble, uncertain movements, milky eyes, creaking joints, shaking limbs, trembling lips, toothless mouths, uncontrolled bowels, these are the signs you are in the presence of age. The old are the heralds of death, the trumpeters of the Grim Reaper. No wonder you are eager to drink deep of the consumerist potion and ignore the trumpets. No wonder it is better to pretend that by losing yourself in Consumer-world you can ignore the trumpet when it calls for you. Consumerism sells you a bath in the waters of Lethe, the river of forgetfulness. If you just forget that the monster of death exists, then everything will be all right.

•

Saving the Self

Living with death

Bury death and you bury a part of your self. Denial of death is a denial of your humanity. It is perhaps the greatest of self-deceptions. If you are not truly aware of death, you cannot be complete and you can never find fulfillment.

You cannot accept the beginning of your existence without accepting its end. You cannot live your life meaningfully without accepting it is circumscribed, limited to a fistful of decades, at best a century and change. Birth and death form the covers of your life book. Between these covers lie the blank pages wherein you will write the story of your life.

The path towards self-fulfillment requires acknowledging that every day may be your last, that no matter how many days you have been allotted, one final day will come. It is within these parameters, these uncertain and unascertainable parameters, that you must seek to build your self towards its full potential. It is forbidding and fearsome that you are so vulnerable, that your existence is so fragile, but it is an ineluctable truth. You cannot become a better person if you deny this very basic fact of your existence. You might despair, you might rail, you might struggle against death, but you must admit its inevitability.

Accepting death means accepting a host of corollary matters that consumerism hates. Admitting death means accepting unpredictability, the fact that chance rules your existence as much as anything else. In the perfectly scripted world of consumerism, the element of chance is unacceptable. Consumerism thrives on control, routine, uniformity and predictability. It depends on using such things as the *TV Guide* to program your week. Armed with the knowledge that today might be your last, you will not be as eager to accept living in a preprogrammed Consumer-world.

Knowledge of death is what makes life precious. Knowledge of death is what will push you towards making each day a unique experience, towards cramming as much experience as possible in your brief time on this earth. Far from being a downer, as the multinationals seek to convince us, death is the ultimate motivator. Faced with this ultimate deadline, you will focus on achieving what you consider most important for the self, for personal fulfillment. Knowledge of death catalyzes and propels the individual towards fulfillment.

Death's deadline shatters the myth of immortality peddled by the multinationals. Consumerism thrives on making time worthless, on giving you the impression that time is irrelevant when engaged in consumption. Multinationals have buried death in a perpetual cycle of consumer entertainment and consumer products. Consumerism is designed to convince you that if you just stay cocooned within its synthetic paradise the experience will roll on forever. But once you are alive to death, the illusion of an eternal consumerist existence is roughly stripped away. All that is left before you is the immutable way of the universe: All that is born shall die.

Knowing Death

Illness

Volunteer at your local hospital. Ask to help in palliative care, emergency or cancer centres. By comforting the severely ill, by helping them through their final weeks or months on earth, you will have learned a great deal as to the mortal nature of man, and thus your self. Illness sensitizes you to death, and few places offer a greater harvest to the Grim Reaper than hospital wards. Walk among the ill and you walk among impending doom. They are a nexus to mortality, closer to death's door than most others. Shut away in hospitals and hospices, the ill do not partake in the consumer society; they have withdrawn from Consumer-world. Walking among them is thus a walk into freedom.

The self learns and progresses among the corridors filled with the dying. Those who face death can teach you the meaning of acceptance and imbue you with the needed courage to accept your own mortality. It is a bitter fruit, this knowledge, it is an unhappy lesson perhaps, but it is a necessary one to strengthen and prepare the self for death. It will temper your actions this newfound knowledge, and yet it could bring enormous satisfaction, joy and appreciation for the self. Above all, it brings freedom, for you know that your health is the greatest of all gifts, and all you desire in terms of consumer things is meaningless, and will be meaningless if you do not work to protect your health.

Despite the dreariness of it all, despite the depression of illness, despite the pain of suffering that seems to darken the brightest sunlight, know that you will find joy among the ill. It is the joy of offering your self and seeing it appreciated, rewarded with gratitude.[49]

Funerals

Do not shirk away from the dead. Fear of death can only be overcome by facing it head on. Facing death requires more than just attending the funeral of a relative or a friend. Facing death means seeing the dead, means being in the presence of death for a prolonged period of time. A closed casket lowered in the ground is unlikely to shake you from your consumer stupor. The experience of death requires the courage to interact with the dead person. That means staying beside the open casket for more than a few brief seconds and that means staying in the room itself, in the inescapable presence of death. You must see death, you must touch death; you must acquire both a sensory and a temporal comprehension of death.

Funerals are not only important for teaching the meaning of death, but also for personalizing it. In hospitals you might be exposed to death, but at funerals you will not only see death, but you will see the death of someone you know and presumably cared for. You will see the body juxtaposed to your memory of the living being that used to animate it. It is a painful lesson, seeing how death changes the body, how different it is from life; it is a lesson that must be learned. Only in the presence of a dead person that you knew while alive will you understand and appreciate your own life. Only then will you understand how beautiful

---

49. While volunteering at the palliative care unit of a local hospital, I comforted a woman dying of cancer. A few weeks later, after she had passed away, I ended up in the elevator with her sister, who had come from England to be with her in her final moments. Noticing my name tag, she proceeded to tell me how the woman had spoken glowingly of me in their final telephone conversations. The sheer joy of being I experienced knowing I had done something of use brought tears to my eyes.

and precious your own self is, and how it must be fructified before it vacates its mortal shell.

Age

Live with your elders; bring your parents or grandparents closer to you. Living with the aged means living with the knowledge of death. They can transmit that knowledge to you. The aged have learned of death in two ways:

Death through their body: The aged are not only the trumpeters of death, but their impending end and the slow deterioration of their body has taught them the wisdom of death. They feel death stalking them in their bones, in their ailments, in their fading powers. It's inescapability is something they live with every day, although far from being a source of weakness it is a source of strength. Death concentrates their mind on that most important thing, which is sucking the maximum benefit from every living moment. The aged can find fulfillment in every second of their existence precisely because they know its importance.

Exposure to death: The aged have been exposed to death more than others. They have buried friends, relatives, spouses and even children. Some have fought in wars, and have stared death in the face on a daily basis.

It is more than just the death of individuals to which the aged are habituated. Their whole world, the world of their youth, has vanished. All that they knew, their way of life, their society, no longer exists. Rapid technological advances have changed society beyond recognition from their heyday. From their perspective, the eternal nature of Consumerworld is an illusion. Change is the only constant in their world, and death is the agent of change. The aged know that all that surrounds you will soon pass, and that the struggles to achieve an earthly consumer Nirvana are mere folly. Having been privy to enormous societal changes, they have learned the importance of improving the self rather than sacrificing its needs for flitting consumerist successes. Make sure they pass on their wisdom to you.

Death, giver of life

Witnessing death

You have no right to eat meat unless you witness the transformation whereby a living being becomes food. You must bear witness to the slaughter. Start with a trip to an abattoir. Every single human being that includes meat in their diet must know where their hamburger comes from. It is not enough to see pictures or even videos of animals killed. Just like a human death, the video will not give you the complete picture. The smell, the sounds of a dying being, the sheer proximity and the ability to touch the creature in its final shudder all are present in the assembly line of this butchery. Every person must experience it, this daily holocaust of domestic animals. The killing that goes on and on and on and never stops though you think the stench of death obscures heaven itself. It is all done in your name. It is your burden to bear. The very least you can do is witness the transformation of a living being into a grocery product.

The necessity of killing

Do not eat what you cannot or will not kill yourself. You have no right to eat meat unless you have participated in the transformation process yourself.

After you've seen the death of animals, if you are still carnivorously inclined, then it is time to do it. Only then will you rise to the level of every other carnivorous beast on this planet. Get a knife, get a live beast. Can you kill? And not just once, but over and over again. Every single time you need meat. Can you butcher an animal? If you cannot, then do not eat flesh ever again. Killing is the responsibility of the carnivore. It cannot, must not, be forsaken. In many countries people kill animals daily in order to feed their families. These people have a moral right to eat meat. Unless you can do the same, you don't.

This is not a vegetarian call to arms. It is a call to you to assume the mantle of responsibility for your food choices. That responsibility includes killing, includes death. Killing animals on a regular basis, for the purposes of feeding yourself and your family, provides an education in death. It will familiarize you with death, and with familiarity comes acceptance. It will impart a knowledge of death, a new-found maturity that will counter the superficiality of your consumerist existence. Taking the life of a living being, even if only a chicken or a pig, is an act that will make the consumerist experience pale by comparison. It is nothing less than an affirmation of the harsh truths of the universe.

Killing will give you a greater respect for life. At first glance, this statement seems paradoxical. However, only killing teaches you that a life had to perish so that you could live.

Only through killing are you truly alerted to the fact that every day living beings give their lives for you. The knowledge of this death, the sacrifice that is required so that you may walk the earth, inevitably makes one realize the importance of those creatures we depend upon. It is no wonder that those closest to nature, the world's native peoples who live off nature's bounty, are both killers and preservers, practicing conservation long before the notion crept into the vocabulary of the "civilized world." For it is these people, who meet and deal death every day, that most revere the animals that keep them alive, and know that the beast's survival and flourishing is integral to their own existence. Only those who do not know death can allow, participate in and ignore the death of the whole planet. Cocooned in the consumerist paradise it is easy to forget that an episode of "Friends" won't fill your stomach, and that food does not come from McDonald's, but is only served there.

Aging with grace

Acceptance: Just as you must accept death, so you must acknowledge the constant aging process that occurs within your body. You must have the courage to accept the wrinkles, the sagging, the slow deterioration of the body. Acceptance is not an act of despair or self-abandonment. Acceptance of aging does not mean that you should neglect your body. On the contrary, strive with all of your might to keep your body in tip-top condition. The importance of bodily maintenance and healthy living increases with age. Keeping mentally and physically fit is more important than ever in your golden years. But that fitness is within the parameters of your age, within the limits imposed by the passage of time.

Do not confuse acts of self-preservation with consumer anti-aging treatments. Prolonging your life by natural methods such as exercise and diet is not the same as cosmetic treatments to undo the physical effects of age. Age is about healthy living not surgical procedures. Plastic surgery will not make you healthier. Botox injections will not extend your life span. Multinational cosmetic products cannot make you reach the century mark. Consumer anti-aging procedures and products merely distort the self by creating an artificial physical image of you. Despite their claims, cosmetic surgery cannot mask your age. A 70-year old with cosmetic surgery does not look like a 50-year old. He or she simply looks like a 70-year old with cosmetic surgery. Rejoice in your self and concentrate on quality of living rather than external appearances.

The Beauty of Age: The obsession with looking younger via consumer treatments also points out the failure to realize the beauty of age. Age is beautiful both from a physical and mental aspect. Physically, while your body is deteriorating, slowing down means you will put less stress on the body. You are also more likely to care for your body in order to ensure its well-being. Retirement eliminates work stresses from your life and allows your body to exist in a healthier environment. Grown-up children mean no further need to concern your self with their upkeep and maintenance.

Age also relaxes the mind. Knowing you are approaching the end of your life, you are apt to take greater interest and joy in the world around you. When you have no artificial goals such as job promotions to look forward to, you live for the moment. Age teaches the joy of living, even if it means living within the limits of your body. There is no more hurry and hassle, no more running around to realize your self within Consumer-world. Age brings the desire for true realization, for true self-fulfillment.

Age is also timeless. The golden years and their impending sunset make time irrelevant. You grow closer to the cycle of nature and to the self. Age brings you the opportunity to reminisce on what was and to contemplate what will be. Above all, it offers the chance to explore and discover your innermost self. Your final years are a time of reflection and of self-revelation. It is a time when you take your greatest strides towards fulfillment, not through physical actions or great works within society, but by simply pondering the self. It is a time for making peace with both the world and your self. The aged are the most capable of acknowledging and working with the true self. The young are most likely to war with their self by imposing upon it artificial and harmful consumer needs.

Chapter 20

Not a Conclusion, but a Beginning

In every end, there is a beginning.

Practical limits of self-expression

Consumerism has permeated society to such an extent that finding non-consumer solutions has become increasingly difficult. While I have touched on some aspects of consumerism's effect upon you, the fact remains that in certain cases it is virtually impossible to avoid the consumerist influence. In terms of choosing your personal transportation, the battle has already been lost. You are invariably forced to purchase your car from a multinational. Independent family-owned car manufacturers simply do not exist. The situation is similar for public forms of transport such as buses and airplanes. Your transportation choices have been consumerized. An essential aspect of your freedom has been taken away from you.

So how are you to save the self from consumer transport? Making your own vehicle is impossible; establishing a vehicle manufacturing business from scratch would probably cost billions. Some non-multinational bike manufacturers still exist, and there is always that old standby, the horse, but the fact remains that, at the moment, you do not have a choice. It's either the multinationals' way or the highway. And the highway on foot is not a very smart proposition.

While certain portions of your freedoms have seen consumer encroachment, there is still time to preserve what you have left. You still have the opportunity to save the self if you make the conscious decision to stop being a consumer slave.

Learned helplessness and self-sufficiency

It is a tragic irony that America, defender and champion of independence and personal freedom, possesses the world's most enslaved people.[50] Aside from the consumerist freedom of choice, the freedom to choose between competing brands, Americans are essentially incapable of making choices in their life. The reason? The average American is utterly helpless, totally dependent on consumerism to care for his needs. It is this consumerist slavery that the multinationals seek to establish all over the planet under the guise of freedom.

Consumerism teaches you how to be helpless. As long as you are utterly incapable of doing anything for yourself, as long as you believe multinational handouts are the best way to exist (and a helpless person merely exists but does not live), then you are well on your way to becoming a perfect consumer.

Self-sufficiency provides the best method of breaking free from the cycle of consumer dependency. The self-sufficient person relies on the self to generate and fulfil needs. The more you can rely on the self to determine and care for your needs, the less you will need to rely on others. In taking personal responsibility for your self, you have taken the reins of destiny in your hands.

Embracing self-sufficiency will also bring you closer to your natural self, to the expression of your natural potential. For nature made you whole and complete and gave you all the tools necessary to care for your earthly needs: a mind and a body. Consumerism has only taught you how to squander your gifts.

If you wish to see the polar opposite of the consumer existence, look no further than nature. There, the struggle for survival is paramount, and each day lived is a triumph for the innumerable species of the biosphere. Animals live simple lives but they are complete in themselves. They can account for all of their needs. If these lesser beings are completely self-sufficient, are you, most gifted by far of all the species on the planet, inferior? If a lowly rat can survive and prosper without relying on multinationals why can't you do without them? Why have you become more helpless and dependent than the lowliest creatures that walk the earth?

As consumerism gathers strength, self-sufficiency is on the wane. You have become increasingly incapable of caring for your needs. You might be competent in the narrow field of your profession but can do

50. If New Hampshire's state motto of 'live free or die' were made into law and ruthlessly applied, a lot of Americans would find themselves on death row with no hope of parole.

little else. Instead of developing new skills or unearthing hidden talents, you choose the vacuous offerings of the consumer universe. You crave the convenience of the consumer lifestyle, its unmitigated ease and constant accessibility. But what if society stopped being so convenient? What if you could not have access to all of life's necessities (or at least what you have brainwashed into thinking are life's necessities) with a mere telephone call? Are you capable of leading a self-sufficient life, of growing your own food, of finding or building shelter, of fashioning clothes? When the gas runs out of the SUV, when the batteries fail on the cell phone, when the power is cut to the house, could you survive a week? A month? A year?[51]

What is the likelihood of there being a complete breakdown of Western society? Multinationals would politely laugh off self-sufficiency as utterly irrelevant in today's world, practiced only by loners, tree-huggers and right-wing militias who subscribe to apocalyptic visions of the future. However condescendingly multinationals dismiss self-sufficiency and offer up soothing consumerist pap to keep you quiescent, the fact remains that such skills are nothing less than acts of self-emancipation. Self-sufficiency is not only about surviving. Self-sufficiency is about freedom. The consumerist giants fear nothing more than a free human being. Freedom places you beyond their grasp. If you can take care of all your needs, you do not need consumer products.

Consumerism cannot provide genuine joy. The fountain of happiness rests in the self. Achieving a personal goal is infinitely more satisfying then any television show or any brand name product. Seek pleasure in fulfilling your self, in human companionship and in nature rather than in artificial consumption. For the pleasures of consumerism are limited, repetitious, mind numbing and tedious but the joys of self-development are as varied and infinite as your imagination.

Saving the self is not easy. The distance you must travel to achieve your full potential, to become the superior being that lies dormant within you, is vast. The journey usually ends in death, far from the destination point. Few are those who know how far they must travel on that road. Fewer still are those who do fulfil all that lies within them. Have the courage embark on that journey, freeing the self so that it may propel you higher on the scale of being. In the end, no matter far you have traveled down that road, it is better to perish in the attempt than to die in a numb consumerist stupor, unaware of the chance you have wasted, the chance called life.

---

51. Look at the panic and chaos that erupted during the blackout of August 14, 2003. And that blackout was barely one day long.

The journey of earthly salvation will have many missteps, many deviations, many errors. After all, you are only human. There will be times when you will vegetate in front of the TV. There will be times when you get a craving for really bad junk food that you just have to satisfy. There will be times when you will be reading the tabloids in the line-up at the grocery store. They are natural human failings, as natural as lying to your best friend to protect their feelings, or cheating on a test or exam. Everyone sins. Whether it's a moral sin or a consumer one, none of us are perfect. The important thing is to keep on the path, for that is the only true path you can take.

The greater picture

Saving the self might seem a selfish act, but acting in your interests is not selfish at all. Consumerism is selfishness. Consumer selfishness redefines well-being, achievement, satisfaction, joy and happiness to fit within the prison of your fears. Through consumerism, you escape the universe for an artificial Consumer-world, a world that seemingly cares only for you, except that it only cares to use you for its profit. In using consumerism to distort reality, you are only harming your self. The paradox of consumer selfishness is that the more selfish you are, the more you are harming your self. Rather than help you get ahead, consumer selfishness leaves you dead in your tracks.

Saving the self requires not only living in the real world, but acknowledging your dependence upon that world. The fulfillment of the planet is necessary to your own personal fulfillment. In realizing your self, you will need the realization of mankind. Your well being cannot be separated from that of the objective world.

There is no escape from the fact your fulfillment is dependent on the whole of this planet. Some think they can buy escape through reclusive retreats, or large estates, fortified against the outside world. However, no matter how far you go or how you try to isolate yourself you can never be "far from the Madding crowd." The very poorest among us influence the richest and most powerful just as surely as the rich and powerful influence the poor.

The illusion of consumer escape from planetary realities was tragically exposed in 1986. The Chernobyl nuclear accident showed Western Europe how the most stringent laws, the greatest safety precautions and the most rigorous inspection standards for their nuclear industry were all in vain when a decrepit and poorly-regulated Soviet nuclear power station had a meltdown. Similarly, September 11, 2001 showed Americans that no matter how much they deluded themselves on their invulnerability, no matter how much they chose to isolate themselves from the outside world, the world still came to them in a violent and horrible way.

Saving the self is also an act of charity. In fulfilling your self, you are more charitable than the most venerated holy man. How is that possible? The relationship between you and mankind is a two-way street. The self-fulfillment of every single individual on this planet is dependent upon you. Perhaps the effect is minimal, but it's there. I need you. We all need you. In helping better your self, you are helping all of us in our own quest for self-fulfillment. Humanity can only fulfil its destiny when the absolute potential of each human being is realized. The six billion souls on this planet might walk their own individual path, but we are all dependent on each other to ensure that everybody reaches their desired end.

Remedy the inequalities in your mind, body and soul and you will help remedy those of the planet. Act in your best interests and you will act in the planet's best interests. Let self-fulfillment perpetuate a virtuous cycle; in helping your self, help the whole of mankind, which in turn will help you.

All of this might sound fine and dandy, but is it practicable? My answer is that it is both practicable and natural. This is the way of the world. Look how the rest of the planet operates. Look at the natural world.

There is no waste within nature, none of the destruction and pollution created by human selfishness. But there is no altruism either. Nature's denizens do not act for a global purpose, but for an individual one. Birds, for instance, do not eat insects to control bug populations and thus keep the ecosystem in balance; birds eat insects because they are hungry. Every single individual being in nature acts in its own self-interest, struggling to survive; and yet, paradoxically, every living organism helps keep the local and global ecosystem in balance through these self-same acts. All of nature benefits through the sum total of these infinite individual actions.

Similarly, you need not undertake an action because of the beneficial effects it may have upon mankind, although it will have such effects; perform the action according to your needs. By discovering your true needs, you will see that they are in concordance with those of your fellow man, with those of the biosphere itself. Nature, of which you are an integral part, was conceived so that each individual's attempt towards self-realization is congruent with the planet's attempt towards self-realization.[52] This is a wonderful, magical truth of our existence, and yet

---

52. What the purpose of this planet is, aside from being a dance in time, we do not know. One thing is for sure: it is not up to man to upset the tremendous symphony

it is one we constantly deny. Only the selfish and the ignorant might think it to their advantage that others starve or are miserable, and only the pusillanimous will throw their hands up in the air and say they are helpless to affect global problems. The way of the world, despite our attempts to deny it, is this: Do good unto your self, and you will invariably do good unto others.

---

of infinite complexity that is life on Terra. The rise and fall of life on the planet, the evolution of organisms and its interaction with the universe is an awe-inspiring wonder, subject of human contemplation. It is not to be callously and ignorantly destroyed and replaced with our artificial constructs, ruins by comparison. For we are the merchants of death, with our artifice, our cement highways that pave over life, our skyscrapers that wound the sky, our machines that gnaw at the earth and plunder the sea. We kill all that we survey. We are not the masters of this world. We are its executioners.

References

4 *multinationals not accountable to human beings* As GM's failure to recall defective autos shows. See Jamie Court. *Corporateering: How Corporate Power Steals Your Personal Freedom... And what You Can Do About It.* New York: Tarcher Putnam, 2003, pp. 16-17.

4 *your existence reduced to numbers* Ibid. 18-19.

5 *Consumer-world* Ibid. 54-55. Court points to the corporations' attempt to create a "commercial world."

5 *consumerism controls every aspect of existence* Jean Baudrillard. "Consumer Society." in Martin Poster ed. *Jean Baudrillard: Selected Writings.* Cambridge: Polity Press 1988, p. 33-34.

5 *existence dependent upon consumption* Douglas J. Goodman and Mirelle Cohen. *Consumer Culture: A Reference Handbook.* Santa Barbara: ABC-Clio, 2000, pp. 93-94.

6 *working to consume* Thomas Hine. *I want That: How We All Became Shoppers.* New York: Harper Collins, 2002, p.18.

7 *pressure to consume* Douglas J. Goodman and Mirelle Cohen. *Consumer Culture: A Reference Handbook.* Santa Barbara: ABC-Clio, 2000, pp. 93-94

7 *artificial needs for consumer products* Celia Lury. *Consumer Culture.* New Brunswick: Rutgers University Press. 1996, pp. 62-64

15 *Suburban Hell* The problem with soulless municipal planning and the lack of community was addressed by Jacobs. See Jane Jacobs. *The Death and Life of American Cities.* New York: Vintage, 1992

16 *separation of commercial residential districts* James S. Russell "Privatized Lives: On the embattled 'burbs" *Harvard Design Magazine*, 12, Fall 2000;

http://www.jsrussellwriter.com/embattledburbs.html

16 *distance* Ibid.

16 *lack of amenities* Ibid.

17 *Migration and immigration* William H. Frey. *Melting Pot Suburbs: A Census 2000 Study of Suburban Diversity.* The Brookings Institution Census 2000 Series, June 2001 p. 1.

17 *social mobility* Richard Morin. "The New GREAT DIVIDE: More and more, where you live depends on what you're worth" *Washington Post* Sunday, January 18, 1998; p. W14 .

17 *geographic mobility* According to the U.S. government 45.9 % of U.S. citizens changed residence in a five year period (1995-2000). Jason P. Schachter, Rachel S. Franklin and Marc J. Perry "Migration and Geographic Mobility in Metropolitan and Nonmetropolitan America: 1995 to 2000" U.S. Census Bureau August 2003 p. 2

18 *difficult immigrant integration* Brian Ray. *Immigrant Integration: Building to Opportunity.* Migration Policy Institute. October 1, 2002; http://www.migrationinformation.org/Feature/display.cfm?ID=57

18-19 *technology substituted for community* Richard J. Barnet and John Cavanagh. *Global Dreams: Imperial Corporations and the New World Order.* New York: Simon & Schuster, 1994, p. 38

19 *mall prevents community spirit* Joel Bakan. *The Corporation: The Pathological Pursuit of Profit and Power*. New York: Free Press, 2004, p. 131.

19 *malls impersonal creations* Laura Byrne Paquet *The Urge To Splurge: A Social History of Shopping*. Toronto: ECW Press, 2003, p. 98.

19 *malls want to attract people from far away* According to the Department of American Studies at Eastern Connecticut State University Shopping Mall Studies, malls with more than 100 stores seek to attract customers from within at least a 100 mile radius.
http://www.easternct.edu/depts/amerst/MallsTerms.htm

19 *high turnover for malls* According to Paquet, the Mall of America attracts 600,000 – 900, 000 visits per week. Laura Byrne Paquet. *The Urge To Splurge: A Social History of Shopping*. Toronto: ECW Press, 2003, p. 97.

26 *artificial need for multinational products* Food as entertainment is one way of selling product. Susan Linn. *Consuming Kids*. New York: The New Press, 2004 pp.99-101; Richard J. Barnet, John Cavanagh *Global Dreams: Imperial Corporations and the New World Order* Simon & Schuster New York 1994, pp. 241-242.

26 *attracting kids with giveaways* Susan Linn. "Electronic marketing: 'Here, kiddie, kiddie!' " *Boston Sunday Globe*, January 16, 2000.

26 *over 30,000 outlets* http://www.mcdonalds.com/corp/about.html

27 *multi-billion dollar advertising campaigns* According to a republican Public Committee of the U.S. Senate McDonald's spent US$1, 644 billion advertising Big Macs and French Fries during the 1995-1996 period. See Jade West. *Are We Spending Too Much to Elect Congress? Advertising Costs and Congressional Campaigns* May 13, 1997; http://rpc.senate.gov/~rpc/releases/1997/Fec-ads2.lo.htm

29 *consumer food problems (high fat, salt)* "Junk Food"; http://www.betterhealth.vic.gov.au/bhcv2/bhcarticles.nsf/pages/Junk_food?OpenDocument

29 *gastrointestinal problems epidemic* Reza Malekzadeh MD•, Siavosh Nasseri-Moghaddam MD, Masoud Sotoudeh MD "GastroEsophageal Reflux Disease: The New Epidemic"; http://www.ams.ac.ir/AIM/0362/0362127.htm

29 *heart disease number one killer* Fighting Heart Disease and Stroke Locally September 11, 2004; http://www.americanheart.org/presenter.jhtml?identifier=1200247&division=NEA115

29 *obesity-related diabetes* Erin McClam "Diabetes 'Epidemic' in the US: Disease of the Elderly Now Afflicts the Young" *The Associated Press* Jan. 26, 2001; http://abcnews.go.com/sections/living/DailyNews/Diabetes012601.html; Editorial. "Selling to – and selling out – Children". *The Lancet 360* (September 28, 2002): 959.

32 *obesity in France* "France: Map and Tourism and Travel Facts France in a Nutshell — find essential information on traveling to France using our map and resources"; http://goeurope.about.com/cs/france/l/bl_france_map.htm

32 *French women life-expectancy* "France"; http://www.nationmaster.com/graph-T/hea_lif_exp_fem_hea_yea

33 *Asian and Europeans slimmer than U.S.* Gaetan Lafortune. "Weighty problem." *OECD Observer,* July 2003, pp.20-21.

34 *increasing number can't cook* "Growing Number of Americans Don't Have The Time or Know How to Cook, New Survey Reveals." Meat AMI.com Press Release, November 18, 1996; *http://www.meatami.com/Template.cfm?Section=Archived&template=PressReleaseDisplay.cfm&PressReleaseID=138*

36 *urban centres have open door markets* Paquet comments on the revival of farmer's markets in North America. Laura Byrne Paquet. *The Urge To Splurge: A Social History of Shopping* Toronto: ECW Press, 2003, p.51.

38-39 *Jean Georges serving chickweed* Jean Georges website; http://www.allinfo.net/jg/jean_georges.htm.

41 *KFC claims its fried chicken is healthy* "KFC Sets the Record Straight Fried Chicken Can Be Part of a Healthy, Balanced Diet." KFC Press Release, Oct. 28, 2003; http://www.kfc.com/about/pr/102803.htm

41 *sedentary lifestyles* Ray Dunne, "Obesity: Who is to blame?" *BBC News Online health*, March 14, 2004; http://news.bbc.co.uk/1/hi/health/3501512.stm

41 *fat is not a health issue* Clare Matheson. "Food lobby weighs in on obesity debate" *BBC News Online business.* 27 May, 2004; *http://news.bbc.co.uk/1/hi/business/3750127.stm;* Charles E. Henderson. "Subconscious Confusion between Fat and Health"; http://www.bcx.net/hypnosis/hlth_fat.htm

42 *multinationals support embracing fat* Such as the misguided attempt of African-Americans to affirm themselves against white domination through obesity. See Greg Critser. *Fat Land.* New York: Houghton Mifflin, 2003, pp.118-119.

42 *fat is beautiful* Thus, when people rebelled against skinny models, plus size models were trotted out. See "Plus-Size People, Plus-Size Stuff," *Associated Press* Nov. 10, 2003; http://www.cbsnews.com/stories/2003/12/01/health/main586142.shtml

44 *90% regain weight* "Weight Loss Program — Part 8 Maintaining Weight Loss, The Long-Term Plan"; http://www.thedietchannel.com/weightloss8.htm

51 *air's beneficial qualities* V. Voiculescu. *Ginduri Albe.* Bucuresti: Cartea Romaneasca, 1986 pp. 231-232.

52 *common hydrotherapies* Anonymous. "Hydrotherapy." *Holistic Online.com* ; http://www.holistic-online.com/hydrotherapy.htm); Dian Dincin Buchman. *The Complete Book of Water Therapy* New Canaan, Connecticut: Keats Publishing, 1994; Paula Anne Ford-Martin. "Hydrotherapy" in *Encyclopedia*; http://www.healthatoz.com/healthatoz/Atoz/ency/hydrotherapy.html

52-53 *baths used since time of ancient Greeks and Romans* Dian Dincin Buchman. *The Complete Book of Water Therapy* New Canaan, Connecticut: Keats Publishing, 1994, p. 8.

53 *Heliotherapy in Ancient Egypt* Robert M. Oliva "Sunlight: The Great Healer" July 15, 2000;
http://www.suite101.com/article.cfm/healthy_aging/43857

53 *moderate exposure beneficial* Phyllis A. Balch. *Prescription for Herbal Healing.* New York: Avery, 2002, p. 419.

53-54 *beneficial effects of sunlight* Robert M. Oliva "Sunlight: The Great Healer" July 15, 2000;
http://www.suite101.com/article.cfm/healthy_aging/43857;
Richard Ruhling. "Be Your Own Doctor!"
http://www.chattanooga.net/membersites/totalhealth/3HlthFrm.htm

54 *sun sets biological clock* Richard Ruhling. "Be Your Own Doctor!"
http://www.chattanooga.net/membersites/totalhealth/3HlthFrm.htm

54 *natural products root of consumer medicine* According to Balch about 75% of common drugs are just refinements of direct medicines. See Phyllis A. Balch. *Prescription for Herbal Healing* New York: Avery, 2002, p. 8.

55 *Herbal Products last resort* Karen Wolfe, "Herbal Remedies" in *Health Encyclopedia*;
http://www.northmemorial.com/healthencyclopedia/content/3137.asp

55-56 *preparing healing herbs* Phyllis A. Balch. *Prescription for Herbal Healing* New York: Avery, 2002, pp. 424-434; Jadwiga Zajaczkowa, "Making Herbal Preparation";
http://www.lehigh.edu/~jahb/herbs/preparations.html; Karen Wolfe "Herbal Remedies", in *Health Encyclopedia*;
http://www.northmemorial.com/healthencyclopedia/content/3137.asp

56 *illnesses combated through basic foods* Anonymous. *Medicinal Benefits of Whole Foods*; http://www.naturalways.com/medValFd.htm.

57 *no herbal treatments prior to surgery* Karen Wolfe, "Herbal Remedies" in *Health Encyclopedia*;
http://www.northmemorial.com/healthencyclopedia/content/3137.asp

60 *television stunting kids development* Lawrence Kelemen. "The truth about TV: What they don't want you to know about television and videos";

http://www.aish.com/societyWork/society/The_Truth_about_Television.asp

60 *the importance of play* Susan Linn. *Consuming Kids*. New York: The New Press, 2004 pp. 61-74; Lawrence Kelemen. The truth about TV: What they don't want you to know about television and videos"; http://www.aish.com/societyWork/society/The_Truth_about_Television.asp

61 *television principal source for advertising* Arthur Asa Berger. *Ads, Fads and Consumer Culture: Advertising's Impact on American Character.* Latham: Rowman & Littlefield, 2004, pp. 40-42.

65 *living in the Information Age* Stuart Ewen and Elizabeth Ewen. *Channels of Desire: Mass Images and the Shaping of American Consciousness Revised*. Minneapolis: University of Minnesota Press, 1992, p. 210.

66 *ignorance is revered* Ibid. pp. 210-211.

68 *fitting in means forfeiting intellectual pursuits* Mary Pipher. *Reviving Ophelia: Saving the Selves of Adolescent Girls.* New York: Ballantine Books, 1994, p.64.

68 *self-worth tied to spending, prestige* Karen Kersting. "Consumerism Driving teen egos—and buying—through 'branding.'" *Volume Monitor on Psychology* 35 (June 2004): 60-63.

68 *fitting in means embracing consumer entertainment* Mary Pipher. *Reviving Ophelia: Saving the Selves of Adolescent Girls.* New York: Ballantine Books, 1994, pp. 242-244.

69-70 *the concept of cool* Klein points out how cool was redefined to mean consumer brands. Naomi Klein *No Logo*, New York: Picador 1999. pp.72-76.

70 *consumerizing rebellion* Douglas J. Goodman and Mirelle Cohen. *Consumer Culture: A Reference Handbook.* Santa Barbara: ABC-Clio, 2000, pp. 54-55.

70-71 *multinationals control music of rebellion* The Big Four record labels hold over 75% of market share. http://encyclopedia.thefreedictionary.com/Big%20Five%20record%20labels

77 *Consumer vernacular* The online Urban Dictionary has collected some of the terms that form Consumer-speak. See Urban Dictionary http://www.urbandictionary.com/

80 *Shakespeare irrelevant* The assault upon classic literature by misguided academics is amply discussed in John M. Ellis *Literature Lost: Social Agendas and the Corruption of the Humanities* New Haven: Yale University Press, 1997.

80 *Simpson course* Ryan E. Smith. "Bart, Homer assist search for wisdom at Siena Heights," *Toledo Blade,* Monday, February 4, 2002. *http://www.toledoblade.com/apps/pbcs.dll/article?Site=TO&Date=20020204&Category=NEWS21&ArtNo=102040022&Ref=AR*

80 *video games* Scott Carlson. "Can Grand Theft Auto Inspire Professors?" *The Chronicle of Higher education* August 15, 2003; http://chronicle.com/free/v49/i49/49a03101.htm

83 *poor financial rewards of arts & humanities grads* Alicia C. Dowd. "Return to Field of study and Institutional type among elite graduates." Presented at the Cornell Higher education Institute Higher Education Policy Research Centre, October 15-16, 1999, p.4; http://www.ilr.cornell.edu/cheri/conf/chericonf1999/chericonf1999_07.pdf ; Andrew Norton "Curtail the Glut of Arts Graduates" *The Australian* July 19, 2000; http://www.cis.org.au/Media/OpEds/opeds2000/E190700a.htm

85 *multinationals extend their domain in classroom* Joel Bakan *The Corporation: The Pathological Pursuit of Profit and Power*. New York: Free Press, 2004, pp. 128-129; Mark Walsh "Commercial Invasion of Schools Growing, Report Charges" *Education Week on the Web* April 26, 1995; http://www.edweek.org/ew/vol-14/31commer.h14

85 *Educational television* Naomi Klein *No Logo*, New York: Picador 1999, pp. 89-93; Joel Bakan *The Corporation: The Pathological Pursuit of Profit and Power*. New York: Free Press, 2004, pp. 128-129;

89 *elevation to sainthood of athletes* Klein discusses the creation of sports heroes. Naomi Klein *No Logo*, New York: Picador 1999, p.52.

90 *Super Bowl ads* There is even a website dedicated to these ads. See http://www.superbowl-ads.com/

91 *Rangers owned by Cablevision and Fox Sports* See http://www.hoovers.com/new-york-rangers/—ID__46757—/free-co-factsheet.xhtml

91 *Manchester United and Borussia Dortmund listed companies* Andrew Ellson. "Kenyon questions PLC logic for Utd" *The Times* June 9, 2004; "BVB's going public: Borussia's future has started" October 31, 2000; http://borussia-dortmund.lycos.de/?%9E_%1B%E4%F4%9D

92 *NHL sunbelt expansion and consequences* Jason La Canfora, and Thomas Heath."The Coming Ice Age." *Washington Post*, Saturday, January 17, 2004; Page D01

93 *Manchester and Yankees global teams* "Man Utd top Europe sports brand" *CNN.com* February 19, 2001 http://www.cnn.com/2001/WORLD/europe/02/19/manutd.brand/

94 *Brazil Nike scandal "Are Nike calling the shots in football?"* Evading Standards June 18, 1999 http://www.urban75.org/archive/news055.html ; Tim Vickery, "Dream partnership turned sour" *BBC Sport* Monday, 15 January, 2001; http://news.bbc.co.uk/sport1/hi/football/1118247.stm

94 *Kim Clijsters* Raf Casert. "Clijsters to boycott Olympics if she cannot play in outfit of her choice." http://www.usta.com/protennis/fullstory.sps?iNewsID=46904&itype=&iCategoryID= - 11/21/03

94 *value of Beckham* Marcel Fenez. "The value of David Beckham." September 2, 2003 http://www.hollywoodreporter.com/thr/pwc/talking_display.jsp?vnu_content_id=1964244

95 *Italian Serie A in financial trouble* Gerard Kiely. "A league of their own," *The Sunday Business Post online,* September 5, 2004; http://www.thepost.ie/web/The%20Newspaper/Sundays%20Paper/index.asp

107 *McDonalds on Champs Elysee* Cris Yabes. "French Food Still Resisting Globalization," *Pacific News Service,* December 20, 2000; http://www.pacificnews.org/jinn/stories/6.25/001220-french.html

107 *consumer travelling* The spreading cancer of theme parks is addressed in Richard J. Barnet and John Cavanagh *Global Dreams: Imperial Corpoations and the New World Order* Simon & Schuster New York 1994, pp. 30-32.

113 *consumerism erases culture* Levitt addresses multinational-led global homogenization. Theodore Levitt. *The Marketing Imagination.* London: Collier Macmillan, 1983, pp. 22-28.

113 *world's youth becoming consumer clones* My anecdotal evidence is backed up by Heaven and Tubridy in their report. Cara Heaven and Matthew Tubridy, "Global Youth Culture and Youth Identity," in *Highly Affected, Rarely Considered: the International Youth Parliament Commission's report on the impacts of globalisation on young people.* Sydney: Oxfam, 2003 pp.149-154

113 *same consumer test tube* MTV is one of the creators of the consumer test tube. See Marc Levinson, "It's an MTV World," *Newsweek* 24 April 1995, pp.45-49.

114 *America hated for, defined by consumer culture* Adam Garfinkle "Anti-Americanism, U.S. Foreign Policy, and the War on Terrorism," in Adam Garfinkle ed. *A Practical Guide to Winning the War on Terrorism* Stanford: Hoover Press, 2004, pp. 205-206.

114 *American immigrant identity* Ewen and Ewen trace the origins of the consumerization of American identity. Stuart Ewen and Elizabeth Ewen. *Channels of Desire: Mass Images and the Shaping of American Consciousness Revised.* Minneapolis: University of Minnesota Press, 1992, p. 33.

118 *white teens emulate hip-hop* According to one hip-hop mogul, 80% of rap audience is white. "Russell Simmons, Unplugged." *CBS News,* February 11, 2004;
http://www.cbsnews.com/stories/2004/02/09/60II/main598970.shtml

118 *Afro-Americans resent cultural appropriation* Maria T. Padilla "African-American presence influences mainstream from music to advertising," *The Orlando Sentinel*;
http://www.blackvoices.com/feature/cross_culture/

118 *American Indian cultural appropriation* Terri Jean "When honoring and borrowing one's cultural identity turns into thievery," *Awakened Woman,* August 19, 2001;
http://www.awakenedwoman.com/cultural_theft.htm

132 *no utensils* Ritzer points out the simplification of food by the consumer food industry. George Ritzer. *The McDonaldization of Society.* Thousand Oaks: Pine Forge Press, 1996, pp.39-40.

133 *food availability causes obesity* Linda Russell, " *Obesity in Childhood: Our New Epidemic" Jacksonville Medicine* June/July 2002.

136 *cultured dining avoiding heartburn* "Self-Care Tips"
http://www.heartburnalliance.org/section3/1020.jsp

137 *consumer-controlled concept of rebeliousness* Naomi Klein. *No Logo*. New York: Picador, 1998, pp. 118-119; The appropriation of subculture is also dealt with in Cara Heaven and Matthew Tubridy. "Global Youth Culture and Youth Identity" in *Highly Affected, Rarely Considered: the International Youth Parliament Commission's report on the impacts of globalisation on young people* Sydney: Oxfam, 2003 p.151.

140 *denigration of women* Thulani Davis. "The Height of Disrespect" *The Village Voice*. March 17 - 23, 2004; www.villagevoice.com/issues/0411/davis.php

140 *mistreating men* Debbie Schlussel. "Pop princesses' jihad on men." *WorldNetDaily.com,* 2002; http://www.worldnetdaily.com/news/article.asp?ARTICLE_ID=26047

142 *consumer-wear promotes freedom* Lindsay Rowan "The revolution will not go better with Coke" *Resistance Magazine* 3, February/March, 2004; http://www.resistance.org.au/res_mag/issue1/res1-30.shtm

143 *consumer-wear as social emancipation* Ibid.

143 *promotes self-expression undermining traditional dress* Jordan Tylor, Nyssa Shawstad, Naila Ahmed "Fashion and Globalisation" in *Globalisation and Communication: People, profits, and Production.* Anke Bartl and Ben Pyman eds. http://www.ssn.flinders.edu.au/global/glob1002/2003book/contents/contents.htm

154 *economies of scale* See Richard J. Barnet and John Cavanagh *Global Dreams: Imperial Corpoations and the New World Order* Simon & Schuster New York 1994, p. 315.

154 *perform task without deviation* Ritzer refers to the control exerted upon workers in McDonaldized organizations. George Ritzer. *The McDonaldization of Society.* Thousand Oaks: Pine Forge Press, 1996, p.11.

154 *cog in the machine* Despite claims of multitasking and other cosmetic changes to the mass production industry, the repetitive mindnumbing aspect of mass production has not changed. See Eric Schlosser *Fast Food Nation: The Dark Side of the All-American Meal* New York: Perennial, 2002, p. 174.

155 *detailed training programs* Robin Leidner *Fast Food Fast Talk: Service Work and the Routinization of Everyday Life* Berkley: California 1993, pp. 55-60.

155 *becoming the multinational product* Disney Cruise lines gives its employees a Disney Look Book; http://www.dcljobs.com/diff-male.htm; McDonald's tries to "mass-produce friendliness" according to Robin Leidner. See Robin Leidner. *Fast Food Fast Talk: Service Work and the Routinization of Everyday Life* Berkley: U. of California Pub, 1993, p.46.

155 *Disney facial hair* In a major change, moustaches have been permitted since 2000 but not beards. Ben Fenton "Hair today as Disney lifts rule on shaving." *Daily Telegraph,* March 27, 2000.

155 *multinationals act like mini-states* Southwest Airlines' success rests in part to the corporatization of its employees using the Orwellian-sounding Culture Committee. See Adolf Haasen and Gordon F. Shea. *New Corporate Cultures That Motivate.* Westport: Praeger Publishers, 2003, pp. 98-102.

160 *credit card debt* Credit card balances in the U.S. grew from $3000 in 1990 to $8,100 in September 2001. See Jamie Court. *Corporateering: How Corporate Power Steals Your Personal Freedom... And what You Can Do About It.* New York: Tarcher Putnam 2003, p.144.

167 *rapid employee turnover* According to Leidner, McDonald's employee turnover in 1985 averaged 205 per cent. See Robin Leidner *Fast Food Fast Talk: Service Work and the Routinization of Everyday Life* Berkley: California 1993, p.51.

168 *multinationals control marketing and distribution* Paul Du Gay ed. *Production of Culture/Cultures of Production.* Sage Publications: Thousand Oaks, 1997, pp.78-81.

172 *multinationals destroying environmentalism* Two books that deal at length with this issue are Andrew Rowell's *Green Backlash - Global Subversion of the Environmental Movement*. London, New York: Routledge, 1996, and Sharon Beder. *Global Spin: the Corporate Assault on Environmentalism.* White River Junction, Vt.: Chelsea Green Publishing, 1998.

173 *chemical cleaners cause cancer and allergies* Rebecca K. Reynolds. "The Safe Way to Clean." *Balanced Living Magazine,* March/April, 2004.

174 *lawns waste water* Neil Strassman. "Region's water consumption cause for concern" *Fort Worth Star Telegram*; http://www.texaswatermatters.org/pdfs/news_09.pdf.

174 *America's low water supply* Mort Rosenblum. "America's Water Supplies Are Drying Up, Despite warnings, politicians still see the glass half full"; http://www.ulct.org/news/across_utah/2001/desnews_051501.html

174 *lawns polluting* Environmental media services "Yard Appliances and Pollution" May 30, 2001; http://www.ems.org/lawncare/appliances.htm

174 *lawn weakling* Stevie Daniels. "Introduction: The New American Lawn"; http://www.bbg.org/gar2/topics/sustainable/handbooks/lawns/1.html

174 *allergies and pesticides* "Allergy and Pesticides: Ten Questions and Answers" Division of Public Health and Public Service Agromedicine Program / OEM Department of Family Medicine; http://www.musc.edu/oem/pestallr.html;
Wayne Sinclair, Richard Pressinger. "Chemical pesticides health effects research."; http://www.chem-tox.com/pesticides/index.htm

175 *sterilized environment causes sickness* Stuart B. Levy. "Antibacterial Household Products: Cause for Concern." *Suppl.Emerging Infectious Diseases 7(3)* (2001): 512-515.

176 *bedrock of farming corporate* Debra Bendis. "Field of corporate dreams - Farming Without The Farmer." *Christian Century*, June 19, 2002, pp. 8-9.

176 *multinationals directly or indirectly control food supplies* Tom Hanahoe. *America Rules.* Dingle: Brandon, 2003, pp.29-32.

177 *pesticides cause sterility* A.R. Greenlee, T.E. Arbuckle and P.H. Chyou. "Risk factors for female infertility in an agricultural region". *Epidemiology 14* (2003):429-436; *"Pesticides and male infertility: is there a link?"* Farm family health 3(1) *(Spring 1995)*:6.

177 *pesticides cause cancer* Alavanja MCR, Samanic C, Dosemeci M, Lubin J, Tarone R, Lynch CF, et al. "Use of agricultural pesticides and prostate cancer risk in the Agricultural Health Study cohort," *Am J Epidemiol 157* (2003): 800-814.

178 *hormones and early puberty* Sherrill Sellman "The Problems of Precocious Puberty" *Nexus Magazine 11(3)* (April-May 2004); http://www.nexusmagazine.com/articles/puberty.html;
Sandy Slater "The meat we eat: Would you like a Side of Hormones and Antibiotics with that Steak?" *Capital News Online* Nov. 1, 2002; http://temagami.carleton.ca/jmc/cnews/01112002/c2.shtml;
Michael Lamm "Beef, Chicken, and Fish," 2002; http://www.lammd.com/A3R_brief_in_doc_format/2002-No2-Beef ChickenorFish.cfm

178 *food with antibiotics* Deborah MacKenzie "Gut reaction: Could a mechanical gourmet help us digest a GM future?" *New Scientist* 30 January, 1999, p.4; Charles Q Choi "California OKs GM pharm crops" *The Scientist*, April 8, 2004; http://www.biomedcentral.com/news/20040408/04

179 *Mexican corn* John Ross. "Nasty Niblets: Mexico's Ancient Corn Threatened by Fake Species"; http://www.nowtoronto.com/issues/2002-02-28/news_story3.php; "Mexicans angered by spread of GM corn" *Asheville global report,* No. 155, Jan. 3-9, 2002; http://www.agrnews.org/issues/155/environment.html

179 *Canadian farmers sue* Craig Wong. "Saskatchewan Organic Farmers File Lawsuit Against Monsanto and Aventis." *The Canadian Press*, January 10, 2004; http://www.mindfully.org/Farm/2004/Monsanto-Saskatchewan-Organic10jan04.htm

180 *55-60% of the human body is water* "The Water Page: Water Basics." http://www.thewaterpage.com/waterbasics.htm

180 *tap water chemical composition* Joseph Keon *Whole Health: The Guide to Wellness of Mind and Body*, Mill Valley, CA: Parissound Pub, 1997.

181 *Walkerton deaths* Erik Marcus. "E. coli Tragedy in Walkerton, Ontario: Everyone Gets Sued, Except the People Directly Responsible." *Vegan.com,* June 2000; http://www.vegan.com/issues/2000/jun00/walkerton.htm

181 *water filters won't eliminate all impurities* Don Vandervort "Water Filters: Making a Choice"; http://www.hometips.com/cs-protected/guides/waterfilters.html

181 *chemical filters* "Filter Types: Advantages & Disadvantages"; http://www.ewater.com/water/info/filtertypes.htm

181 *can't filter bacteria* "Water Filters." http://www.cmhc-schl.gc.ca/en/burema/gesein/abhose/abhose_041c.cfm; "E. coli 0157:H7 in drinking water." US EPA; http://www.epa.gov/safewater/ecoli.html

181-182 *global water pollution* Hillary Mayell. "UN Highlights World Water Crisis" *National Geographic News*, June 5, 2003; news.nationalgeographic.com/ news/2003/06/0605_030605_watercrisis.html - 43k -

182 *soda fountains contain tap water* "Soft Drink Syrup" http://www.ezp.novem.nl/english/toon.asp?id=4

182 *annual deaths in Toronto* Barbara Yaffe. "In Toronto 1700, annual premature deaths are blamed on air pollutants." *Toronto Staff Report*, June 29, 2004, p.5.

183 *jury out on air purifiers* EPA Office of Air and Radiation (OAR) "Residential Air Cleaning Devices: A Summary of Available Information" *EPA 400/1-90-002*, February 1990; B.C. Ministry of Health Services "Indoor Air Quality Combustion By-products," Health File #65c, April 1998.

183 *rural air worse than city* "Pollution count: rural drives may be worse than urban cruises" January 31, 2000; http://www.cnn.com/2000/NATURE/01/31/rural.pollution.enn/

186 *plant native species* "Water- Efficient Landscaping: Preventing Pollution & Using Water Resources Wisely," p. 5; http://www.epa.gov/owm/water-efficiency/final_final.pdf.

190 *sex as currency* Cameron Weston "'Enjo Kosai' – Sex, Schoolgirls and Consumerism in Japan" *Crikey* July 9, 2004; http://www.crikey.com.au/columnists/2004/07/09-0005.html

190 *young girls need boys who will buy them stuff* Richard J. Estes, Neil Alan Weiner. *The Commercial Sexual Exploitation of Children Living in the U.S., Mexico and Canada.* U.S. National Study, 2001, p. 69.

193 *obesity lowers libido, causes erectile problems* "Big-bellied men have flagging libido"; http://www.health24.com/medical/Condition_centres/777-792-1446-1872,12617.asp

194 *psychology of obesity, sex* "Understanding Adult Obesity"; http://www.niddk.nih.gov/health/nutrit/pubs/unders.htm#psychosocial;

J.F. Kinzl, E. Trefalt, M. Fiala, A. Hotter, W. Biebl, F. Aigner. "Partnership, sexuality, and sexual disorders in morbidly obese women: consequences of weight loss after gastric banding." *1: Obes Surg*. 2001 Aug;11(4):455-8; Michael W. Wiederman. "Body size, physical attractiveness, and body image among young adult women: relationships to sexual experience and sexual esteem" *Journal of Sex Research* (August 1998): 272-281.

194 *TV in the bedroom* Christine Guy Fischer. "Coitus Non-Existus." *Today's Parent*. October 1999, p. 68.

195 *fantasizing over idealized images* Arthur Asa Berger *Ads, Fads and Consumer Culture: Advertising's Impact on American Character* Latham: Rowman & Littlefield, p. 59.

197 *arousal a matter of abuse, violence* Gargi Bhattacharyya. *Sexuality and Society.* London: Routledge 2002, p.130.

197 *women exist to satisfy men's needs* Ibid. 136.

197 *porn encourages treatment of women as objects* Ibid. 131.

199 *get an education* Ibid. 140.

209 *burying death* George Ritzer. *The McDonaldization of Society.* Thousand Oaks: Pine Forge Press, 1996, p. 172.

210 *how Big Macs started out* Schlosser gives an account of the consumerized butchery. See Eric Schlosser *Fast Food Nation: The Dark Side of the All-American Meal* New York: Perennial, 2002, pp. 169-172.

210-211 *diminution of death* J. McMurtry "The New World Order: The Hidden war of values," in *The New World Order: Corporate Agenda and Parallel Reality* Gordana Yovanovich ed., McGill-Queens: Montreal-Kingston, 2003, pp. 32-33

212 *electronic death* Video games parallel army simulators in teaching how to kill reflexively. Dave Grossman, and Gloria DeGaetano, *Stop Teaching Our Kids to Kill: A Call to Action Against TV, Movie and Video Game Violence*, New York: Crown Books, 1999, pp.73-75

212 *divorcing death from emotional response* Ibid.73-75.

212 *ignorant youth enact killing sprees* Ibid. 75-77.

213 *consumerism the new faith* David Loy and Jonathan Watts. "The religion of consumption: a Buddhist rebuttle(*sic*)." *Development 41(1)* (March 1998): Bruce Bower. "Buyer beware: some psychologists see

danger in excessive materialism." *Science News*, Sept 6, 2003, pp. 152-154;

213 *consumerism and the desire for immortality* Bill McKibben. "Do We Really Want to Live Forever?"; http://www.beliefnet.com/story/147/story_14779_1.html

214 *die with dignity* Ritzer points out medicine's mandate to keep people alive regardless of condition. George Ritzer. *The McDonaldization of Society.* Thousand Oaks: Pine Forge Press, 1996, p. 170.

214 *age removed from consumerism* Thomas R. Cole. "Aging in American Culture Herschel's Vision." *Tikkun,* May/June, 2002.

214 *youth dominates consumer culture* Lorrayne Anthony. "Today's culture offers many alternatives to growing old gracefully." *Canadian Press,* Dec. 17, 2002; mediresource.sympatico.ca/channel_health_news_detail.asp?; Sara Terry. "Saving face: A boom in plastic surgery reflects Americans' growing obsession with youth and discomfort with aging." *Christian Science Monitor,* February 21, 2002, p.15.

215 *marginalization of the old* This process was critiqued by the Vatican. "The Dignity of Older People and Their Mission in the Church and in the World." Pontifical Council for the Laity, October 1, 1998.; http://www.vatican.va/roman_curia/pontifical_councils/laity/documents/rc_pc_laity_doc_05021999_older-people_en.html

Index

Abraham, 202
Adidas, 92
air,
    air filters, 182-183
    healing qualities of, 51
    pollution, 182-183
Alexander the Great, 66
Aristotle, 66, 73
artificial needs, 11-12
artistic creation, 121- 126
artistic labor, 126-128
Aspen, 105

Banff, 171
Beckham, David, 66, 94
Bible, 77
Bocelli, Andrea, 125
Bono, 116 fn26
Borussia Dortmund, 91
Brazil, 94, 109
Brazilian National Soccer Team, 94
Britney Spears, 62, 66, 70, 71, 116fn26
Buddha, 73, 202
Burger King, 31
business ownership, 153-159

Cablevision, 91
Canada, 15
Cancun, 105, 106
Champs-Elysee, 107
Chernobyl, 226
A Christmas Carol 63
Clijsters, Kim, 94
Coca-Cola Company, 61
consumer food, 25, 176-180
    fighting addiction to, 29-31
    GM foods, 178-179
    health effects of, 29
    and obesity, 29
consumer health, 49-51
    chemical basis of, 49
    pills route to health, 50
    shrinking definition of health, 50
consumer porn, 194-197
Consumer-Speak 76-77
consumer
    definition, 5-6
consumerism
    and culture 113-152
    and death, 209-222
    definition, 5
    financing, 149-151
    and high school, 67-71
    and immortality, 213-214
    labor of, 6-7
    and rebellion, 70-71
    and sex, 189-200
    and sport, 89-102
    and travel, 103-113
    and university, 80-85
    and waste, 7-8
Consumer-Wear, 141-143, 146
Consumer-World, 5, 8
cooking, 34-36
    controlling your ingredients, 36-39
courting, consumer, 190-191
culture,
    in America 113-115
    and cosmopolitanism, 117
    and cultural drift, 118
    and dining, 132-136
    and dress, 141-147
    and entertainment, 137-138
    and etiquette, 147-151
    and language, 138-141
    rural, 119
    and the self, 115-118

Dante, 67
Darwin, Charles 73
Daytona Beach, 106
death, 209-222
    and aging, 214-216, 219
    and funerals, 218-219
    and illness, 217-218
    killing, 209-210, 220-221

Delphic Oracle, 66
Descartes, Rene, 73
diets 44-46
    Atkins, 46
    and health 43-44
    perils of, 44
    physician approved 44-46
Dirty Harry, 77
Disney Company, 70, 85, 107, 114, 155,
drinking water, 180-182
Dylan, Robert (Bob), 82

Education
    Arts & humanities, 83-85
    of children, 85-87
    high school, 67-71
    selecting courses, 83
    university, 80-85
Eiffel Tower, 109
Einstein, Albert, 67, 73
Emerson, Ralph Waldo, 114
environment, 171-187
    and consumer improvements, 173-174
    and the self, 183-187
ESPN, 98

faith, 202-203
farming, 38
farmers, 36-37
    buying directly from them, 36-37
finances, 159-169
    cash, 163
    investments, 163-165
food,
    intimacy of, 28
    nutritional value of, 28-29
Ford Lauderdale, 106
Ford Motor Company 3
Fox Sports, 91
Frankenstein, 3
French cuisine, 32-34
Friends, 221

Gap, 68, 189
Gates, William (Bill), 3
Goebbels, Joseph, 61

Hardy, Thomas, 122
Harvard, 177
Healing foods, 56
Heidegger, Martin, 73
heliotherapy, 53-54
herbal remedies 54-56
    preparation of, 55-56
Hilton Hotels, 110
Hippocrates, 56
hydrotherapy, 52-53
holistic food, 31-32

indirect advertising, 26-27
individual expression, 9-11
    and freedom 10-11
Italian soccer league, 95

Jean Georges, 39
Jerry Springer, 60, 63
Jesus Christ, 73, 202, 207
Joyce, James, 68
Jordan, Michael, 67fn15,
Jude the Obscure, 122

Kama Sutra, 199-200
Kant, Immanuel 73
KFC, 41
Kierkegaard, Soren, 73
Knowledge, 65-87
    and consumerism, 65-67
    decline of, 65-67
    and high school, 67-71
    and language, 75-80

language, 75-80
    importance of, 78-79
    steps in learning, 79-80
Lawrence, D.H. 199
Los Angeles Lakers, 91, 101
Louvre, 108

Madonna, 67
Manchester United, 91, 93, 94
Manson, Marilyn, 70
Mao, Zedong 61
Margarita Island, 106
Matrix, 3, 82

McDonald's, 7, 25fn5, 26-27, 29, 35, 39, 44, 81, 103, 107, 114, 132-133, 155-156, 169, 189, 210
MLB, 93
Microsoft, 154fn33
Les Miserables, 63
Mr. Bean, 63
Mohammed, 202
Mona Lisa, 204
Monty Python, 63
Mozart, Wolfgang 67
multinationals,
  and consumer food, 25, 41-43
  in education, 85
  and employment, 154-155
  pharmaceuticals 49-51
  and sex, 189-190
MTV, 85

natural healing, 51-56
  and consulting your doctor 57
Neo, 77
New Kids on the Block, 70-71
Newton, Isaac, 67, 73
New Hampshire, 224n51
New York Rangers, 91
New York Yankees, 91, 93
Nicastro, la Bottega, 167
Nice, 110
Nike, 67fn15, 92, 94, 96,
NBA, 93,
NFL, 90
NHL, 92, 93, 95
Notre-Dame Cathedral, 108

obesity, 41-47
  and advertising, 41-43
  and esthetics 41-43
Olympics, 95
organic produce, 37-38

Paris, 107-110
Pepsi-Cola company, 33, 61, 62, 80, 164
Pepsi Centre, 91
Pepsi 400, 91
Pitt, Brad, 66
Plato, 66, 72, 73
Playboy, 194
Portugal, 110

reading, 71-74
  advantages of, 71
  types of books, 72-74
Real Madrid, 91, 94
restaurants, 38-39
  choosing the right one 39
Ronaldo, 94
Russell, Bertrand 73

St. Lawrence River, 177
St. Martin, 106
St. Tropez, 105
seasonally affective disorder (SAD), 54
September 11, 2001, 213, 226
sex education, 199-200
Shakespeare, 73, 80, 82
Shelley, Mary, 3
The Simpsons, 80
Socrates, 66
Spears, Britney, 62, 66, 70, 71
spirituality, 201-207
Star Trek, 82
Suburbia
  commercial and residential separation, 16
  and consumer technology 18-19
  and lack of community, 15
  distance in, 16
  and the family home, 21-22
  lack of amenities in, 16-17
  local businesses, 20-21
  and the mall, 19-20
  migration and immigration, 17-18
  and neighbours, 22
Super Bowl, 85, 90

Tarantino, Quentin, 138
television, 59-64,
  and children 60
  combatting addiction to 62-64
  commercials 61-62
  and death, 210-211
  effects of 60-64
TV Guide 59, 63, 217

Terminator, 3
travel,
    hotels, 104
    camping, 104-105
    as cultural experience 107-109
    as social experience, 109-111
True needs, 12-13

United States, 15
University of Grenada, 113

Vanilla Ice, 70
Venice, 110-111
video games,
    and death, 212

Washington, George 114
Weight Watchers, 44-46
WWF, 90

Yellowstone, 114, 171

AGMV Marquis
MEMBER OF SCABRINI MEDIA
Quebec, Canada
2005